Acts of Achievement

The Role of Performing Arts Centers in Education

EDITORS:

Barbara Rich, Ed.D

Jane L. Polin

Stephen J. Marcus

D

DANA
PRESS

About Dana

The Dana Foundation, founded in 1950, is a private philanthropic organization with particular interests in science, health, and education. In 2000 the Foundation extended its longtime support of education to fund innovative professional development programs leading to improved teaching of the performing arts in public schools.

Dana's focus is on training for in-school arts specialists and professional artists who teach in the schools. We back up these arts education grants by disseminating information to arts educators, artists in residence, and schools through our symposia, periodicals, and books.

Dana has concentrated on local innovations in public education that can be replicated nationally. In1992 the Foundation established the Dana Center for Educational Innovation at the University of Texas at Austin to strengthen mathematics and science education. The Center continues to develop and identify promising educational innovations for local evaluation emulation across the country.

Our science and health grants support research in neuroscience and immunology. Dana supports brain research through direct grants and by its outreach to the public, which includes books and periodicals from the Dana Press; the international Brain Awareness Week campaign; the Dana Alliance for Brain Initiatives, a nonprofit organization of more than 200 neuroscientists, including ten Nobel laureates, committed to advancing public awareness of the progress of brain research; and the Dana Web site, www.dana.org.

Table of Contents

continued on next page

Table of Contents *continued*

Growth Through Collaboration:
New Opportunities for Educators, Artists, and Presenters

By Janet Eilber,
Principal Arts Consultant,
The Dana Foundation

As a dancer who had the good fortune to work with the legendary Martha Graham, I remember how, despite her own remarkable skill, creativity, and independence, she used to celebrate growth through collaboration. "I am a thief!" Martha would announce, barely suppressing her delight in provocation. "But I only steal from the best."

Collaboration with complementary partners (building on "the best") is, of course, no theft at all, but a win-win enterprise for all participants. Collaboration nurtures those who present the artist's work, as well as the audiences whose hearts and minds the artist and presenter intend to touch, whether in performance centers, in the community, or where it is particularly effective —in schools.

In the rapidly evolving field of arts education, time and resources are limited. Guidelines and success stories that enable an educator, artist and presenter to find ways to exchange ideas and build upon the work of others are hard to come by. Artists and educators responsible for these programs in the classroom often lack the opportunity to document their experiences, especially for a wider audience.

In fact, part of the impetus for this book came from an innocent e-mail the Dana Foundation sent to friends in arts education: "Does anyone have artist residency guidelines?" We sought data about direct interaction among artist, students, and their teachers in a school setting. "Our guidelines need updating," we pointed out. "Does anyone have a good, practical formula?"

Responses flooded back, showing that we were not alone:

"Artist residency guidelines? We've been looking for some for months. Forward any that you uncover."

"We need them, too, both for artists and the schools."

"We're looking for guidelines that include performing arts centers."

"Please send us a copy of any and all—even old ones."

The need for facilitating educator/artist/presenter collaboration was brought home again. Dana's grants and outreach, though relatively new on the scene, seemed to be filling this gap in arts education funding. But there was a long way to go.

Dana's support of education dates from the Foundation's beginnings in 1950. Its interest in arts education began in 2000, with an initiative to improve the quality of arts in the schools by training teaching artists and in-school arts specialists.

We have reinforced this mission in several ways. In 2001, the Foundation held a symposium in Washington, DC to explore the options, resources, and best practices available to planners of K-12 schools with an arts focus. The information from that stimulating symposium was turned into a free publication, *Planning an Arts-Centered School: A Handbook.* The demand for the book required a second printing of 10,000 copies within three months. Dana also produced or participated in workshops and panels; established an arts education section on the Foundation's Web site; created "The Arts and the Brain" for the syndicated radio series, *Gray Matters;* and began publishing a new quarterly, *Arts Education in the News.*

The enthusiastic response to these coordinated efforts spurred the planning of a second national conference, "Acts of Achievement," (held April 9-10, 2003, at the Dana Center in Washington, DC, and the John F. Kennedy Center for the Performing Arts) and this companion publication.

We set a series of specific goals for the 2003 symposium:

• First, we aimed to address issues which most concern our Dana grantees. Arts providers, presenters, and other arts organizations typically ask:

– How do we involve school leadership in arts education?

– How do we develop a symbiotic relationship between teaching artist and classroom teacher?

– How do we involve parents and secure grass-roots community support?

– What elements make artist residencies in schools successful?

• Our second goal was to build on pioneering work in this area of arts education. *Creating Capacity: A Framework for Providing Professional Development Opportunities for Teaching Artists,* a publication prepared by The National Conversation on Artist Professional Development and Training, provided an excellent foundation. Creative resources such as the Kennedy Center's *A Community Audit for Arts Education: Better Schools, Better Skills, Better Communities* were invaluable.

• Finally, we determined that the participants at the symposium should represent a "critical mass" of diverse members of the arts education and presentation communities who could advance this field by their interaction.

These goals shaped the symposium, aided by the guidance of philanthropic advisor Jane L. Polin, and the active involvement of Sandra Gibson (president and CEO of the Association of Performing Arts Presenters), and Derek E. Gordon (senior vice president at the Kennedy Center). The wide-ranging effort, under the administrative leadership of Barbara Rich (a Dana vice president with a doctorate in education) produced a dynamic exchange in which many participants explored uncharted areas and generated new ideas.

This book provides several ways to make use of the resources created in conjunction with the 2003 symposium, "Acts of Achievement: The Role of Performing Arts Presenters in Education."

The Executive Summary provides an overview; even the most seasoned arts education professionals at the conference remarked on the freshness of the information exchanged about practical experiences. The goal of achieving "critical mass" with a complementary group of participants was not only reached, but was exceeded. It became a central feature of the event. The summary, written by Polin, reviews this interchange of ideas and is enriched by the author's expert observations and recommendations.

• The Case Studies and Profiles of arts presenter institutions are designed as a practical guide for others who are initiating, assessing, refining, or revamping arts education programs of their own. The profiles, which examine the work of presenters across the nation, offer a variety of curricula and approaches to learning organized to encourage local adaptation and national advancement. The detailed case studies do the same in greater depth.

• Lynne B. Silverstein's essay, "Artist Residencies: Evolving Educational Experiences," is a step-by-step guide for educators and artists planning to work together for students'—and each others'—benefit. Using research, interviews, and insights derived from the Acts of Achievement forum, this article provides ten "elements of success" for artist residencies and an appendix of checklists for each type of participant. The purpose of this essay is to demystify and illuminate the artist residency process.

The participants in the "Acts of Achievement" forum—school administrators, teachers, experienced teaching artists, and arts presenters—are the central authors of this book. We hope the reader will continue this "growth through collaboration" by taking advantage of the many ideas in its pages.

And for those looking for artist residency guidelines—as we at Dana were—here they are. Feel free to make good use of them, refine and adapt them, and share them with colleagues and partners. In the Martha Graham tradition, you'll be building on the best.

Acts of Achievement:
The Role of Performing Arts Centers in Education
Executive Summary

By Jane L. Polin,
Philanthropic Advisor

In Anytown, USA, 11-year-old Bobby attends a performance of *Revelations,* the signature work of the Alvin Ailey American Dance Theater, with his middle school class at a local performing arts center. He is amazed, having never seen anything like this before. How do those guys jump so high in the "Sinner Man" scene? And why are they running? The lighting on stage keeps changing—how do they do that? The gospel music is both happy and sad; and the sounds remind him of the hip-hop that his older brother often plays. Religion certainly seems to be central in the lives of these people, and the women appear to be in charge of everything. Finally, why does everyone in the audience start clapping rhythmically during the last scene, even before the piece is over?

Although the individuals portrayed in *Revelations* are from a different time and place, they have so much to say to Bobby. These characters are believable human beings, not just figures in a video game. But where do their portrayers come from? And how did they learn to do what they do? Soon he and his classmates actually interview the dancers, who answer some of his questions. Back at school, Bobby even gets to dance with them, and learns of the cultural and social conditions of the Deep South that inspired Alvin Ailey to choreograph this American classic. Afterward, Bobby writes about this extraordinary experience for his social studies class.

The local performing arts center has become a true partner of Bobby's school. They prepared the teachers for this specific performance, but the center's education department staff also provides guidance and resources in numerous other ways throughout the year. Together, the performing arts center and the school are focused on one thing: student achievement. As partners they are collaborating to perform "acts of achievement" for Bobby and many other students across the nation.

"Audience Development" Comes of Age

At the turn of the 20th century, many music halls, opera houses, and theaters were built across America as places of entertainment. For example, the Colonial Theatre in Pittsfield, Mass., built in 1903, was typical of "a time when almost every community had a showplace like this, a place where you could walk in from the street and be transported to a world far removed from the mundane rituals of everyday life." (2001: National Geographic Society, *Saving America's Treasures.*) These showplaces were deemed "magical venues with names like Grand or Tivoli or Majestic." In the mid-20th century, the Colonial and similar sites were often reconfigured for the primary entertainment of the day: moving pictures.

As the century drew to a close, another building boom throughout the country created large numbers of performing arts centers to serve as homes for local performing arts companies and havens for touring enterprises. Once again, these places became vehicles for civic identity. But the evolving expectation was that the centers would serve not as "roadhouses" but rather as "community centers." While still transporting audiences to faraway places, they would also develop programs that addressed local needs, especially those involving the economy and education. The new performing arts centers would now play a critical role in developing a capable, caring citizenry.

"Audience development" had admittedly been a major preoccupation of these centers' leaders, who long recognized that contributions—a vital element —were directly related to income earned from the purchase of tickets and related products. These centers came up with marketing strategies to fill their halls with arts lovers young and old, but young ticket buyers were especially desirable; viewed as institutional "annuities," they were people who could provide steady income to the performing arts center over their lifetimes.

Meanwhile, a crisis in K-12 public education was declared. Ever since the U.S. Department of Education's release a generation ago of *A Nation At Risk,* educators had been struggling to reinvent schools and raise student achievement. In many places, performing arts centers joined other school reformers to improve K-12 public education.

Their innovative activities had the added benefit of expanding young audiences. The recent report *The Capacity of Performing Arts Presenting Organizations* (2002: The Urban Institute) found that 76.9 percent of these organizations were using "programs and performances for K-12" as an "audience-development strategy." For organizations with small budgets, 69 percent were using this strategy, while 93 percent of large organizations were engaged in K-12 outreach.

These activities consisted of more than just selling or subsidizing tickets. As noted in *Toward Cultural Interdependence: The Fourth Phase of the Performing Arts in America* (2002: Association of Performing Arts Presenters), "audience development" soon grew to have a more complex meaning. Its four major aspects were:

• Establishing new forms of partnership

• Making up for the loss of arts education at every level

• Improving the quality and quantity of teaching artists

• Involving new audiences by developing new, non-traditional venues

For the best K-12 education programs established by performing arts centers, narrowly defined audience development was not the focus but rather a byproduct. Leaders in the field were now focusing on student learning.

Acts of Achievement—The National Forum

On April 9-10, 2003, leaders from the arts, education, performing arts centers, and related professional communities participated in "Acts of Achievement," a national invitational forum on performing arts centers in K-12 education. Performing arts centers nationwide were also invited to submit profiles describing their respective programs. The Dana Foundation sponsored the forum, in partnership with the John F. Kennedy Center for the Performing Arts—a critical national force and resource for increasing student success through arts learning—and the Association of Performing Arts Presenters.

Welcoming Remarks

The 145 participants from 25 states who convened at the Kennedy Center were welcomed by Michael Kaiser, president; Derek Gordon, senior vice president; and Alma Powell, vice chair of the board.

In describing the current and future education programs of the Kennedy Center, Kaiser noted that "at the heart we think of ourselves as an educational institution." The Center is heavily involved in "enriching the lives of children and allowing children to express themselves through the arts," he said. "We believe the audiences will be developed if we do that work. But our primary focus is on enhancing the lives of young children."

Powell added: "I salute you who are here today to exchange ideas about the arts for children, because it is certainly a very vital part of our children's development. Quite simply, the arts are what civilize us."

Interview

William Safire, chairman of the Dana Foundation, provided a brief overview of Dana's half century of work in education, neuroscience, and, most recently, arts education. To further set the stage for the day, *The New York Times* columnist said:

"I like the idea of getting the most for your buck in education. But in the movement to measure, in the movement to make sure that you can put your finger on what's happening to students in school, we all too often go for the easy-to-measure—reading comprehension, science, math. This has impressed a lot of budgetary types, but at the same time it denigrates the power of arts in education because you can't quite measure it."

Safire then conducted an interview with Warren Simmons, executive director of Brown University's Annenberg Institute for School Reform. Their dialogue included:

• The state of urban school reform

• The importance of participation in the performing arts for all students

• Standards-based reform and student assessment

• The relationship of education to the economy and to other purposes ("democratic citizenship, cultural well-being, individual fulfillment, family and community development"), according to Simmons

• Direct and indirect effects of the arts on learning

• Opportunities to interconnect multiple school reforms now underway

• Support systems that include the arts.

Simmons encouraged the leaders of performing arts centers, and other stakeholders, to become "part of a larger system that provides continuous support for [the] arts and other forms of development as part of school-based and community-based activities." He also described the building of such systems as "the most exciting opportunity to join top-down reform with bottom-up reform and

have the two be mutually reinforcing." Based on his own experience with the Rhode Island Governor's Task Force on Literacy in the Arts, Simmons cited the need to map arts resources and school needs; to identify funding and coordination mechanisms; and to develop governing structures to ensure high-quality practice.

Safire and Simmons then extended their lively conversation to include the forum audience. The following issues, among others, were raised:

• Arts standards

• Preparation of teaching artists

• The need to gather evidence to improve arts education

• How the arts can reduce school violence and address student fears during crises

• Career opportunities in the arts "behind the scenes"

• Methods for assessing student learning

• The imperative to build community and financial support for proven solutions, with public accountability

• Curriculum frameworks that can support learning in and through the arts

Excerpts both from the interview and the follow-up exchange can be found on page 23.

Three Panels

Following the interview, three research questions—each addressed by a panel of experts—framed the rest of the day's presentations and discussions:

• What do you consider to be the critical factors for success in artist residencies?

• What can performing arts centers do to better prepare teaching artists?

• How can performing arts centers provide more and better professional-development opportunities for K-12 leaders—including teachers, principals, superintendents, school board members, and others?

Panel One: The Role of Artist Residencies

Ken Fischer, *University of Michigan (moderator)*

Nnenna Freelon, *jazz singer and educator*

James Catterall, *UCLA Center for Imagination*

Rob Smith, *superintendent of Arlington, VA schools*

Because artist residencies are a basic education offering of virtually all performing arts centers, moderator Fischer, University of Michigan, and his panelists examined critical factors for success and explored the evolution of the artist residency from a "diversion" to a fully integrated learning experience for students, artists, and teachers.

As the leader of a high-achieving school system, Superintendent Smith spoke about "the importance for children of engaging in life through the arts, as they do through literature, as they do through mathematics, as they do through scientific experimentation, as they do through studies of history and social science, or as they do through athletics. I believe it's part of a well-balanced curriculum, which is a phrase that's not heard a lot these days."

The jazz performer and educator Freelon described lessons learned from her experiences as a teaching artist over the past 15 years, and she emphasized that strong communication is an essential ingredient before, during, and after the artist residency. "You have to allow [students] the opportunity to experience your art and to experience themselves in the doing and making of the art as well. That's how you really transform lives, which is what I really see myself doing."

Researcher Catterall spoke about artist-teacher partnerships in the context of integrated instruction, and he made several observations about effective practice. Catterall described the dynamic between the artists and teachers involved (it's "about relationship development [and the] development of skills and curriculum in practice"), and "mutual adaptation" (a term coined by Stanford University scholar Milbrey McLaughlin) for the partnering institutions. He also noted the current gap between arts standards and the testing agenda, and he urged the forum participants to consider sustainability as a key asset in developing longer-term partnerships through their artist residencies.

Panel Two: The Preparation of Teaching Artists

Frank Hodsoll, *Center for Arts & Culture (moderator)*

Ella Baff, *Jacob's Pillow Dance Festival*

Daniel Bernard Roumain, *composer, violinist, and educator*

Libby Lai-Bun Chiu, *Urban Gateways*

During this session, moderator Hodsoll, Center for Arts and Culture, encouraged his panelists to describe how their own particular work addresses teaching artists' advancement.

Composer, violinist, and educator Roumain told the forum participants about his own "rules and tools" for artist residencies, which involve eight factors: program design, flexibility within the program, a structure that creates a system, the power of conversation, the connections that provide validations, relevancy and respect for the participants, goals that generate gains, and the entertainment value of the residency. He also observed that fun is fundamental.

Baff, Jacob's Pillow Dance Festival, described various elements of the Pillow's programs that nurture teaching artists in dance. These include: the basic desires of the artist; a personalized approach to his or her needs; the development of skills through preparation and practice; the issues of problem-solving and translation; the replication of individual efforts to a larger scale; the management of broad and multiple concepts; the ability to improvise; and the willingness of the curious to create, regardless of domain.

As one of the leaders of the "National Conversation on Artists' Professional Development & Training", Chiu, Urban Gateways, referred to the publication *Creating Capacity: A Framework for Providing Professional Development Opportunities for Teaching Artists* (2001), which articulates six basic elements of teaching-artist training: philosophy of arts education, theories and models of arts education, teaching methods and the content of instruction, collaboration with educators, effective assessment, and knowledge of school culture. She also defined a continuum for the role of the teaching artist—presenting artist, interacting artist, collaborating artist, and master instructional artist—and described how the "healthy child concept" and the "encounter, engage, and reflect" methodology help guide Urban Gateways' training programs for teaching artists.

Panel Three: Professional Development of K-12 Teachers

Uri Treisman, *Dana Foundation, Director of the Dana Center, University of Texas at Austin (moderator)*

Gail Burnaford, *Northwestern University*

Jose Colchado, *Northern Arizona University*

Steve Seidel, *Harvard Project Zero*

Within the context of the "No Child Left Behind"

> **"The emerging artist residency model is an informed partnership—a collaborative effort of the teaching artist and classroom teacher..."**

federal legislation, moderator Treisman, Dana Center, University of Texas, at Austin, asked panelists to comment on the issue of competency—what do teachers need to know and be able to do in the arts?—and on how performing arts centers, higher-education institutions, and other organizations can support learning in and through the arts for these teachers.

Burnaford, Northwestern University, spoke about the need to understand the work "one classroom at a time." She drew attention to the role of arts specialists within schools and raised the issues of teacher certification, the expectations for content knowledge and instructional experience, and the impact of decisions by state policymakers on current and future practice. She urged others to document their work, share proven practices, and promote collaborative learning among teachers as well as students.

Telling the story of his own journey to achievement through the arts, Colchado, Northern Arizona

University, described how they can form a "spiral of success" for students, particularly minority and poor students, and especially those with language deficiencies. He said that teachers "should know what it feels like to be involved in the creative process. They should know the joy of making art." Colchado cautioned that you can have a learning objective and assess that particular objective—without critiquing the entire work of art. He also encouraged greater political activism, and endorsed a more influential role for higher education through curriculum change in pre-service teacher training.

Seidel, Harvard Project Zero, noted that understanding what students need to know and be able to do should inform what teachers should know and be able to do—and that this basic premise should not be taken for granted. To stimulate the "leap into learning" for teachers, Seidel cited the value of bringing teachers together with artists as fellow explorers of "new territories." He decried the "disposable" nature of student work when both teachers and students have much to learn from creating a body of work, as in the portfolio assessment model. Seidel also spoke about the need to transform schools from "institutions" into "communities," and pointed out that arts learning can contribute to this process. A commitment to arts learning shows the community's "desire to open the doors and invite people in, both to see your work and to help you do what you do better."

Acts of Achievement—The Book

Artist Residencies: Evolving Educational Experiences

In preparing for the "Acts of Achievement" forum and book, we listened to teaching artists, classroom teachers, and others who work at the local level—and heard a distinct request for help in doing artist residencies. The "old" model—basically a client/customer relationship between teaching artist and teacher—was changing, but practitioners were unsure how to modify their programs accordingly. As a result, arts education consultant Lynne Silverstein was invited to research and write an essay that would offer practical guidance for the key players in artist residencies: the classroom teacher, the teaching artist, the arts organization coordinator, and the school coordinator.

The emerging artist residency model is an informed partnership—a collaborative effort of the teaching

> ## "...education, both for the young and the young at heart, is one of the best ways to give to the community."

artist and classroom teacher, often mediated by the program and school coordinators. Together, they try to focus on learning in and through the arts for young people, whether in a single classroom session, a day, a week, or over a much longer period.

Silverstein's excellent essay, "Artist Residencies: Evolving Educational Experiences," addresses three core topics: the instructional purposes of artist residencies; the factors that are critical for artist residencies' success; and residency checklists for artists, teachers, arts organization coordinators, and school coordinators. This book presents that essay in its entirety.

A Sampling of Programs: 74 Profiles

The "Acts of Achievement" initiative was the first nationwide attempt to document the size and scope of these fast-growing K-12 education programs at performing arts centers. Dana issued an open call and received 138 qualifying profile submissions from centers located in 37 states. Seventy-four of them, some serving fewer than 20 schools and others serving hundreds of schools, were selected for inclusion in this book, based on ratings established by our advisory committee.

Note the relative youth of many of these. Exactly half or 37 were instituted after 1990. Only 20 pre-date 1983, and the remaining 17 were created between 1983 and 1990. The rapid development of such programs in recent years is clearly the result of community expectations and political commitment, backed by new or increased financial support.

The K-12 education programs of 66 of these performing arts centers are profiled here, and eight more are presented in "case history" detail. The eight are presented in-depth not only for their acknowledged quality, but also for the range of institution and program types they represent:

- The Bushnell Center for the Performing Arts (Hartford, CT) is an 84-year old institution in a mid-sized city.

- Cal Performances (Berkeley, CA) is based at a major research university.

- Flynn Center for the Performing Arts (Burlington, VT) is serving a largely rural population

- Jacob's Pillow Dance Festival (Lee, MA) is a national professional center focused on a single performing arts discipline.

- The John F. Kennedy Center for the Performing Arts (Washington, DC) is a center addressing both local and national arts education needs.

- The Kentucky Center (Louisville, KY) is operating on both a local and statewide basis.

- Maui Arts & Cultural Center (Kahului, HI) is a new center located in a rural setting.

- Scottsdale Center for the Arts (Scottsdale, AZ) is a 16-year old center in a fast-growing metropolitan area.

Celebrating the Contributions, and Aiming for More

The explosive growth of performing arts organizations—dance ensembles, symphony orchestras, theater companies, and others—throughout the 1960s was often made possible with support from the Ford Foundation, the single largest arts funder of the time. The visionary Mac Lowry, who led Ford's arts philanthropy work, saw that involvement with the performing arts was a vital experience for all Americans and that access to quality performances should not be an accident of geography.

An important mentor to this author, Lowry stressed the importance of nurturing a partnership between the local performing arts organization and its community. During one of our final conversations before his death in 1993, Lowry said: "Any organization that takes the name of a city into [its] name has a responsibility to give to, not just take from, that community." And he believed in particular that education, both for the young and the young at heart, is one of the best ways to give to the community.

Performing arts centers, those of long-standing as well as those of recent vintage, are indeed recognizing that K-12 education is an enterprise to which they can contribute in their communities. That investment will yield long-term benefits, for these institutions and their communities alike, beyond the short-term gain of filling seats with young people.

To raise the quality and quantity of their K-12 education programs, performing arts center leaders and their partners might consider the following actions as potential next steps:

• *Utilize* "*A Community Audit for Arts Education: Better Schools, Better Skills, Better Communities*" (2001: Kennedy Center Alliance for Arts Education Network). This research-based audit tool enables groups or even individuals to examine the state of arts education in their communities and set measurable objectives for improving available programs.

• *Establish relationships* with university-based schools of education and schools of the arts, the primary sources of teachers and teaching artists. The pre-service and in-service programs of these institutions can be powerful partners in developing a cadre of capable professionals for programs both in and out of schools. Local colleges and universities can also be a technical resource for evaluation and research efforts.

• *Learn from the experiences* of others in the field. This publication provides a new tool for that learning. Also look to national resources such as the Arts Education Partnership and the John F. Kennedy

Center for the Performing Arts, as well as to discipline-based service organizations. Contact information for many of these groups is contained in this book's resource listing.

• *Engage the entire community* in the development of an arts education program. The strongest programs, many of them described in these pages, thrive from the active participation of individuals with diverse backgrounds and experiences.

• *Launch internships and residencies* for teachers and other educators within performing arts centers. Residencies, after all, do not need to be limited to teaching artists alone. Performing arts centers and their education programs would undoubtedly benefit from the on-site involvement of local teachers, principals, and others in structured learning experiences.

• *Document the learning.* As performing arts centers begin to exchange information on their K-12 education practices, the ability of teaching artists, teachers, and program coordinators to access a significant knowledge base will depend on their colleagues elsewhere having communicated their own successes (and disappointments).

• *Build sustained support* for these programs through targeted advocacy efforts. Just as students demonstrate their knowledge through performance, performing arts center leaders and their partners need to make visible the results of their education programs to decision makers and opinion makers—school-board and center-board members, elected officials, the media, and others.

Through the national forum and this publication, *Acts of Achievement: The Role of Performing Art Centers in Education* celebrates the considerable contributions of performing arts institutions to K-12 education in recent years. We are grateful to them for pursuing or supporting this important work, and we applaud their own acts of achievement that bring the performing arts into the lives of young people.

Artist Residencies:
Evolving Educational Experiences

By Lynne B. Silverstein

At schools, community centers, and arts venues across the nation, we see students choreographing and performing compositions guided by professional dancers, teachers learning methods to help students examine American history through theater, aspiring opera singers taking master classes, future stage managers helping to build sets, and the voices of middle school choruses rising because of their work with professional jazz vocalists. Such activities are all becoming increasingly familiar as artists come together with students and teachers for the purpose of learning in, through, and about the arts.

The programs that make these activities possible are referred to as "artist residencies"—direct interactions between artist and students, with their teachers in a school setting. They are developed by arts organizations in partnership with school administrators and teachers, and they supplement and extend schools' arts programs. Whether residencies consist of one visit or a series of visits across a week, a month, or several months, there are basic principles that apply to them all.

> ### "Arts organizations have responded by developing residencies that rely more and more on collaborative relationships with school-system administrators, teachers, and arts specialists..."

Artist residency programs as we now know them began during the 1960s,[i] and they continue to be a significant part of arts organizations' education programs today. For the 1998-99 school year 38 percent of public elementary schools reported that they hosted at least one short-term artist residency (one week or less) and 22 percent had hosted at least one longer residency. During the same school year, 34 percent of public secondary schools hosted at least one short-term residency and 18 percent hosted longer residencies.[ii]

Such residencies must necessarily be of high quality and relevant to schools' curricula. As accountability looms large, administrators and teachers are scrutinizing how student time is spent and how activities align with content standards; they are increasingly concerned with results—what students will know and be able to do. Arts organizations have responded by developing residencies that rely more and more on collaborative relationships with school-system administrators, teachers, and arts specialists in order to best reflect the system's priorities and ensure success.

Winning Hearts and Minds

Residencies have three distinct instructional purposes. (In practice, however, these same residencies may serve more than one purpose.)

To spark students' interest in the arts.
This is usually accomplished through "performance residencies" planned by artists in consultation with arts organizations, which work with teachers and in-school or school system arts specialists to align the performance residencies with applicable standards and students' learning needs.

Residencies have a variety of objectives. For example, performance residencies may introduce students to the collaborative nature of the performing arts, to the arts of a particular culture, or to the arts as a professional career. They may be organized as a sampler series of different art forms or as a series that introduces different genres within one art form. Series invite comparisons between or among the performances. Such residencies are strengthened by active student participation and the distribution in advance of printed or online materials that give students information about the artists, the art forms, and the performances they will see.

As defined in *Creating Capacity*,[iii] the artists who lead these residencies tend to be both "presenting artists" who perform for student audiences, and "interacting artists" who, through their performances or lecture-demonstrations, make connections to the curriculum and engage students in pre- or post-performance discussions or activities.

Characteristics of performance residencies include:

• A focus on a topic or theme related to specific goals

• A structure with a well-defined introduction, body, and conclusion

• Strategies for engaging students' curiosity and interest

• Guidance to students on what to look and listen for in the performance

• Clear, jargon-free language that does not assume specialized arts knowledge

• Instruction to help students learn their roles and responsibilities as audience members

• Opportunities for students to interact with performers

• Supplemental resource materials (e.g., print, Web site, compact discs) that prepare students and help teachers extend the learning in the classroom

Through technology, performance residencies extend their reach to wider audiences of students and teachers. Some performance residencies are broadcast, real time by satellite, to outlying sites throughout a state, region, or the nation. Provision for live question-and-answer sessions gives these hook-ups an interactive component. In addition, online bulletin boards provide forums for discussions among students, teachers, and performing artists.

To develop students' knowledge and skills in the arts and/or help them learn other subject areas through the arts.
These "in-classroom instructional residencies" are planned with or adapted to student needs identified by participating teachers. Although these residen-

cies have an indirect benefit for teachers, their primary focus is on students. The teaching artist provides instruction using specialized arts techniques generally outside the expertise of classroom teachers. By contrast, residencies focused on teachers' professional development (see below), teaching artists use and share techniques that can be replicated and adapted by teachers.

In-classroom instructional residencies focusing on particular art forms are intended to help students learn the creative process; acquire technical abilities; apply the arts process to other areas of study; and develop a variety of learning skills (such as practice, exploration and experimentation, reworking and revising ideas, getting feedback, and working collaboratively as well as independently). The residencies may be designed for students who have limited experience with the art form or for those who have achieved a certain level of expertise. The latter take the form of master classes or clinics, and are usually planned in collaboration with arts specialists.

In-classroom instructional residencies focusing on integrating arts with other parts of the curriculum meet objectives in both the art form and the subject area. In addition to art skills, they help develop students' learning skills (e.g., listening and concentration), social skills (cooperation and collaboration, for example), and emotional skills (such as empathy). The teaching artists who lead these residencies are "collaborating artists" or "master instructional artists."[iv] In addition to having the skills to perform and engage students in discussions, they work in partnership with school administrators and teachers to plan and lead appropriate instruction and assessment.

A school's first experience with a teaching artist provides an opportunity to become acquainted, begin to develop a trusting relationship, and understand the potential that residency work holds for engaging students in powerful learning. When successful, these initial residencies can lead to invitations for artists to return for future residencies in which they collaborate more fully with teachers. In addition, arts organizations are using technology to expand the reach of in-classroom instructional residencies. These "cyberspace instructional residencies" are linking teaching artists with students and teachers in distant locations.

Characteristics of in-classroom residencies include:

• Carefully developed plans to increase students' knowledge, skills, and appreciation of the arts

• Authentic connections between the arts and other areas of study

• Strategies that inspire and motivate students

• Hands-on opportunities that develop students' abilities to use the arts process confidently and creatively

• Use of appropriate art-form vocabulary

• Sound educational practices, such as accommodations for a variety of learning styles and intelligences, as well as questioning techniques that require higher-order thinking

• Learning activities that are age appropriate and interesting to students, clearly related to instructional goals and objectives, and appropriately sequenced to build students' knowledge and skill incrementally

To build teachers' capacity to teach in, through, and about the arts.
Teaching artists who lead residencies are increasingly being asked to include, or focus exclusively on, professional development—to raise teachers' awareness and enhance their knowledge and skills. Through professional development, teachers are able to continue using the arts on their own long after the residency is over.

Teaching artists plan professional development programs in collaboration with arts organization program staff, school district professional development specialists, school arts specialists, or university faculty. These residencies may include: workshops that provide an introduction to the teaching artist's upcoming interactions with students; courses that provide information and strategies for teaching in and through the arts, taking local, state, and national standards into account; teachers' application of what they've learned in workshops and courses to their classroom lesson/unit planning; and classroom "laboratory" opportunities in which teachers develop their arts teaching expertise with the teaching artist acting as mentor.[v] In some residencies, master teachers participate as reciprocal mentors for teaching artists.

Efforts to influence teacher attitudes and refine practice require time for building relationships between teacher and teaching artist, and time for practice, reflection, and transfer. As a result, programs focusing on professional development may include a series of opportunities within a year and across years. Professional development efforts are also supported by a variety of other activities: study groups in which teachers discuss related articles,

> **"Teaching artists who lead residencies are increasingly being asked to...raise teachers' awareness and enhance their knowledge and skills."**

videotapes, or books; networking sessions during which teachers share what they are learning; online data banks through which teachers share their successful lessons/units with others within or outside the school; and action research in the classroom. Teachers' participation in professional development is encouraged by the availability of in-service or university credit and public recognition of their efforts.

Teaching artists who lead professional development residencies are called "master instructional artists."[vi] They have similar skills as "presenting," "interacting," and "collaborating" artists but in addition have the ability to plan curriculum and teach teachers.

Characteristics of professional development residencies include:

• Enhancement of teachers' knowledge and appreciation of the arts

• Demonstration of connections between an art form and other parts of the curriculum

• A clear focus and careful planning

• Instructional examples targeted to the appropriate grade levels and aligned with state/local standards

• Examples of model classroom practice and reflection on that practice

• Active teacher involvement

- Opportunities to raise teachers' levels of confidence and comfort about including the arts in their teaching

- Resource materials to guide classroom practice

- Accommodations for the needs of teachers as adult learners [vii]

The Elements of Success

Ten factors are key to successful artist residencies: [viii]

1. Begin with a Reality Check.

Teachers, artists, and arts organization coordinators all bring assumptions and misconceptions to the table. Some beliefs have developed from negative encounters, while others have little foundation in personal experience but are simply accepted as true. Residencies are most successful when planners take their partners' assumptions and misconceptions about residencies into account; an understanding of the various perspectives allows planners to anticipate problems and develop strategies for addressing them.

The following assumptions and misconceptions, not uncommon among teachers, should be addressed: "talent" is mysteriously bestowed on some individuals rather than the result of learning, practice, commitment, and hard work; in a teacher/artist collaboration, the artist alone is the "creative expert"; residencies are fun but do not provide "real" learning; artists get students overexcited and ruin carefully established classroom practices.

Artists and arts organization coordinators also come to residencies with assumptions and misconceptions, which participants must deal with if they hope to be successful in their collaboration. Artists may assume that: participating teachers already see the value of residency for their students; teachers do not participate in the classroom because they do not care about the residency; their residency is the teacher's or school administrator's foremost concern; school schedules and routines are requirements for teachers but not for artists. Arts organization coordinators may assume that: residency artists and teachers already understand and support the residency's purpose and that their understandings are consistent; teachers have plenty of time to plan with residency artists; the teachers are the learners and the artists are the sole teachers.

2. Focus on Student Learning Needs.

Although the teaching artist is fundamental to the residency experience, residencies are student-centered, not artist-centered. Regardless of the residency's purpose, school objectives for student learning are the priority. Teaching artists' and arts organizations' residency plans, responsive to those needs, are drafted with results in mind: what will students know, be able to do, and appreciate as a result of participating in the residency? And during that residency, the focus remains on the students—what information they need to learn or skills to develop; how well they are learning; and their degree of mastery, level of confidence, and engagement with the work. Even in professional development residencies, the focus is still on student learning—what do teachers need to know, be able to do, and appreciate to help their students learn?

> "Although the teaching artist is fundamental to the residency experience, residencies are student-centered, not artist-centered."

3. Have Clear Purposes and Set Achievable Goals.

Successful residency programs are clear about their purposes—to spark students' interest, build students' knowledge and skills, or develop teacher capacity—and the partners jointly set realistic goals both short- and long-term. Meeting short-term goals provides a sense of accomplishment and progress, and gives impetus to future work. Meanwhile, keeping an eye on progress toward long-term goals supports thoughtful planning, self-assessment, and reflection; it also acknowledges and respects the amount of time required for programs to grow and mature. Having clear intent and setting achievable goals imbues the arts organization and its school partners with a common vision, helps to guide program decisions, and serves as a basis for evaluation.

4. Assure Effective Leadership and Support.
Successful residency programs are guided by leaders in arts organizations, schools, and school systems who are personally committed to the residency work, can articulate the program's benefits to a variety of constituencies, and can ensure an appropriate level of financial support. Effective leaders play various roles: visionary, strategist, facilitator, organizer, and taskmaster.

As visionaries, leaders understand the program's potential and what the partners can ultimately achieve. They motivate key people to give time and resources to support the work that will become an integral part of each organization's plans. As strategists, leaders develop both long- and short-term plans; aim at "targets of opportunity" as they arise; clearly identify the pluses and minuses of various plans; anticipate obstacles and proceed accordingly; and devise ways to institutionalize the residency programs in the school, school district, and arts organization.

As facilitators, leaders take into account all points of view and balance multiple needs; ensure joint action on key decisions so that every partner has a stake in carrying out the work; know how to seek input from, and provide support to, all involved; and enjoy the trust and respect of all partners. As organizers, leaders have a grasp of the day-to-day workings of residencies and arrange for systems that allow them to run effectively while keeping everyone's efforts coordinated. As taskmasters, leaders are persistent in holding individuals accountable for turning plans into realities.

5. Implement Careful Coordination and Effective Communication.
Although maintaining coordination and communication is a nuts-and-bolts job, it has powerful and far-reaching consequences that can enhance or undermine a residency's success. The arts organization and school coordinators must work together to maintain regular contact, solve unanticipated problems, and provide overall support to the artist and participating teachers. Whether school coordinators are teachers, administrators, or parents, they are the artists' ambassadors to the school. As such, their ability to set a positive tone and work collegially with all involved is critical.

Effective coordination and communication result in the residency artist feeling welcome at the school from Day One. Instead of facing blank stares upon arrival at a school, the teaching artist finds administrators, teachers, school secretaries, parents, and school custodians who know the purpose of the work, want to see the program succeed, and are willing to help ensure that the residency runs smoothly. Effective coordination and communication allows students, artists, and teachers to be focused so that learning is maximized.

6. Emphasize Teacher Participation and Teacher-Artist Collaboration.
Successful residencies rely on the active involvement of teachers in planning, implementation, and evaluation. Teachers' willingness to participate is increased when they:

• Have a role in determining the residency focus and selecting the artist

• Understand the benefits of the residency for student learning

• Are invited, rather than assigned, to participate

• Help plan the residency focus with the teaching artist

• Understand and agree to their roles and responsibilities

• Are asked to provide continual feedback to the teaching artist about the residency's progress

• Play a role in documenting the residency

• Enable the teaching artist to plan ways to assess student learning

• Assist in evaluating the residency

Teacher participation is positively influenced by the availability of well-conceived, appropriate resource materials that help teachers prepare students for residency experiences, lead lessons between artist's visits, and guide pre- and post-residency activities. Similarly, residencies benefit from involving school arts specialists (when available) in the project; their expertise and leadership are valuable additions.[ix]

Teacher-artist collaborations have powerful effects on attitudes as well as on instruction. When teachers and artists work together with mutual respect, they develop relationships in which they are valued colleagues who benefit from each other's advice and support. On a more personal level, teachers and artists report that collaboration decreases feelings of isolation; they each appreciate company on "the journey."

7. Make the Residency Visible and Develop Messages Tailored to a Variety of Needs.

A residency relies on support from numerous constituencies, and making its work visible to all of them is a critical requirement. But, visibility is considered strategically—it requires matching the audience with a message crafted for them.

Every residency has many "stories" to tell; deciding on which one, and for whom, are important strategic decisions. Activities such as family nights, showcases of student work, radio interviews, and receptions may be used to relate a selected story and tailor a message for a particular constituency. For example, in addressing such audiences as school officials, arts organization leaders, funders, or parents, the message(s) specifically crafted for them may stress the residency's impact on student learning, knowledge of the arts, development of learning skills, or growth in creativity, among other things.

Effective programs seek help from teachers, parents, university students, and others to document student learnng. They collect a variety of evidence, such as narrative descriptions of the residency; photographs or videotapes of program activities; examples of student work; interviews with students, teachers, and artists; and anecdotes.

8. Continually Refine Programs through Feedback, Assessment, and Evaluation.

Residency programs are strong when participants view their efforts, even well-established ones, as "works in progress." Continuing feedback, assessment of student growth, and evaluation from the perspective of artists, teachers, students, arts organization coordinators, school coordinators, and others are valuable in guiding improvement not only for the effectiveness of any one residency, but for the entire program.

Planning for systematic feedback and collection and review of data is critical. Regular assessments help residency programs determine to what extent the content and skills that artists thought they were teaching were indeed learned. Results help shape instruction. Securing these assessments can be as simple as embedding questions to students within lessons, making informal observations, or conducting interviews with students or parents.

9. Be Concerned with Impact.

Whether the teaching artist visits a school for a short performance residency, or an extended in-classroom instructional residency, planners want it to make a difference.

Residency programs are sometimes set in fertile ground and at other times in less welcoming environments. But it is no surprise that residencies have a greater impact if placed in schools where administration and staff members value the arts, school-improvement goals include the arts, there is an ongoing arts program, and a relationship with the arts organization or the artist already exists. When relationships are built and rapport and trust are established, the school's "readiness" is advanced and the potential impact of residencies increases.

The impact of performance residencies, for example, is heightened when program planners work together to link different artists into series or when performances are extended with in-classroom instruction led by the performing artists or local artists.

In-classroom instructional residencies increase their impact when teaching artists work with core groups of students. This is not always obvious to administrators, who typically plan their first in-classroom instructional residencies to serve as many students as possible. This leads to schedules that give only a little of the teaching artist's time to each of a large number of students—and results in reduced impact. But teaching artists report that school administrators soon come to realize how much more can be accomplished when core groups of students are able to work with the artist on a repeated and relatively intense basis.

Similarly, the impact of professional development residencies is enhanced when artists work with a critical mass of teachers—a subset of the faculty—from one school. This allows teachers to support each other by working collaboratively in their school thereafter to make a large enough improvement in practice that it attracts the attention and support of teaching colleagues and school administrators.

In addition to having fertile ground in which to "plant" the residency, linking individual visits into series, and working with core groups of students or teachers, impact is obviously influenced by program quality—both in artistry and teaching. In that spirit, there is growing recognition of the need to provide professional development for teaching artists themselves.

10. Work with Artists Who Have Expertise both in Their Art Form and Teaching.

In addition to manifesting artistic excellence, residency artists must be well versed in teaching and be able to establish positive relationships with students and teachers.

Successful teaching artists are clear about the purpose, goals, and objectives of the residency and are well-prepared. They are familiar with related curriculum and content standards and are able to design residency sessions and assessments, understand students' developmental stages, use questioning strategies that engage students in higher levels of thinking, motivate and actively involve students, and effectively manage student behavior (whether as audience members or in the classroom). The artists participate in professional development programs that assist them in furthering their understanding of education, and they keep up with current research in various theories and models of arts education.[x]

Teaching artists possess positive attitudes. They encourage the expression of ideas, are open to different points of view, have a sense of humor, and are optimistic, flexible, and patient. They have high expectations and throughout the residency give stu-

dents and teachers numerous opportunities to reflect on and improve their work. Teaching artists care deeply about young people and their instructors, are enthusiastic about working with them, and seek ways to empower them. Teaching artists have respect for teachers as professional colleagues who can play an important role in bringing the arts to students. They work collaboratively and collegially with teachers, invite feedback, and make appropriate adjustments to residency plans based on that feedback. The teaching artist works with the partnering teacher to plan for and assess student progress, and uses assessment results to further improve the teaching plan.

Making the Arts Central to Learning

In sum, artist residencies are designed to meet one or more purposes: to spark students' interest in the arts through performance series, to develop students' knowledge and skills in and through the arts by means of in-classroom instruction, and to develop teachers' capacity to include the arts in their teaching with the aid of professional-development efforts.

As residency purposes vary, so too, do the skills that artists need to lead them. Arts organizations that offer residency programs thus recognize the critical need for the continuing professional development of teaching artists.[xi] Many arts organizations are working on their own or in collaboration with school systems, arts service organizations, or universities to develop initiatives for strengthening the knowledge and skills of experienced teaching artists as well as of artists who are new to residency work.

Residency programs that have clear purposes, and that rely on the expertise of skilled teaching artists who work in partnership with teachers, can contribute greatly to making the arts central to learning. As education reform efforts open doors, arts organizations must be ready and clear about what artist residencies can accomplish and certain about the skills of those they entrust to implement their programs.

Appendix to "Artist Residencies"
Artist Residency Checklists

Here are four checklists,[xii] one each for arts organization coordinators, artists, teachers, and school coordinators. The checklists are written for in-classroom instructional residencies and should thus be adapted to meet the needs of performance residencies or professional development residencies.

Checklist for Arts Organization Coordinators

1. Select Residency Artists

• Establish criteria. Observe artists doing what they will be hired to do. Invite other teaching artists in your program to help assess their work.

2. Secure commitments

• Begin early. School budgets and plans are often set during the winter/spring of the previous school year.

• Identify school partners and plan residency programs that meet their needs. Some schools may apply to participate; applicants should describe school needs and how a particular residency will help them address those needs.

• Sign letters of agreement with school administrators that outline respective school and arts organization responsibilities, and indicate the residency artist, the residency program, the date and time.

• Assume change in school staffing. Before the new school year, check to see if the same teachers and administrators with whom you signed letters of agreement, are at the school. If there is a new principal or new teachers, provide information and garner support. If necessary, sign a new letter of agreement.

• Prepare a list of responsibilities for the school residency coordinator; discuss with principal the qualifications for the school coordinator; ask principal to designate the coordinator.

3. Meet with the principal, school coordinator, and other key individuals (e.g., parents, arts specialists) to:

• Do a reality check; ensure understanding and agreement about the residency purposes and procedures.

• Discuss/clarify coordinator's responsibilities.

• Ask the principal to make arrangements for interested teachers to self-select for residency participation. (As the residency progresses and news of its success spreads, other teachers will ask to be included the next time).

• Agree to use the best methods for communication among principal, arts organization coordinator, school coordinator, artist, and teachers.

• Discuss the value of the artist working with core groups of students and how it impacts scheduling.

• Confirm planning time for teacher and artist. Consider possibilities for leveraging time through schedule adjustments or other methods.

• Provide time during the residency for teacher and artist to engage in ongoing dialogue to evaluate how well the residency is meeting their objectives and to plan adjustments.

• Plan for a school-wide orientation to clarify residency objectives and activities.

• Arrange for principal to attend residency activities.

4. Do a Reality Check with Artists

• Ensure that artists understand the residency purposes and plans.

5. Attend to Residency Content

• Share your expectations with artists about residency design.

• Review and provide feedback on residency plans. Assist in further development, as needed.

• Observe residencies in progress. Determine to what extent the instruction correlates with initial and revised plans.

6. Arrange for Effective Communication

• Prepare a summary of residency information. Include such things as residency title, artist name, residency dates, and contact information for participating teachers, arts organization coordinator, and school coordinator.

• Agree to the best methods and timing for communication.

• Contact school coordinator regularly about residency needs and progress.

7. Attend to Logistics

• Discuss logistical needs with artist and communicate them to school coordinator.

• Check back with school coordinator to determine if there are any problems in securing needed resources/materials/equipment.

• Review schedules prepared by school coordinator.

• Arrange for timely payments to artists.

8. Be Visible and Helpful

• Visit programs and observe their progress.

• Check in regularly. Talk to the participating teachers, school coordinator, artist, and principal. Ask them how things are going and listen to their answers. Help solve problems.

9. Make the Program Visible

Working with principal, school coordinator, teachers, and artist:

• Plan ways to identify which residency "stories" to tell and to whom to tell them.

• Design messages targeted to various constituencies.

• Plan a variety of strategies for delivering the targeted messages.

• Determine methods of program documentation.

• Prepare "messengers."

10. Provide Professional Development Opportunities for Teaching Artists

• Plan and implement orientations for residency artists.

• Assess artists' needs and create appropriate professional development opportunities that draw on the expertise of master instructional artists within your program, the school district, or universities.

11. Plan and Implement Program Assessment and Evaluation

• With school partner, plan appropriate evaluation measures that collect information from a variety of perspectives.

• Encourage participating teachers, school coordinator, and artist to self-assess their work in the residency program.

• Review and analyze self-assessments and other evaluation results with school partner.

• Hold a post-residency evaluation discussion with the artist. Invite the artist to talk about his or her self-assessment and together review evaluation results. Discuss ways to improve the residency.

• Communicate evaluation results.

Checklist for Artists

1. Do a Reality Check: Clarify Expectations

• Compare your understanding of the residency with that of the arts organization. Identify any discrepancies.

• Contact participating teachers to introduce yourself and express your excitement about the upcoming residency. Ask about their understanding of the residency. Clarify, if needed. Tell teachers you are interested in developing the residency with their help. Arrange for time to plan.

2. Conduct Residency Planning Sessions with Teachers

• Find out what students are studying and work with teachers to plan ways the residency can help meet student needs. Discuss possible curriculum connections and borrow resources (e.g., textbooks and teacher guides) that will provide information about the related content area. If the residency focuses on integrating the arts with another subject, clarify that the arts are disciplines with content and skills that are learned along with other curriculum content.

- Develop realistic plans.

- Identify ways to work with teachers in assessing student learning on a steady basis.

- Find out if there are students with special needs. Determine if any accommodations are needed.

- Discuss your expectations for teacher participation. Will the teacher be expected to: participate with the students, provide feedback about student progress, document the residency, help assess student learning, help with classroom management/discipline, and lead agreed-upon activities between artist visits?

- Find out about established classroom rules and, if appropriate, discuss needed adjustments.

- Develop resource materials for teachers or students that will help them prepare for the residency as well as lead or participate in learning activities between and after residency sessions.

3. Get to Know the School; Attend to Logistics

- Get an orientation to the school facility and check the residency locations.

- Meet key people. Introduce yourself to the school residency coordinator, the school support staff who are important sources of information to others in the school, and also the school custodian, who can help you with access to rooms, equipment, and materials.

- Confirm schedules and requirements with school coordinator. Check back regularly with school coordinator and teachers for schedule changes.

- Recognize that teachers are extremely busy. Whenever possible, arrange for logistical details on your own.

4. Communication and Coordination

- Make plans with school coordinator for the most effective ways to provide residency information to teachers, school administration, office personnel, and support staff.

- Get contact information from arts organization coordinator for all key people.

5. Invite Feedback on an Ongoing Basis

- Regularly assess with teachers how the residency is progressing. Invite teacher observations about both class and individual-student progress; adjust plans as needed.

- Regularly invite questions from teachers.

6. Document the Residency

- Make plans with teachers, school coordinator, and arts organization coordinator for ways to document the residency. Select together the most appropriate plans and agree to responsibilities.

7. Respect Established School Procedures

- Learn about the school procedures (e.g., bell schedules, lunch times, security sign-in at the school, parking) and respect them.

- Follow school schedules.

8. Participate in Residency Evaluation

- During the residency, keep notes about what activities worked well and how they could be strengthened.

- Prepare a self-assessment of your residency. Discuss it with the arts organization coordinator.

- Complete residency evaluations.

Checklist for Teachers

1. Do a Reality Check: Clarify Expectations

- Compare your understanding of the residency with that of the artist.

2. Assist in Residency Planning

- Get acquainted with the artist. Start by introducing yourself.

- Assist in planning residency goals and objectives that meet student learning needs; identify possible curriculum connections.

- Suggest ways to assess student learning throughout the residency.

• Share information about students with special needs. Discuss appropriate adaptations.

• Describe classroom rules and expectations. Find out if the residency work will require adjustments to rules.

• Clarify your role during the residency. What type of participation is expected: Participating with students? Helping students make connections to other areas of study? Leading activities before/during/after the residency? Documenting the residency? Helping assess student learning? Assisting with classroom management?

• Discuss schedule and logistics.

3. Attend to Communication and Coordination

• Confirm with school coordinator that other teachers, school administration, office personnel, and support staff are informed about the residency.

• Get contact information for all key people.

• Check back regularly with school coordinator and artist about schedule changes.

• Arrange to meet regularly with the artist to discuss residency progress.

4. Make the Most of the Time that Students Have with the Artist

• Prepare students for the residency. Provide information about the artist; explain the purpose of the residency, and what students will learn.

• Maximize teaching time with artist by preparing students and having the room set up before artist arrives.

• If the residency is not conducted in the classroom, bring your class to the location prior to the start time so that the work proceeds on schedule.

• Clean up and re-set furniture after the artist leaves.

5. Participate in the Residency

• Participate as agreed upon during planning with the artist. Will you participate with the students? Document the residency? Help assess student learning? Help with classroom management/discipline? Lead agreed-upon activities prior to or between artist visits?

6. Provide Feedback to the Artist about Student Progress

• Share your observations about how the residency is progressing (i.e., what students understand, where they need further explanation).

7. Make the Residency Visible

• Plan ways to make the residency visible to other teachers as well as to parents and the community. Think about which residency "stories" are significant to tell and to whom to tell them.

• Select ways to document the stories (e.g., photographs, videotaped interviews with students, descriptions of lessons and interactions, journals in which students record experiences at each session).

• Determine the most appropriate ways to tell the stories (e.g., a bulletin board "message center" about the residency, letters to parents describing what their children are learning, invitations to attend special residency events, a post-residency showcase of student work accompanied by descriptions of the learning that resulted in the work, articles for school or school-district newsletters).

8. Get Something for Yourself

• Document what you are learning throughout the residency. Take notes about each lesson, the skills taught, the processes used, the vocabulary. Reflect on how you might use this knowledge in your classroom in the future.

9. Participate in Residency Evaluation

• During the residency, keep notes about what activities worked well, what didn't, and how they all could be strengthened.

• Do a self-assessment of your role in the residency; review it with the arts organization coordinator.

• Complete residency evaluations.

Checklist for School Coordinators

1. Check Assumptions

• Check that your understanding of the residency's purposes is consistent with that of the arts organization coordinator.

2. Plan with Principal and Arts Organization Coordinator

• Review your responsibilities related to residency coordination.

• Help plan the residency schedule.

• Agree to best methods for communication between you and the arts organization coordinator with the artist.

• Assist principal in making arrangements for interested teachers to participate as a result of self-selection rather than assignment.

• Aid principal in making arrangements for artist-teacher planning time before the residency. Consider possibilities for leveraging time through schedule adjustments or other methods.

• Facilitate arrangements for ongoing artist-teacher feedback and planning during the residency.

3. Draft Schedules and Arrange for Logistics

• Speak to arts organization coordinator and artist about scheduling, space, and materials needs. Draft schedule. Make arrangements for appropriate space and materials.

• Orient artist to the school facility and residency locations.

• Provide information to artist about school schedules and protocols.

• Check with artist about needs throughout the residency.

4. Communication: Keep Everyone Informed Before and Throughout

• Make plans for a school-wide orientation to inform everyone about residency objectives and activities.

• Keep everyone at the school continually informed about the residency's progress.

• Update participating teachers about schedule changes.

5. Be the Artist's Ambassador to the School

• Get to know the artist. Introduce him or her to school staff and members of the community through a variety of means (e.g., meet-the-artist reception, orientation session at staff meeting).

• Maintain a positive tone.

• Keep tabs on how things are going. Anticipate problems and find creative solutions to address participants' needs.

6. Help to Make the Residency Visible

• Develop plans with the artist, teachers, and arts organization coordinator to make the residency visible to other teachers, parents, and the community. Help select residency "stories" that are significant and decide to whom to tell them.

• Create ways to document the stories (e.g., photographs, videotaped interviews with students, descriptions of lessons and interactions, journals in which students' record experiences at each session).

• Determine with others the most appropriate ways to tell the stories (e.g., a bulletin board "message center" about the residency, letters to parents describing what their children are learning, invitations to attend special residency events, a post-residency showcase of student work accompanied by descriptions of the learning that resulted in the work, articles for school or school-district newsletters).

7. Participate in Residency Assessment and Evaluation

• Keep notes about what went well during the residency, what didn't, and what aspects would benefit from changes.

• Do a self-assessment of your work as coordinator. Review it with the arts-organization coordinator and your principal.

• Complete residency evaluations.

"Artist Residencies" Notes

Thanks to the following people for sharing ideas and resources related to residencies:

Jane Polin, Dana Foundation advisor; Derek E. Gordon, Senior Vice President, The John F. Kennedy Center for the Performing Arts; Linda Bamford, North Carolina Arts Council; Eric Booth, arts and education consultant and teaching artist; Kimberli Boyd, teaching artist, Dancing Between the Lines; Sherilyn Brown, Rhode Island State Council on the Arts; Deb Brzoska, arts and education consultant; Chris Cowan, Maui Arts and Cultural Center; Amy Duma, The Kennedy Center; Karen Erickson, teaching artist, Creative Directions of Illinois; Miriam Flaherty, Wolf Trap Institute for Early Learning Through the Arts; Doug Herbert, National Endowment for the Arts; Lenore Blank Kelner, teaching artist, InterAct Story Theatre; Sean Layne, teaching artist; Kathi Levin, The Kennedy Center; Greg McCaslin, The Center for Arts Education; Jeanette McCune, The Kennedy Center; Beck McLaughlin, Montana Arts Council; Jan Norman, Young Audiences; Joan Robinson, The Flynn Center for the Performing Arts; R. Virginia Rogers, The Kennedy Center; Debbie Shannon, The Kentucky Center; Barbara Shepherd, The Kennedy Center, Jenni Taylor Swain, Walton Arts Center; and Ellen Westkaemper, The Peace Center for the Performing Arts.

i Jane Remer, "Artist-Educators In Context: A Brief History of Artists in K-12 American Public Schooling," *Teaching Artist Journal*, 1, (2) (2003): 71-72.

ii U.S. Department of Education, National Center for Educational Statistics. *Arts Education in Public Elementary and Secondary Schools: 1999-2000. Nancy Carey*, Brian Kleiner, Rebecca Porch, and Elizabeth Farris. Project Officer: Shelley Burns. (Washington, DC: NCES, 2002) 5, 37.

iii Melissa Ford Gradel, *Creating Capacity: A Framework for Providing Professional Development Opportunities for Teaching Artists*, (Washington DC: The John F. Kennedy Center for the Performing Arts, 2001) 11-15.

iv Gradel, 11-15.

v Laura Lipton and Bruce Wellman, *Mentoring Matters: A Practical Guide to Learning-Focused Relationships*, (Sherman, CT: MiraVia, 2001)

vi Gradel, 11-15.

vii Teaching artists recognize that teachers expect respect for their maturity and experience; prefer to be active in learning situations; prefer learning experiences relate to classroom realities and be immediately applicable; prefer to collaborate with their peers; prefer to engage in self-evaluation; and expect comfortable learning environments. Lynne B. Silverstein, Barbara Shepherd, and Amy Duma, *Partners in Education: Building Partnerships for Teachers' Professional Development in the Arts* (Washington, DC: The Kennedy Center. 2001) 11.

viii A number of the success factors are consistent with descriptions of successful partnerships included in works by Dreeszen and Seidel and Maryann Marrapodi, *Promising Practices: The Arts and School Improvement* (NY: The Center for Arts Education, 2000).

ix Remer. 298.

x Carol Ponder, "The Dual Career of Teaching Artists," *Creating Capacity: A Framework for Providing Professional Development for Teaching Artists* (Washington, DC: The John F. Kennedy Center for the Performing Arts, 2001) 17-18.

xi Judith M. Burton, "Natural Allies, Part 2: Children, Teachers and Artists," in Remer. 391-321.

xii Residency Checklists are adapted from a variety of residency guides and from conversations: *Arts Residency Handbook for Teachers, Arts Residency Handbook for Artists*, and *Arts; Activities Handbook for Project Coordinators, 2002-2003*. (New York: P.S. 107, 2002); *Artist-in-Residence Grants, 2002-2003* (Greenville, SC: The Peace Center for the Performing Arts, 2002); *Residency Planning Guide* (North Carolina Arts Council, 2000); *Ohio State Arts Council's Arts in Education Handbook*, online at www.oac.state.oh.us/aie/handbook.html; *Resource Manual: Artists in the Schools and Communities*, (Montana Arts Council); *An Artist in our Midst: Kentucky's Artists in Residence Programs and What Makes then Work, FY 2003-2004*. (Frankfort, KY: Kentucky Arts Council, 2003)

Interview Excerpts:
Simmons and Safire

Excerpts from an interview by William Safire, chairman of the Dana Foundation, with Warren Simmons, executive director of the Annenberg Institute for School Reform, Brown University. The interview was the keynote at the symposium, "Acts of Achievement," April 10, 2003.

William Safire: How do you see the study of, or the participation in, the performing arts in a school? How does it help a student do better in school? Or does it?

Warren Simmons: I think there's lots of evidence that the arts have a very positive impact on learning, but it is not evidence that you can glean from cheap, large-scale standardized tests. As long as we continue to use large-scale assessments and standardized tests as the primary, if not the sole, basis for determining when learning is occurring, we're going to have difficulty showing the impact and effectiveness of the arts. I think standards-based reform, as a movement, began by saying that large-scale assessments should only be one of the indicators, and that there was a need for multiple indicators and forms of evidence to demonstrate learning. The opportunity now, at the local level at least, is to talk about the indicators and evidence that you would put alongside of standardized tests to make the convincing argument that the arts produce learning.

Safire: If standardized tests are only a small part of the answer, what's the big part?

Simmons: What *A Nation At Risk* did was to paint the challenge of urban school reform—and school reform at large—as one that was a threat to the nation's economy. While certainly economic well-being is one important purpose for education, there are others that are equally as important. When you surface the economic purpose as singular, and when you hold schools accountable for achievement that spurs on the economy, I think you tend to focus on subjects that are directly related in our minds to economic well-being, which leads you to mathematics and reading.

There are other purposes that people are attending to, and have always attended to, in education. Education should be an effort that strengthens our democracy; that should equip citizens with the skills they need to participate effectively and make informed choices. Education should contribute to cultural well-being; it should allow us all to feel we can not only participate in our mainstream culture and home cultures, but also help construct that culture itself.

If we broaden the lens or use multiple lenses, we'll make it clearer to people that the arts are a fundamental discipline for what it means to be a competent, effective person; and we need to emphasize that the arts have both direct and indirect effects on learning.

Safire: How about when you were a student?

Simmons: By doing work in the arts and progressing, it helped me understand that through discipline, through practice, and through adequate support, I could do well in the arts. And that gave me the confidence and understanding that through discipline, practice, and hard work, I could do well in mathematics and literacy as well.

In cognitive science we would call what my arts education did was to give me a stronger set of meta-cognitive skills. The arts helped me understand how to monitor, how to be evaluated, how to develop my own learning. And by doing so, I was able to transfer my meta-cognitive skills and awareness to my mathematics, to my English language, or to my social studies.

Also, the arts helped me understand that achievement was effort-based, not just ability-based. That is, I thought that you had to be naturally good at mathematics. And I wasn't naturally good at mathematics, in part, because I didn't do my homework. But I didn't do my homework because I thought you had to be naturally good at it. What arts education emphasizes is you come with some talent, but in order to realize that talent, you have to practice. Once I understood that in the arts, it was easier for me to understand that though I was initially struggling with mathematics, practice had a good deal to do with heightening my achievement.

Safire: That's the old story of the Texan who was walking down 57th Street in New York City and says to a little man, "Excuse me, can you tell me how I get to Carnegie Hall?" And he replies, "Practice, practice."

We've got people here who are on the frontlines of getting audiences into performance halls. What can they do that will help arts education?

Simmons: Urban schools are beset by multiple reform initiatives right now, and I'll give them some labels. There continues to be the current version of standards-based reform, with an emphasis on increased assessment. We have to get all children to high standards. Next, the Gates Foundation is encouraging many communities to invest in taking large schools and dividing them up into small learning communities, or creating autonomous small schools with inter-disciplinary curriculum. A third strand of work is growing out of the recognition that school reform will never be taken to all schools if we approach it school by school and classroom by classroom. In addition to transforming schools, we also have to transform the systems that govern schools.

The question is not just what kinds of schools do we need, but what kinds of school systems. We have to think about and help communities build a local education support system. Not just redesigning the district as it currently exists with a central office, but thinking about all the resources that are available in the community, and how you create an infrastructure that coordinates those resources so that young people have pathways of continuous learning, both in and out of school.

The performing arts community has to figure out how to think about itself and organize itself as part of a larger system that provides continuous supports for the arts and other forms of development as part of school-based activities and community-based activities. It's the most exciting opportunity to join top-down reform with bottoms-up reform, and have the two be mutually reinforcing.

What I have in mind is what the Rhode Island Governor's Task Force on Literacy in the Arts did on behalf of the state and local communities. First, you map the arts resources that are available in the community—their quality, their quantity, their nature—and you map the needs of the schools. Then you develop funding and coordination mechanisms so that schools, no matter where they're located and what communities they serve, have access to support from arts specialists to integrate the arts in the schools; and students have access to arts opportunities out of school in a systematic way, not in the episodic way that work occurs now. That's going to require cities and funders to rethink funding streams and how they can be combined, and rethink governing structures so that people in school systems and community-based organizations can align strategic planning. And also rethink all of this based on a vision of what it should look like on the ground, not based on a vision of a policy maker or researcher, who can come up with a vision very quickly, but it wouldn't be customized and suitable in local communities.

How do you organize communities to get policymakers to devote time and attention to this work? How do you build evidence that would allow you to improve practice? When I brought together a group of funders, they realized that one of the mistakes we've made in education reform is that we've invested a lot in evaluation studies. What evaluation studies do is give a grant to somebody who watches what you do for about three years and never says anything. At the end, they show you all the mistakes you've made, which is not a good use of resources. So what reformers and philanthropists now understand is that, in addition to doing evaluation studies, they need to do documentation studies, where researchers work along with practitioners, and share lessons along the way, so that you can modify practice.

Warren Simmons, executive director of the Annenberg Institute for School Reform, and William Safire, chairman of the Dana Foundation, in discussion during the keynote at the "Acts of Achievement" symposium, April 2003.

Safire: I would think that the rise in violence in schools cannot be cured by the introduction of more performance art in schools. I think it would be far more deeply influenced by public disapproval of violence on television, not censorship of it, but just a wrinkling up of a lot of parents' noses at kids watching or playing those violent games on video equipment. But you have a different view?

Simmons: A complementary view. There are multiple sources and reasons for a rise in violence in schools, and one of them has to do with the sense of cultural alienation that you have when you don't experience efficacy. So, if you are in an environment where you experience nothing but failure early on, one response is to withdraw and one response is to depersonalize your relationship with not only the adults in that community, but also with other youth in that community. I think that it is far more difficult to engage in violence when you feel effective and when you feel connected. And I think what the arts do is that they create heterogeneous learning communities.

When I was in my academic courses, I was usually the only African-American in the room. When I was in the arts and music and recreational activities, the community was far more diverse. As a result, I felt safer and people felt more accepting

of me. Academic divisions that cause alienation or lack of efficacy underscore and support violence. Anything that schools can do to create cultural well-being and connectedness, especially through the arts, has a positive impact on reducing violence.

Safire: The arts can have an impact on the mood of schools. Right after September 11th, dancers from the Martha Graham Center performed "Lamentations" in New York City schools. The Dana Foundation and other foundations chipped into The New York Times Foundation, which went out to arts groups, who then sent artists into schools to let kids see and participate in dramatic performances that helped them confront the crisis.

Simmons: What I did not get in my arts education was an understanding of how I could continue in the arts as a profession, even though I wasn't going to be a performing artist playing the viola. I think the extent to which we can help children understand the arts and all of its performance aspects—business, political, legal—would allow students to, first of all, make more connections between the arts and other areas of the curriculum. But we would also allow them to see ways in which they can continue to work in the arts, though perhaps not as a performing artist.

Safire: We've got a question here on funding this work.

Simmons: I think what the larger foundations have done is recognize that their investments have to be made over a longer period of time, and so they have stretched from three-year grants to five-year grants and beyond. What they have also recognized is that external funding is no substitute for adequate resources for education. A number of them (foundations) are turning their attention to the issue of school finance equity. As we approach the 50th anniversary of Brown vs. Board of Education, I know foundations that are interested in organizing national and local conversations about the local vision for schools and education, which occur not just in schools, but also in the community. How can that vision be resourced, and what is the local, state, and federal contribution to that effort? Funders had this model that if they just invested in exemplars and demonstrations, then the existence proofs would lead to adequate funding. This has not been the case, which means that we have to mobilize and organize ourselves to be advocates for adequate funding. The existence proof, in and of itself, doesn't guarantee the support. Most urban systems and schools are inundated with solutions. So, one issue is how do you build a consensus about prioritization, given limited resources?

Safire: You touched on something earlier of what presenters and people who are interested in the arts can do for education. And that is to rally community support for greater public support of the schools.

Simmons: I would say it's a rallying of community support for a new vision of learning, and the need to not only transform schools, but also examine all community resources. I think that's what New York City is on the verge of doing. If you look at their small schools effort, they are attempting to design small schools that are operated in partnership with community-based organizations. Now they realize in order to pull that off, they will have to have a system for identifying community organizations that have the wherewithal to operate either individual schools or networks of schools. They have to have a system to adequately resource those organizations, because they can't do it with just their grant dollars. That notion of creating a portfolio of schools that works in partnership with community organizations is forcing them to rethink the larger system.

Safire: What about the use of dramatic and poetic and musical techniques in teaching other academic courses?

Simmons: One of the challenges we face is this issue of how you create a K-12 developmental progression that is not what I would call a curriculum, but rather a curriculum framework that specifies what kinds of learning activities support learning through the arts versus learning in the arts. I've experienced being in the divisive, dichotomized, polarized battle about whether it should be at all times learning in the arts versus learning through the arts. I think that it is both, and in other discipline areas, it's always been both.

We're moving away from the notion of tracking, but we also have to understand how in the arts you need to have a curriculum framework that helps community and school people arrange the learning activities. At all levels, we need to provide some activities that are relative to the core curriculum of learning through the arts, while also allowing for the existence of learning in the arts.

I don't understand why this is easier for us to think about in sports than in almost any other discipline. If you think about the sports infrastructure, you have opportunities for students in elementary, middle and high school—both in school and out of school—for people who are very talented to get very intensive recreational support and development. At the same time, we give opportunities to those who have the interest, but not necessarily the talent, to continue to engage in sports at any level of interest and ability for the rest of their lives, on into adulthood. Those kinds of infrastructures exist. Somehow, that's easier for us to figure out how to do with recreation. We get into battles when we think about the same kind of infrastructures in mathematics, science, and certainly in the arts.

CASE STUDIES

*Following are in-depth examinations
of eight Performing Art Centers
and their role in education.*

Scottsdale Center for the Arts

Scottsdale, AZ   www.scottsdalearts.org

- School districts served per year: 15
- Elementary schools served per year: 38
- High schools served per year: 18
- K-12 students served per year: 31,000

CASE STUDY

The mission of the Scottsdale Center for the Arts is to present high quality traditional and contemporary arts to the citizens of Scottsdale, Maricopa County, and the State of Arizona; create events of worldwide interest; offer opportunities for audiences to have thought provoking experiences and interactions with artists and speakers; and foster creative expression, diversity in thought, and awareness of cultural heritage.

The Scottsdale Center is proud of its long history of administering arts education programs, in particular, and attributes its success to three factors:

• *Establishing trust and building foundations.* The Center recognizes the critical importance of bridging cultural barriers by securing participants' confidence.

• *Flexibility and adaptability.* In response to the changing constraints on school systems, staff members continually seek alternative, creative ways to accomplish program goals.

• *Tenacity and persistence.* Program leaders' commitment and steady efforts help ensure that good ideas become useful realities.

Intercultural Project with Native American Students

The centerpiece of the Scottsdale Center's outreach program is the longstanding relationship with the Salt River Pima Maricopa Indian Community. Although rich urban Scottsdale and the neighboring Indian farming community had mistrusted each other for generations, in 1994 the Scottsdale Center approached the tribe as an apolitical entity offering an intercultural project to bring Native American and Scottsdale students together through Circus Arts. Out of that humble beginning, a community dialogue between city and tribal officials has been established.

Over time the Circus Arts project has grown. Today teaching artists work with every student at Salt River Community schools in residencies of three to eight weeks, during which students develop original writing and photography, compose and record lyrics, and learn storytelling. Hundreds of students have participated in these residency projects over the years, spending time in activities that direct them toward positive behaviors and cultural pride.

Professional Development for Teachers

Participatory workshops (providing re-certification credit), in which educator teams learn about techniques for integrating the arts in their content areas and across the curriculum, are now offered to all 75 teachers and aides at Salt River Schools. During the next phase of workshops, visual and performing teaching artists will partner with traditional Native American artists who work in the same arts discipline. In this way, Native arts may also be introduced across the curriculum.

Following the Salt River model of working with middle school teachers, the Scottsdale Center has developed a relationship with Sacaton Middle School in the Gila River Indian Community. Serving the teaching staff in these Indian communities, the arts programs are designed to help teachers improve student self-confidence and self-esteem and prepare them to mainstream into the society-at-large.

Arts Workshops for Hispanic Students

Scottsdale is recognized for its lush golf courses and posh resorts, but all too frequently those residents responsible for the upkeep of the hospitality industry are forgotten. The Paiute Neighborhood Center was Scottsdale's first neighborhood enhancement center providing services to a primarily Hispanic population. The Scottsdale Center has worked hand-in-hand with Paiute to offer arts workshops to youth at the teen center and at after school and

PAIUTE NEIGHBORHOOD CENTER

Paiute Neighborhood Center Day Program Summer 2002 – Mask-making

summer programs. Last year 130 neighborhood youngsters, ages 6-18, participated on multiple occasions in 11 workshops (each of them three to six weeks in length) in mask making, theater, art, dance, and creative writing. Parents remark how these workshops build a sense of self-worth and cultural pride in youth who, away from the country of their birth, frequently feel disenfranchised.

Within this same Hispanic neighborhood, new summer programs are being offered to students transitioning from middle to high school. Camps Coronado and Guadalupe complement morning summer school classes with afternoon workshops in theater, creative writing, and photography. Beyond instruction in the subject at hand, these workshops are also designed to improve students' life skills in such areas as interpersonal communication, decision making, goal setting, problem solving, and conflict resolution. In addition, working collaboratively on a unified theme (e.g., community pride) with mutually established goals has also benefited teaching artists, who expect to continue working in this format.

"Cultural Connections Through the Arts"

The startling recognition that "fear of each other" is common to white Scottsdale and inner city Phoenix students alike motivated the Center to develop its signature program, Cultural Connections Through the Arts. The year 2003 marks the 13th season of this program in which the arts promote racial tolerance, multicultural understanding, and friendship among high school students of diverse backgrounds. Since its inception, more than 2,400 students have participated. Recognizing the benefits for students and the community-at-large, a similar program was started in 2001 for middle school youngsters in six Scottsdale Boys and Girls Clubs. The program brings Hispanic, Indian, and Scottsdale Anglo clubs together to celebrate diversity and explore cross-cultural similarities through photography, creative writing, and theater arts. More than 150 young people participated during the 2002-2003 school year. A comparable activity will begin shortly with area YMCA programs.

Artist Residencies

Each performance season, the Scottsdale Center identifies at least one national or international artist or company to lead a one-week residency. Program partners (e.g., schools, school districts, or community or social service agencies) are fully involved in the planning process, and the result is that artists are placed in schools, communities, or after school programs where they are best suited and will provide the most benefit to participating youth. For example, the Cleo Parker Robinson Dance Ensemble recently undertook such a residency in the Gila River Indian Community. There the Dance Ensemble worked with middle school students on basic dance vocabulary, development of self-confidence and poise, and appreciation of diversity. Students then attended the Ensemble's matinee performance at the Center, followed by a workshop in a professional environment on stage. Additionally, the Ensemble met with middle school faculty members for discussions about the challenges of teaching on a rural reservation and ways to integrate the arts into the curriculum.

Children with Disabilities; Children in Early Childhood Programs

Diversity at the Scottsdale Center for the Arts is not limited to ethnicity and economics. The annual Celebration of the Arts for Children with Disabilities, which includes student participation in a variety of arts workshops during a half-day outdoor event, serves more than 500 children with special needs and their teachers. In addition, the Scottsdale Center hosts the Arizona Wolf Trap program (a regional presentation of the Wolf Trap Institute for Early Learning Through the Arts) to bring the arts into the lives of children in Head Start programs.

Performances for Student Audiences

School performances offer nationally known artists to K-12 audiences. During the 2002-03 season, 25,000 students attended productions at the Scottsdale Center that included Momix, Ballet

Senegal, Mark Morris, *The Belle of Amherst*, and Alvin Ailey. Students in the Scottsdale Unified School District attend courtesy of the parent-run Arts-in-Education Council, which raises funds to support annual attendance by every student in grades one through eight. And as part of the Scottsdale Center's continuing emphasis on making the arts accessible to all members of society, selected Center performances are sign language interpreted for patrons with hearing impairments and audio-described for patrons with low vision or blindness.

Arts Advocacy

The Scottsdale Arts Breakfast serves youth in the community, but in an indirect manner, by focusing on the importance and impact of arts-in-education programs. The Arts Breakfast, served on stage at the Scottsdale Center for the Arts, is a biannual event that is co-sponsored by the Center, the Scottsdale Museum of Contemporary Art, and the Arizona Alliance for Arts Education. Its primary focus is to encourage community leaders, educators, and administrators to support arts education in their communities and to provide them with appropriate tools. The Arts Breakfast features a speech by the Mayor as well as student performances and demonstrations.

Summer Arts Camps

Although school-based arts programming diminishes during the summer months, activities at the Center do not. An annual summer camp for 7 to 13 year olds, consisting of activities in drama, art, music, creative writing, character development, tennis, and swimming, has been enthusiastically embraced for nearly ten years. This program offers nine weekly sessions each summer, with a total enrollment of approximately 650 youngsters. The final two week session culminates in an original student theatrical performance. The camp's success has led to a newly formed partnership, with the Paradise Valley School District, which aims to replicate it.

Cal Performances

Berkeley, CA   www.calperfs.berkeley.edu

- School districts served per year: 35
- Elementary schools served per year: 117
- High schools served per year: 8
- K-12 students served per year: 16,000

CASE STUDY

Located on the campus of the University of California, Berkeley, Cal Performances is not only the largest performing arts presenter in Northern California, but also is recognized internationally as one of the most influential. It offers a variety of art forms and cultures—from early music and classical ballet to modern dance and avant-garde theater—and draws on material from ancient China and Greece to modern day Argentina. The mission of Cal Performances is "to inspire, nurture, and sustain a lifelong appreciation of the performing arts." It does this by presenting, producing, and commissioning outstanding artists, both renowned and emerging, to serve the university, K-12 schools, and the broader public through performances as well as through education and community programs.

Because studies have shown that arts education improves children's school attendance, levels of engagement, achievement, and graduation rates while also increasing parental involvement, educational programming gets top priority at Cal Performances. The organization does not enjoy the benefit of a resident company or family of artists, but Cal Performances' education programs have evolved by finding ways to utilize its resources to the best advantage of schools and the community.

SchoolTime

Since 1986, the cornerstone of Cal Performances' educational initiative has been SchoolTime, which offers daytime performances on the Zellerbach Hall stage to public and private school students.

Through outstanding productions of modern and classical dance, theater, and all forms of musical expression by the same internationally acclaimed artists who appear during Cal Performances' main season, SchoolTime introduces young people to cultures and performing arts from all over the world. Grade-appropriate study guides, sent to all schools in advance of the artists' visit, include pre- and post-performance exercises; background on the artists, art forms, and cultures; and learning activities designed to incorporate requirements of the Reading/Language Arts and Visual and Performing Arts Frameworks for California Public Schools.

Cal Performances in the Classroom

In 2001, Cal Performances and the Berkeley Unified School District established a partnership and were invited to join the John F. Kennedy Center for the Performing Arts' Partners in Education program. Combining resources and expertise to support arts education, the team created Cal Performances in the Classroom, which provides an in-depth experience with the arts and cultures exemplified by the artists performing in the SchoolTime series.

Cal Performances in the Classroom includes:

- *Professional Development Workshops for Teachers.* In three hour participatory workshops with professional performing artists and area curriculum specialists, teachers learn ways to effectively integrate into the curriuculum the arts presented at SchoolTime performances. Teachers also receive extensive workbooks (see below) that provide information about the artists and art form; classroom connections and lessons; and resource materials, such as videotapes, slides, audiotapes, or compact discs for classroom use.

- *In-School Participatory Sessions for Students.* Prior to attendance at SchoolTime performances, local artists (the same ones who lead the workshops for teachers) go into the classroom, and side by side with teachers, lead the students in dance, music, or theater activities and provide culturally specific background on the performance. These in-school sessions with artists complement the teachers' professional development workshops and give students hands-on experience of the art form they will see on the stage.

• *Attendance at a SchoolTime Performance.* Each Cal Performances in the Classroom unit culminates with attendance at a professional production on the Zellerbach Hall stage. Following the performance, students may visit with the artists or demonstrate the skills they have learned in school.

• *Comprehensive workshop guides.* Examples of workbooks related to SchoolTime performances that have been developed for teachers' use in the classroom include:

– African-American history through modern dance. This guide, in preparation for seeing the Alvin Ailey American Dance Theater, examined slavery and emancipation through the music and lyrics of spirituals, the writings of Ernest Gaines, The Autobiography of Miss Jane Pittman, and Alvin Ailey's *Revelations.*

– A history of the Silk Road and its signficance to Western culture. In preparation for seeing Yo-Yo Ma and the Silk Road Ensemble with storyteller Ben Haggarty, this unit explored the transmission of cultural ideas, economics, and religion along the Silk Road.

– Understanding the Irish culture's various winter solstice traditions. In preparation for seeing a seasonal program by Ireland's musical group Altan, this guide shed light on Irish history and culture through music, dance, and mumming in pagan and Christian Celtic celebrations.

– A study of Balinese music, dance, and storytelling. In preparation for a new work by Gamelan Sekar Jaya (a troupe devoted to the study and presentation of traditional and contemporary Balinese performing arts), this guide helped teachers instruct students in creating characters, using Balinese dance, music, masks, and shadow puppets, to stage their own stories.

Berkeley/Oakland AileyCamp at Cal Performances

Outside of its hometown of New York City, the Alvin Ailey American Dance Theater annually gives more performances in Berkeley than anywhere else. The company is continually seeking ways to engage the community with the dancers and their expertise.

In 2002, Cal Performances established the first West Coast site of the Alvin Ailey American Dance Theater's summer education program. This Berkeley/Oakland AileyCamp at Cal Performances is a six-week program in dance instruction also designed to develop self-esteem, self-discipline, creative expression, and critical thinking skills in youths aged 11-14. AileyCamp is not a professional dance training program. It targets students with academic, social, and domestic problems that often increase a child's risk of dropping out of school. An important aspect of the program's success is its provision of positive adult and peer role models for these often underserved youths.

In general, AileyCamp welcomes students, whether at risk or not, with an interest in the arts and potential to improve their academic performance. Following recruitment presentations in schools, individual applicants are interviewed by AileyCamp staffers and volunteer community leaders, many of whom are members of Cal Performances' Board of Trustees. All campers receive full tuition scholarships, meals, camp uniforms, dance clothing, and, in many cases, transportation. The AileyCamp curriculum includes daily technique classes in ballet, Horton-based modern dance, jazz, and West

KEN FRIEDMAN

Alvin Ailey American Dance Theater Rehearsal Director, Ronni Favors, teaching section of Revelations to students at Willard Middle School in Berkeley, California

African music and dance. Classes in Performance Skills and Creative Communications (writing, poetry, photography, and studio art) deepen the students' awareness of their potential for self-expression; and Personal Development classes provide counseling in nutrition, conflict resolution, drug-abuse prevention, decision making, and goal setting. The camp is supplemented with weekly field trips to educational, cultural, and recreational venues.

The 75 middle school students from Berkeley and Oakland who participate in AileyCamp conclude their summer training in a grand performance on the The Zellerbach Hall stage. At the end of camp, students leave with valuable life skills and a sense of accomplishment before they enter the challenging high school years. It is hoped that by providing a positive experience in a university setting (AileyCamp is held in Zellerbach Hall and adjacent buildings on the UC Berkeley campus), youths will consider pursuing higher education as a personal goal.

Short-term In-School Residencies

Cal Performances works with teachers and schools who seek help augmenting lesson plans, want to develop curriculum, or make special requests for in-school residencies. For after school programs in dance, music, or theater programs, visiting artists may provide successive master classes during a week's visit. For schools that provide arts instruction as part of the required curriculum, artists work with students during the school day.

Life-long Learning.

Throughout the year, lectures and colloquia are offered to the public, including K-12 students. Sightlines events, which are pre- and post-performance discussions, provide a view of history, biography, and artistic practice from the the perspective of internationally acclaimed artists and scholars. Visiting artists regularly offer master classes, open rehearsals, and campus residencies to students. Conferences, demonstrations, and symposia are co-sponsored by the Consortium for the Arts at the university, and all UC Berkeley students can receive half-price tickets to performances.

The Bushnell Center for the Performing Arts

Hartford, CT   www.bushnell.org

- School districts served per year: 14
- Elementary schools served per year: 33
- High schools served per year: 4
- K-12 students served per year: 5,000

CASE STUDY

The Bushnell Center has had a commitment to education since its inception in 1919. The current vision statement conveys this commitment:

To present, create, inspire, and share the best in the performing arts and, in partnership with others, deploy the arts as major catalysts to advance education, to promote economic development, and to build a sense of community in Central Connecticut.

The Bushnell's history reveals a long list of educational programming: public lectures, seminars, community forums, and debates featuring such visionaries as Eleanor Roosevelt, Winston Churchill, Helen Keller, and Martin Luther King, Jr. Over the years, diverse activities such as spelling bees, cooking classes, and state political conventions have offered education at the Bushnell with multiple dimensions.

One of its educational traditions aimed directly at youngsters is the Bushnell Children's Theatre. Founded in 1973, BCT provides live theatrical experiences for students in kindergarten through high school. BCT brings more than 13,000 students annually to the William H. Mortensen Hall, offering performances based on historical fiction, the classics, and popular children's literature.

A Ten-Year Overview of PARTNERS®

The strongest and most visible manifestation of the Bushnell's commitment to education is its school-

The annual Language Arts Festival is a culminating activity for children in The PARTNERS® program.

based arts education program, PARTNERS (Partners in Arts and Education Revitalizing Schools), which was inaugurated in 1993 as a pilot program for eight elementary schools in three school districts, beginning with the first grade. A grade level was added each year until PARTNERS' services were reaching all elementary grades (1-6) in the pilot schools.

In 1996, through the support of General Electric and the GE Fund, the Bushnell expanded PARTNERS into another school system in Plainville, CT. This program featured a K-12 district-wide approach that was implemented in multiple grades in multiple schools during the same year. The program also incorporated GE-employee volunteers as regular visitors in each classroom for one-on-one "read aloud" sessions.

During the 1997-98 school year, PARTNERS expanded into middle schools with a variety of interdisciplinary programs (English, social studies, and the arts). Fifth and sixth grade students began to work with teaching artists in short-term poetry or playwriting residencies (one to four visits). Teams of seventh and eighth grade English and social studies teachers began teaching interdisciplinary units that integrated arts resources.

In 1999, the John G. Martin Foundation of Farmington, CT, supported the Bushnell's efforts to demonstrate, document, and disseminate the PARTNERS Approach® and expand the program into the Torrington school district. In 2000, the PARTNERS program began a collaboration with the Capital Region Education Council to implement an arts-focused, interdistrict "sister school" program in which students from urban and suburban schools work together in arts-learning activities.

The 2002-2003 school year marked the tenth year of the PARTNERS' program, which now serves nearly 5,000 students in grades K-12, in 37 schools from 14 districts in the Greater Hartford region.

A Program and a Process

PARTNERS offers a series of classroom-based, arts-infused unit outlines, integrated into the school curriculum and linked to state and national standards. The goals are to improve literacy, enhance self-confidence, encourage creativity, and foster understanding and appreciation of diverse cultures. Each unit outline combines social studies and language arts with a variety of arts disciplines to reach specific learning goals; and each unit uses literature as the focal point, draws on a variety of arts resources (artists, performances, the community), and concludes with family involvement activities. The program is supported by professional development for teachers and artists, and by evaluation.

For example, the outline for an interdisciplinary study, "The Civil War Seen Through Many Eyes," lists required literature for student reading, the unit's "big idea," concepts, themes, related standards, student learning outcomes, a range of artist-led activities, and related performances and exhibits.

Participating teachers first meet for multiple planning sessions to develop unit outlines and participate in a full day professional development workshop in which they examine the arts resources available, meet the teaching artists, and engage in the same learning activities their students will experience.

In the classroom, teachers lead the social studies or language arts instruction and use activity guides developed specially for student readings. An artistic partner (either a teaching artist working directly in the classroom or a presenting artist conducting a grade-level assembly) then uses the literature, along with his or her particular art discipline, to present a hands-on activity or performance at the school or at the Bushnell. Artist visits range from one to five classroom periods. Later, on a designated date, students participate in full day workshops with teaching artists and then extend the connections between the arts and their studies through teacher-led writing activities. At a culminating event for families, students showcase the work they created and explain its links to their studies. After the unit is completed, teachers meet to review and evaluate the program and make plans for the following year.

PARTNERS' programs are also held after school, on weekends and during school vacation weeks at library sites, and in the summer either at school sites or in conjunction with local park and recreation organizations. One example is String Break, a series of classical music performances in the community that culminates with a full day open-house event at the Bushnell for young people and their families. The weekend event features free performances and participatory activities in both the visual and performing arts presented by various arts organizations.

The Promenade Gallery, located in the Bushnell's main-stage lobby, annually presents the works of professional Connecticut artists, as well as historical and interpretive exhibits. Area high school students view the exhibits and participate in talks with the artists. Moreover, PARTNERS' student artwork is recognized in dedicated exhibits, held periodically throughout the school year at the Bushnell, as well as at other public sites.

As a process, PARTNERS offers an inclusive, collaborative planning and implementation model that can mobilize the arts, the schools, and funders to plan, design, build, and sustain cost-effective, quality arts education programs. The application of the process is unique to each school community. As the process moves forward, the community begins to recognize the ways the arts can foster multicultural understanding, promote greater family involvement in the schools, and enrich and enhance the curriculum. This happens only when the focus and extensive commitment of many individuals and organizations in the community are woven together with adequate financial support to:

• Identify, encourage, and sustain passionate, visionary leadership

• Involve stakeholders in significant ways

• Design comprehensive, cost-effective programs that meet local needs

• Ensure stability and continuity of administration and management

• Refine and revamp programs to meet changing needs

PARTNERS has been recognized as a National Endowment for the Arts Program Model, and has received two two-year grants— in 1999 and 2002— from the Fund for the Improvement of Education, administered by the U. S. Department of Education. Most recently, the Bushnell received the Connecticut Quality Improvement Award's 2002 Gold Innovation Prize for its unique approach to learning—arts organizations, educators, and businesses joined together to enhance schools, give students high quality learning experiences, and build bridges between schools and the larger community.

Maui Arts & Cultural Center

Kahului, HI   www.mauiarts.org

- School districts served per year: One (only one in the state)
- Elementary schools served per year: 35
- Intermediate schools served per year: 6
- High schools served per year: 9
- K-12 students served per year: 25,000

CASE STUDY

Since opening in 1994, the Maui Arts & Cultural Center (MACC) has become an active participant in school renewal throughout Hawaii. This state-of-the-art, comprehensive arts facility grew out of community initiative and the need for professional arts venues. One of MACC's core values of is that "arts are essential to the complete education of children." Key components of the Center's success are the development of viable partnerships, support of strong and stable leadership, and a deep commitment to arts education by the MACC staff and Board of Directors. These beliefs and practices encourage MACC to act as a catalyst for learning in, through, and about the arts for every school on Maui.

Performances, Participatory Arts Workshops for Students, and Art Exhibitions

Planning for its education programs began two years before the MACC even opened. Teachers were on-site in hard hats making arrangements for the first student art exhibit, "Celebrating the Artist In Us," which featured artwork from throughout Maui County and offered teacher workshops on the creation, selection, and presentation of visual art. This exhibit has now become an annual event.

A series of performances designed specifically for students began when MACC opened in 1994. In 1995-96, *CanDo! Days* were initiated. Today, elementary school students and their teachers attend three hour-long participatory sessions in drama, creative movement, and visual arts at MACC. The same students participate annually, allowing their knowledge and skills to grow. Over the years, these initial programs have grown in number and popularity.

Professional Development Opportunities for Classroom Teachers

In 1995, MACC joined with the Hawaii Department of Education (DOE) as participants in the John F. Kennedy Center's Partners in Education program. This partnership has led to an expanded focus on professional development programs in the arts for teachers.

- *Workshops and Institutes.* A series of professional development workshops are offered annually for classroom teachers. Twelve workshops for Maui teachers were offered during the 2002-2003 school year, and six schools requested arts-integration workshops for all their teachers during staff development days. With only a few such days available each year, the requests are evidence of growing administrator and teacher interest in arts education. MACC has also offered week-long summer institutes for teachers since 1998. Some professional development workshops prepare teachers to lead arts activities that relate to performances at MACC. For instance, a workshop series on Chinese culture taught teachers how to lead Chinese ribbon dancing with students prior to attending a performance of Classical and Folk Dances from China.

- *Artist/Teacher Mentoring Program.* In 1999, MACC launched the Art of Standards initiative, which pairs elementary school teachers with teaching artists for ten-hour in-school mentoring programs. Each program begins with attendance at a summer institute in which teachers and artist-mentors learn about the mentoring process, write fine arts curricula, and develop assessments. During the school year, teachers and their mentors develop a unit plan, teach lessons, and assess student progress. The program serves approximately 20 teachers annually, and teacher evaluations indicate that it has a significant impact on their abilities to implement the arts techniques they learn in professional development workshops.

Maui Arts and Cultural Center's CanDo! Day — dance

- *In-Depth Collaborations with Entire Schools.* Teachers' professional development in the arts is a key component of the ArtsPartner program, an in-depth collaboration between MACC and selected schools. ArtsPartner schools sign a letter of agreement with MACC in which both organizations commit to developing the school's arts programs. Each school identifies its needs and sets goals, and MACC offers related professional development for teachers. Schools also host MACC artist residencies tailored to the school's needs. In 1998, through a Goals 2000 grant, four ArtsPartner schools began an 18 month project focusing on the teaching of reading comprehension through drama. Two of those schools went on to win state Arts Excellence Awards in 2000 and were designated in 2003 as honor roll schools for their high achievement in reading and math scores. In 2003, seven schools participated in the program.

- *Continuing Education Credit and Teacher Recognition.* Continuing Education credits are available for participation in professional development workshops. In addition, teachers who complete 32 hours of workshops during a two-year period are recognized with Certificates of Study at an awards dinner. Each year, 18 to 35 teachers are honored at this high profile event. MACC's professional development programs have also built teachers' capacities to be arts education leaders. Teachers who began the

program in 1995 are now presenting workshops for their peers and serving as mentors.

The Preparation of Teaching Artists

Because of Maui's isolation and limited funding, MACC has been training local teaching artists to present professional development workshops for teachers, to write arts curricula, to assess student learning, and to mentor teachers in the classroom. This investment in Maui artists has paid off—a cadre of advanced teaching artists now exists there whose members can both teach the arts and integrate the arts with the curriculum.

Teaching artists have attended the Kennedy Center's two-day seminar "Artists as Educators," offered at MACC, which demonstrates ways for them to find connections between their art-form expertise and the curriculum; it also provides instruction in planning professional development workshops for teachers. Follow-on advanced workshops for teaching artists have been offered as well. Teaching artists learn alongside teachers at summer institutes, in the Art of Standards project, and in the ArtsPartner program. Beginning in the 2002-2003 school year, teaching artists began participating in two workshops each year that focus on the Interstate New Teacher Assessment and Support Consortium Report of 2002.

The Role of the Performing-Artist Residencies

In Fall 1999, when MACC began presenting its own season of performances, a decision was made to select artists based not only on their artistic merit, but also on what they could offer to schools. An artist's experience working with young people is now a major booking consideration, and most artists performing in the school series interact with students or lead workshops for teachers. Approximately half of the artists in MACC's presenting season do residencies in schools and social-service agencies. For example, artists have led two days of dance classes for at-risk youth and a jazz clinic for high school band students.

Partnerships with local arts organizations have been important in all its endeavors. For example, since 2001 MACC has partnered with the Maui Dance Council to provide eight-week dance residencies for middle school students.

Statewide Impact

In 2000, the Hawaii Arts Education Partnership was formed in order to write and implement a strategic plan for arts education in the state. The plan, *ARTS FIRST: Hawaii's Arts Education Strategic Plan 2001,* recommends the Maui Arts & Cultural Center's professional development program for teachers and teaching artists as a model to be implemented throughout Hawaii.

Evaluation

With partial funding from the Kennedy Center, the MACC/DOE team has embarked on an evaluation of its professional development program and that program's effects on students. Phase I (July 2001 - May 2002) found that the artist-teacher mentoring program is increasing teachers' knowledge of the arts and enhancing their abilities to include the arts in their teaching. In the Phase II evaluation, which begins in Fall 2003, a sampling of nine students in each grade level in an elementary school will be followed longitudinally. Teachers will design instruments and collect and analyze data on the effects of arts-integrated curricula on these students' story/reading comprehension skills and attitudes toward reading.

The Kentucky Center

Louisville, KY   www.kentuckycenter.org

- School districts served per year: 150
- Elementary schools served per year: Varies each year
- High schools served per year: Varies each year
- K-12 students served per year: 70,000

CASE STUDY

The Kentucky Center (formerly the Kentucky Center for the Arts) is a performing arts institution whose statewide service is guided by its vision statement:

We believe that the human capacity for art is universal, and that we have been called upon both to present art and to build bridges of understanding and access to it.

Education is the principal means by which the Kentucky Center endeavors to realize that vision.

School Partnerships

The Kentucky Center partners with 13 schools and two other performing arts centers in an in-depth, long-term partnership program, called *Creative Connections,* which aims to achieve school reform through the use of arts and cultural resources. Supported by the GE Fund, this program helps each school create its own unique arts education plan.

In-school artist residencies are provided through *Arts Education Showcases,* one-day events in seven sites across the state. These showcases are designed to familiarize Kentucky educators with performing artists, visual artists, creative writers, arts organizations, and cultural institutions that make programs and other resources available to schools. More than 100 artists/companies participate in showcase events, marketing their programs annually to more than 900 teachers and others who book field trips, in-school performances, and residencies for their schools. Each attending school/organization receives a resource directory that features a full page description of each artist or arts organization. Artists pay a small fee (currently $25) to be included in the showcase and directory.

Hands-on, arts-based professional development opportunities for K-12 teachers—two-week seminars, called "Kentucky Institutes for Arts in Education"; one-week seminars, called "Arts Academies"; and a series of three-hour participatory workshops— are designed to help teachers incorporate the arts into their teaching across the curriculum.

The Kentucky Center provides professional development sessions for teaching artists that are designed to help them connect their work more closely to state and national standards.

Arts in Community Centers

Since 1991, the Kentucky Center's ArtsReach program has been enabling Louisville-area community centers to provide quality arts programs to their constituents, who include youth, adults with disabilities, families, and seniors. ArtsReach offers arts training and resources in the following ways:

• *ArtsReach Institute.* This annual eight-week training session, for staff members from up to 25 community centers, provides opportunities for staff to receive arts resources for their community centers while gaining knowledge of the arts for themselves.

• *ArtsReach Network.* Once participants have completed the ArtsReach Institute, they are invited to join the ArtsReach Network. During monthly meetings, community center staff members have the opportunity to interact with one another, share resources and information that enhance their individual programs, and attend supplementary professional development workshops.

• *ArtsReach Studio.* Through this program, youth receive quality year-round instruction in dance and violin. They are also given opportunities to experience the arts through performances (both as audience and performer), take master classes from nationally/internationally renowned touring artists, and be involved in special projects. ArtsReach has transformed the landscape of local community centers from primarily sports-based models to centers that are rich in arts-based programming as well.

• *Artist Initiated Grants* give local artists and ArtsReach centers the opportunity to partner with each other to do specific projects.

ArtsReach was a 2002 semi-finalist for the Coming Up Taller Awards (presented by the President's Committee on the Arts and Humanities, in partnership with the National Endowment for the Arts, the Institute of Museum and Library Services, and the National Endowment for the Humanities). As a result of the program's proven success locally, the Kentucky Arts Council has enlisted the Kentucky Center to expand ArtsReach statewide. Pilot sites are now operating in the traditionally underserved communities of Paducah, Hopkinsville, and Ashland.

Programs for Talented High School Youth

The Kentucky Governor's School for the Arts (GSA) is best known for its intensive residential program targeted to the needs of talented high school students who are dancers, actors, instrumental or vocal musicians, creative writers, aspiring architects, or visual artists. Specifically, GSA is an arts community of masters and students who join together for three weeks in the summer to explore the discipline and freedom of the creative process. The newest initiative included an international exchange program that brought five students from Northern Ireland to the GSA in the summer of 2003.

By graduating from GSA, alumni earn the opportunity to participate and audition at College and Career Day, which takes place in Louisville every fall. Representatives from nearly 70 institutions of higher learning from around the nation gather at Louisville's Youth Performing Arts School to share information about their schools with GSA students and their parents and to conduct auditions and interviews. Many GSA students have received scholarships as a direct result of these opportunities. Through the Toyota Alumni Performance Fund, GSA is often able to support students' artistic endeavors beyond the summer residential program.

A related, earlier stage program is Artshops, a series of free arts workshops that provide high school students with the opportunity to spend a day at a college or fine arts center in a hands-on arts enrich-

A class photo from Governor's School for the Arts, with a dancer in the foreground

ment opportunity. Artshops include parent/teacher workshops that discuss the GSA summer program, researching college scholarship opportunities, and issues of parenting a gifted child.

Access to Programs for People with Disabilities

With a barrier free facility, assistive listening systems, audio description, and captioned theater available for public shows and student matinees, the Kentucky Center is a leader in arts accessibility. The audio description and captioned theater programs also provide services for other theaters in the community. In addition, the Kentucky Center does training for and loans equipment to organizations throughout Kentucky, and its Access Services Department works to educate other arts institutions by providing workshops and consultancies.

Arts Presenters' Networking Opportunities

The Kentucky Center is a leading convener of groups that might not otherwise be meeting and collaborating regularly for networking opportunities. The Center founded the Kentucky Presenters Network, an organization of performing-arts centers, and it holds a monthly meeting of community centers in the ArtsReach Network program. Most recently, the Kentucky Center formed the Arts Access Forum, which meets monthly to discuss using the arts to better serve people with disabilities, and to provide a means through which member groups can collaborate in new ways.

Performance Series

The Kentucky Center presents a wide variety of performance series in music, dance, and drama, including World Rhythms, a multicultural series with several educational components. World Rhythms features performing arts from around the world, usually focusing on Asian, African, African-American, or Hispanic cultural traditions. Each World Rhythms program includes a student matinee and an evening performance. All schools sending students to the matinee performances receive a standards-based teacher guide, and selected schools also receive an in-school workshop in music or dance of the featured culture, led by local and regional teaching artists. Prior to every World Rhythms evening performance, a Cultural Marketplace is presented, with interactive workshops, demonstrations, and exhibits about the culture spotlighted in the evening program.

In addition to the various programs presented by the Kentucky Center, the facilities are also home to five resident groups (Kentucky Opera, Louisville Orchestra, Louisville Ballet, PNC Broadway in Louisville, and Stage One), each with its own education program. In order to make education performances more affordable, the Kentucky Center Express provides up to half the cost of bus transportation to the Center for student matinees. More than 10,000 students benefit from this program annually.

Jacob's Pillow Dance Festival

Lee, MA   www.jacobspillow.org

- School districts served per year: 11
- Elementary schools served per year: 20-25
- High schools served per year: 2-4
- K-12 students served per year: 1,000

CASE STUDY

Since the "Pillow's" 1933 inception, education has been central to its mission: "To support dance creation, presentation, education, and preservation; and to engage and deepen public appreciation and support for dance."

Education at Jacob's Pillow involves the professional track dancer and the initiate; the artist and the classroom teacher; the aficionado and the new audience member—all desiring to enhance their dance experience.

Jacob's Pillow's multiple entry points enable students, teachers, and artists alike to participate in and reflect on the physical, emotional, intellectual, and inspirational aspects of dance. Program development is always collaborative and art centered, and aimed at helping learners experience dance as a path toward knowledge of self and community.

Four program areas—the School at Jacob's Pillow, the Intern Program, the Community Dance Program, and the Audience Engagement/Free Events Program—nurture the development of each group and provide opportunities for interaction:

• **The School at Jacob's Pillow** is an immersion experience for an international student body of 100 exceptionally skilled pre-professionals and young professionals. In classes no larger than 25, with a high faculty-to-student ratio (averaging 1:6), students receive individualized and comprehensive conservatory style training that prepares them for the demands of a dance career. The curriculum draws on the Pillow's ability to connect young artists with the professional dance world, enabling them to work six

hours per day in a company-like studio environment, perform weekly for Pillow audiences, see three to four dance companies per week, hear artists discuss their work, and complete assigned readings and research in the Pillow's extensive dance archives. The School's five annual two- to three-week programs include ballet, cultural traditions, contemporary, jazz, and choreography.

Within the School's choreography program, artists are offered three types of training for conducting school and community residencies:

– *Professional Development Course,* begun in the 1990s, is designed for artists interested in learning about collaborative and choreographic strategies necessary to build and sustain relationships that support both community and artistic goals. Topics include effective choreographic structures for community settings, stage work created from community interactions, and residency approaches for school aged students.

– *School Residency Teaching Fellows Program* enables an artist with youth teaching experience and strong choreographic ability to serve as an artist-teacher for the Pillow's annual four-week high school residency. Artists participate by invitation only, and must have completed the professional development course described above.

– *Fieldwork Courses about School Residencies* enable artists who lack teaching experience in schools to gain insights into the Pillow's residency approach, called Setting Curriculum in Motion® (see Community Dance Program below). Having completed the professional development course, these artists shadow Pillow residency artists, participating in day-to-day classroom planning and assisting with documentation and evaluation procedures. This fieldwork training may be repeated and can eventually lead to the artists being considered for the Teaching Fellows Program.

• **The Intern Program** provides on-the-job training in nine areas of arts management and technical theater production. Staff-led seminars, field trips to other cultural organizations, and intern-group projects provide key career contacts, insight into the inner workings of international arts productions, and knowledge about current issues critical to the

Jacob's Pillow Artist–Educator Kimberli Boyd leads a 3rd grade science class at Silvio O. Conte Community School.

field. Summer interns lead community dance classes, campus tours, discussions with visiting community groups about artists and works on stage, and other activities designed for K-12 students and teachers. Off-season, interns are integrally involved in Festival planning and the year-round community programs. Intern alumni work at organizations such as the Alvin Ailey American Dance Foundation, American Dance Festival, Ballet Hispanico, Ronald K. Brown/Evidence, Mark Morris Dance Center, Leap…imagination in learning. Six Intern alumni currently serve on the Jacob's Pillow staff.

• **The Community Dance Program** benefits some 3,500 participants each year. More than a dozen community partnerships and alliances engage area schools, after-school programs, elderhostels, special needs participants, and individuals both new to or experienced in dance. Within area schools:

– *Setting Curriculum in Motion* inspires student-developed choreography using K-12 academic topics as source material. The approach has evolved from long-term, committed relationships with area schools and demonstrates dance's important place in the national dialogue about education reform.

Example: Algebra students are guided by their high school teacher and Pillow artist-teacher in creating movement phrases about a key idea in factoring—the process of FOIL (first, outer, inner, last). Students work in quartets, each group demonstrating the four-part idea. For the artist-teacher, breaking down complex material into parts emerges as a theme that can be explored through movement. Students are taught a complex movement phrase as part of the class warm-up, and because factoring occurs both backward and forward, they are asked to reverse the phrase on their own. Excerpts of the original and reversed phrase are then incorporated into each quartet's complex "dance equations."

Example: The Fall semester 2001 included collaboration between an English as Second Language class and a Health class. Students examined the events of September 11 and considered how they related to valued American freedoms and how those freedoms attract others to this country. Students considered misconception, judgment, and variations in interpretation, and used movement to contrast and compare the September 11 event with events from their countries of origin.

Next, students compared these events with the time period and urgency for freedom that led to the writing of the Bill of Rights. Students' written reflections were formed into a text score for the dance's final showing.

– *Professional Development for Classroom Teachers* is offered year-round, in the form of seminars and workshops, as an integral part of school residencies. During Summer Dance Institutes for Educators, established in 1996, participating teachers spend a week at the Pillow being students. They take dance classes, attend lectures, see performances, participate in feedback sessions with artists, and engage in dialogue about classroom applications. The goal is to broaden and deepen teacher understanding of dance and its ability to further student learning—in particular, the academic success of kinesthetic learners.

• **The Audience Engagement/Free Events Program** is central to the Pillow's Festival experience. Every season some 200 free, informal, and informative events provide background about up-and-coming and established artists, new and classic works, and collaborations, many with interdisciplinary or multicultural emphasis. For example:

– The outdoor stage for artists to share works in progress is a popular place for families to introduce children to dance.

– The Pillow's annual Community Day, which creates a family-friendly, celebratory atmosphere for people of all ages, offers performances and participatory dance activities in a full range of dance styles and expressions, and highlights the Pillow's K-12 artists and their work.

– The Pillow Archives, accessible to the public through a multimedia reading room, houses thousands of videos, films, and photos collected over the past century, and inspires a series of annual exhibitions. Drawing on these resources, Pillow education staff members plan "A Day at the Pillow," visits for K-12 students and teachers to learn about the Pillow, its history, and its artists.

Flynn Center for the Performing Arts

Burlington, VT   www.flynncenter.org

- School districts served per year: 27
- Elementary schools served per year: 118
- High schools served per year: 26
- K-12 students served per year: 45,000 (2001-02)

CASE STUDY

The Flynn Center for the Performing Arts is located in Burlington, VT, a city of 40,000 in a county of 120,000, and draws its patrons from within a 100 mile radius. In this bucolic setting, the Flynn's patrons represent the wide range of Vermont experience: urban to rural, industrial to agrarian, progressive to traditional, and high to low levels of education.

The educational mission of the Flynn Center is to provide programs—in the schools, in the community, and at the Center—that engage children, teens, and adults in the artistic process, cultivate appreciation of the performing arts, and make the performing arts an integral part of school and community life. The core strength of these programs comes from their integration with the Flynn's nationally recognized presenting series, which includes a main-stage season of more than 40 music, dance, theater, and multidisciplinary works in the 1,450 seat theater; 25 contemporary and experimental genres in FlynnSpace, the 150 seat black box theater; and more than 35 performances for students on either the main-stage or in FlynnSpace.

The success of these educational programs comes not only from their integration with the Flynn's wide range of performances; additional factors include partnerships with schools and other cultural organizations that extend the Flynn's resources and reach, and the organization's responsiveness to community needs. The programs also offer many different ways for people of all ages to participate at varying skill and commitment levels. The programs' leaders, informed by their own education and arts backgrounds, seek to meet participants where they are and challenge them to go farther.

Student Matinee Series, Study Guides, Teaching Artists in the Classroom

Begun in 1987, the Student Matinee Series offers quality performances to complement the school curriculum and demonstrate the dynamic relationship between the performing arts and history, literature, and world cultures (e.g., *Lindbergh's Ocean Flight, A Midsummer Night's Dream,* and the Peking Opera). The series also includes performances that introduce art forms outside the curriculum, such as Paul Taylor Dance Company, Imago Theatre's *FROGZ,* and jazz vocalist Nnenna Freelon. The Flynn Lead Teacher Network, a volunteer group that represents more than 100 schools and serves as a liaison between the Flynn and the region's teachers, contributes greatly to the series' success. The Network regularly provides information about events and gathers feedback from colleagues about Flynn programs and potential offerings.

To encourage teachers to use the matinee performances as springboards for classroom activities, the Flynn offers free study guides that provide essential background materials and relevant learning activities linked to Vermont standards. In addition, Flynn holds workshops in the classroom before and after attendance at matinees to help students prepare for, reflect on, and extend the performance experience. Typically led by local teaching artists versed in the art form—and, when possible, by the performers themselves—these workshops are highly interactive. In workshops centered on a theatrical production, for example, students might be given a portion of the script to interpret. For a dance performance, they might create movement phrases that express the performance theme. On occasion, these workshops provide the basis for longer-term residencies, in which the teaching artists lead a series of workshops in the classroom to interweave drama and creative movement with content areas. In 2001, the Flynn education department began a three-year project working with the entire staff of a local elementary school to use the arts to improve students' reading comprehension. Flynn teaching artists led a

total of 313 classroom workshops. Paid for by the schools or grants, these workshops have grown in number as a result of the enthusiastic response by teachers and students.

Professional Development for Teachers

For teachers interested in learning more about the arts, the Flynn offers after school workshops in specific art forms (e.g., "West African Dancing," "Storytelling") and in integrating arts into the classroom ("Bringing Books to Life," "Dancing Numbers"). Workshops are held at the Flynn, at schools, and at conferences. Attendance at these workshops is highest, regardless of location, when they are co-sponsored by a school district or another organization. In 2001-02, 287 teachers participated in these professional development offerings. This work with teachers began in 1992, when the Flynn joined the Kennedy Center's Partners in Education program.

College Courses

To offer teachers opportunities for in-depth study, the Flynn partners with the graduate education program of St. Michael's College, in nearby Colchester, VT, to co-sponsor several three credit courses per year (e.g., "Arts: The Creative Process," "Drama as a Teaching Tool," "Aesthetic Education," "Bringing History, Literature, and Arts to Life"). Open to pre-service and practicing teachers; these courses use performances at the Flynn Center as texts and, when possible, include interaction with the performers. Additionally, Flynn education staff members supervise teachers' independent studies in the arts and education (e.g., "Teaching Science through Drama," "Evaluating Arts Activities").

Year-Round Classes for Children, Teens, and Adults

In 1987, to provide the community-at-large with opportunities to participate in the performing arts under the guidance of skilled teaching artists, the Flynn began offering a few classes for children. In 2000, after adding state-of-the-art studios to its facility, FlynnArts, a comprehensive program of year-round classes in theater, dance, and music, was born. The program focuses on topics that relate to the Flynn's main-stage and FlynnSpace presentations. For example, since the Flynn is part of the Doris Duke Charitable Foundation's JazzNet and committed to presenting jazz artists, FlynnArts offers the classes "Jazz Combo" and "Singing Solo Jazz." Similarly, classes in modern dance relate to the Flynn's participation in the National Dance Project. Further, FlynnArts is currently developing an overall curriculum in which performance skills will build upon each other.

Opportunities for students to tour the Flynn theaters, observe rehearsals, and attend Flynn performances and pre- or post-show discussions with visiting performers are available as well.

FlynnArts classes feature entry points at many levels—for the curious, the aspiring, and the proficient—in order to instill a deeper understanding and appreciation of the performing arts while developing increasingly solid artistic skills. For example, FlynnArts students may participate in a

Students work together in a workshop to create shapes from the environment.

one-day workshop, a one-week summer camp, a 12-week course, or audition for a role in an intensive summer theater program.

Fall and spring terms include 12-week classes (e.g., "Ballet for Ice Skaters," "Acting Lab," "Improv Ensemble," "Flamenco Guitar") as well as shorter workshops on topics of particular or specialized interest ("Linklater Voice Technique," "Stage Combat," "Physical Theater") and master classes

linked to main-stage and FlynnSpace events. More advanced students participate in end-of-semester performances in FlynnSpace.

The summer term offers one and two week camps that are open to children and teens of all abilities, as well as programs for more advanced teen students in theater and jazz. In addition, programs of various durations are offered for adults. Summer camps are usually theme-based (e.g., "Tales of the Earth"), and many are offered in collaboration with other local nonprofit cultural organizations (a camp focusing on creating site-specific dances at Shelburne Farms, "Wild and Wacky History" at the Shelburne Museum, "Radio Plays" with Vermont Public Radio). These partnerships were born in 1995, when capital improvements required the Flynn to relocate its summer camps; they continue to flourish, however, because of the mutual and respectful sharing of resources that developed.

FlynnArts offers assistantships and internships through various local colleges and high schools that enable young teaching artists to work under the tutelage of seasoned professionals; this program has been helpful in providing the Flynn with new teaching artists.

Community Residencies

From 1996-2000, thanks to an "Audiences for the Performing Arts Network" grant from the Lila Wallace-Reader's Digest Fund, the Flynn sent artists to three rural towns for in-depth, multiple-week residencies. The Liz Lerman Dance Exchange, for example, drew on stories collected from that experience and created a performance with rural-community participants. The work was performed both for the student matinee and main-stage series in 2000. This residency and other projects have brought working artists who perform in the main-stage season or the Discover Jazz Festival into schools, youth centers, and outlying communities, where they engage Vermont residents in the arts and create new works.

The John F. Kennedy Center for the Performing Arts

Washington, DC   www.kennedy-center.org

Locally

- School districts served per year: 27
- Elementary schools served per year: 475
- High schools served per year: 105
- K-12 students served per year: 855,000

Nationally

The Kennedy Center provides programs and resources to school districts and individual schools in all 50 states.

CASE STUDY

As America's national center for the performing arts, the John F. Kennedy Center is deeply committed to arts education. For more than 30 years, its Education Department has provided quality arts experiences for students, teachers, families, and the public both in the Washington, DC, metropolitan area and throughout the nation. The Kennedy Center's educational programs, which directly serve more than seven million people each year, are focused on three major areas: production and presentation of performing arts for young people and their families; school-based education programs and resources for students, teachers, administrators, and artists; and career development in the arts for young people and professionals.

Production and Presentation

With its commitment to access, diversity, and lifelong learning, the Center continues to provide opportunities for all people to see and learn about performing-arts productions.

- Through the "Imagination Celebration at the Kennedy Center" and "Imagination Celebration On Tour" throughout the nation, the Center presents or produces more than 600 performances for young people and their families in dance, theater, music (classical and jazz), opera, storytelling, and puppetry. Cuesheet performance guides, consistent with guidelines developed from Kennedy Center's three-year study of such materials, help students and teachers familiarize themselves with the performances they will attend.

- Additional programs of the Imagination Celebration type include the Kennedy Center's "Open House," the Prelude and Holiday Festivals, and the Martin Luther King Jr. Celebration.

- Under the auspices of the Education Department, each year the National Symphony Orchestra travels to a different state for an extended residency, which includes performances and extensive educational programs in schools and communities.

- To support the development of new works for young people, every other year New Visions, New Voices brings playwrights, directors, and composers together in a "working forum" to revise promising scripts and produce staged readings for young people and their families. In this week-long residency, the Kennedy Center provides artistic resources, including a full cast, stage managers, and specialists in theatrical presentation for up to eight new plays or musicals.

- Through Performance Plus, the adult public attends demonstrations, discussions, multi-session courses, panels, participatory workshops, and open rehearsals that offer insights into the cultural and historical context of the works presented on stage.

- In an effort to bring its productions to as many people as possible, a free performance is presented daily at 6 p.m. (EST) on the Center's Millennium Stage and is broadcast live over the Internet. These performances are archived on the Center's Web site (www.kennedy-center.org).

School-Based Education Programs and Resources

The Kennedy Center Education Department develops programs that promote student learning in and through the arts; it provides professional development opportunities for artists, teachers, and school and performing arts administrators; and it encourages and supports institutional partnerships across the country that pursue these ends.

CAROL PRATT

The Adventures of Tom Sawyer *by Ken Ludwig*

• A new *DC Arts Education Initiative,* led by the Kennedy Center, is helping to develop a comprehensive K-12 arts education program for the District of Columbia's public and charter schools.

• A partnership with George Washington University and the Duke Ellington High School for the Arts provides a series of arts experiences that extend school-based arts instruction. Students from these partnership institutions, as well as from other schools throughout the Washington, DC, metropolitan area, participate in a weekend program— featuring the Dance Theatre of Harlem—that introduces students to ballet through lecture/ demonstrations, workshops, performances, and training experiences.

• Since 1975, the Kennedy Center has been a classroom for teachers. Each year, more than 1,600 teachers participate in professional-development programs to learn how to integrate the arts with other curricula. For example:

– *Changing Education Through the Arts* is a multi-year partnership with 13 schools in the metropolitan Washington, DC, area that develops, implements, and evaluates the building of teacher capacity to integrate the arts across the curriculum. The program includes arts coaches (teaching artists who mentor teachers in their classrooms), courses focusing on arts integration, and teacher-led study groups.

– The *D.C./Northern Virginia Partnership Program* extends school-based arts education programs with artist residencies in 15 schools.

Teachers who study 30 or more hours at the Center are awarded Certificates of Study; artists who teach in the program participate in professional development training of their own. The experiences gained in this local program are shared nationally through the Partners in Education program (described next).

• The Partners in Education program brings together senior representatives from cultural institutions and neighboring school systems to initiate or develop arts education partnerships with a special emphasis on the professional development of teachers. In 2003, 94 teams in 44 states, Washington, DC, and Mexico participated in the program. In addition to providing leadership for Partnership teams, the program offers a national tour of workshops for teachers, parents, and community members; seminars to assist artists in learning how to plan professional development workshops for teachers; seminars to help arts organizations develop a philosophy and practice for creating performance guides; and a speaker's bureau. The program also offers grants to Partnership teams for supporting collaborative projects with other arts and education institutions throughout their states, and for undertaking research projects that determine project effectiveness.

• The Kennedy Center Alliance for Arts Education Network (KCAAEN), a national network of 46 state-based organizations, endeavors to ensure that the arts are included in the basic education of all children. Through operation, project, and technical assistance grants, as well as various meetings, programs, and publications (e.g., Community Audit for Arts Education: Better Schools, Better Skills, Better Communities), KCAAEN helps communities strengthen and expand their arts education programs.

• A distance learning program, created in association with the Prince William Network (the distance learning arm of the Prince William County Public Schools in Northern Virginia), broadcasts a performing arts series to schools nationally via satellite. This free program provides performances, discussions, and demonstrations by some of the outstanding performing companies and artists appearing at the Kennedy Center (e.g., the Royal Shakespeare Company, Dr. Billy Taylor, Athol Fugard, Suzanne Farrell, and the Turtle Island String Quartet). In addition, teachers can enhance professional development through this distance learning mechanism.

• Through the Kennedy Center's national arts and information network, ARTSEDGE (www.artsedge.kennedy-center.org), teachers and students throughout the nation have access to a variety of quality educational materials about the performing arts. The Web site includes a databank of related lesson plans and links to additional resources, and specific minisites feature topics of special interest (e.g., the Harlem Renaissance, Ireland, the African Diaspora, the Americas). ArtsEdge also participates in the MarcoPolo project (www.marcopolo.worldcom.com)—a partnership with corresponding programs of the American Association for the Advancement of Science, the Council of the Great City Schools, the National Geographic Society, the National Endowment for the Humanities, the National Council on Economic Education, and the National Council of Teachers of Mathematics—to provide quality, standards-based content through the Internet.

Career Development

A variety of programs at the Center provide short- and long-term career development and opportunities for students and young professionals to showcase their talents. Young dancers may study with a prima ballerina, for example; young musicians work with members of a symphony orchestra or leading jazz musicians; young actors, playwrights, directors, critics, and set, costume, and lighting designers learn from appropriate theater professionals; and arts managers are mentored by seasoned and successful management practitioners.

Specific programs include Betty Carter's JazzAhead, the Conservatory Project, Exploring Ballet with Suzanne Farrell, Jazz Ambassadors, Kenan Apprentice Program in Theater, Kennedy Center American College Theater Festival, National Symphony Orchestra (NSO) Summer Music Institute, NSO Youth Fellowship and Young Apprenticeship Programs, and the Vilar Fellowships and Internships in Arts Management.

Each year, more than 1,250 people take advantage of this specialized instruction, and some are selected for performance opportunities.

PROFILES

Following are profiles of the work of 66 Performing Arts Centers and their role in education

UApresents

Tucson, AZ   http://uapresents.arizona.edu

- School districts served per year: 18
- Elementary schools served per year: 50
- High schools served per year: 10
- K-12 students served per year: 13,800

Programs offered:

Performances for K-12 audiences

Short-term in-school residencies (one week or less)

After school or weekend programs for K-12 students

Professional development opportunities for teachers

Professional development opportunities for teaching artists

Summer institute for K-12 teachers

Partnerships with whole schools

Partnerships with whole school districts

Training for school leaders (principals, superintendents, others)

Adult education opportunities

Performances/exhibits by school-based teachers

Performances/exhibits by teaching artists

PROFILE

In this time of budgetary contraints in school districts, inspiring classroom teachers with the concept of the arts as a mechanism for learning is an inexpensive and effective way to encourage creativity and sophisticated thinking, and to reinvigorate the culture of a school. Students not only acquire a deeper understanding of curricular topics through the arts, but also experience the integration of the arts into their lives.

The UApresents School Matinee Program successfully pursues these goals with respect to the performing arts. Nearly 14,000 K-12 students—from public, private, charter, and home schools alike—are given the opportunity to attend a live professional performance each year, many of them for the first time, at Centennial Hall on the campus of the University of Arizona. Six of these matinee performances, featuring world-class artists from a variety of ethnicities and arts disciplines, are presented throughout the year.

In preparation for each School Matinee, local teaching artists present Teacher Inservices, which provide in-depth teacher training in the particular culture and art form being showcased. Moreover, each inservice focuses on themes or lessons connected to the specific Matinee that each teachers' students will attend. Every teacher bringing students to a Matinee is encouraged to attend this free inservice, and approximately 150 teachers participate. They also receive teacher study guides, created by the artists, that provide curricular information and supportive classroom applications.

A select number of schools that attend the Matinees receive an artist's residency for their students. Typically, about 300 students per matinee participate in workshops. In these informative sessions, local artists work with the students in an entertaining and interactive way to further connect the Matinee and performing arts experience to the classroom. The local teaching artists used for the inservices and workshops are themselves trained in these processes, and they receive continuing evaluation from UApresents. The study guides they create, as well as the inservices and on-site workshops are connected to the Arizona Arts Standards.

A week-long Fine Arts Summer Institute for Teachers, which focuses on the School Matinee series, immerses classroom teachers in multifaceted arts explorations that are readily applicable in the classroom. Some 150 teachers participate in multicultural music, movement, drama, and visual-arts workshops each summer. The Principals Forum offers opportunities for administrators; they experience performances and attend meetings to learn more about arts in education, relevant research, arts education resources, and ideas for implementing arts opportunities and programs within their schools.

In 1999, the UApresents School Matinee Program, in a collaborative project with the Tucson Unifed School District, was awarded the Governor's Art Award for Excellence in Arts Education.

Walton Arts Center

Fayetteville, AR   www.waltonartscenter.org

• School districts served per year: 19
• Elementary Schools served per year: 116
• High Schools served per year: 28
• K-12 students served per year: 37,000

Programs offered:

Performances for K-12 audiences

Short-term in-school residencies (one week or less)

Long-term in-school residencies (multiple weeks)

After school or weekend programs for K-12 students

Professional development opportunities for teachers

Professional development opportunities for teaching artists

Summer institute for K-12 teachers

Summer institute for teaching artists

Partnerships with whole schools

Web-based learning opportunities

Programs with parents and/or other adult caregivers

Adult education opportunities

Performances/exhibits by students

Performances/exhibits by teaching artists

Technical/planning assistance

Evaluation methods

PROFILE

The Walton Arts Center (WAC) offers programs in the arts that have evolved over the past 10 years through the collaborative efforts of WAC staff and a diverse community network. WAC enjoys important educational partnerships with the Northwest Arkansas Education Service Cooperative, Ozark Natural Science Center, JASON Foundation, Arts Live Theatre, NOARK Girl Scout Council, and North Arkansas Symphony Orchestra.

The following are the components of WAC's core educational opportunities:

• *Classroom Series Performances.* WAC believes in the special connection that happens in live performances, which speak directly to young people's hearts and minds. Each year WAC presents nearly 40 performances by local, regional, national, and international artists to more than 25,000 students. Examples include the Brenda Angiel Aerial Dance Company, Omaha Theater Company for Young People, and DynamO Theatre of Montreal.

• *Visual Arts Tours.* Interactive tours designed around exhibitions expand students' knowledge and experience. With more than 35 gallery exhibitions each year, students have opportunities to share thoughts in a supportive and respectful exchange, acquire artistic vocabulary, and learn appropriate gallery behavior. More than 250 students participated in docent-led interactive tours last year.

• *School Residency.* WAC residencies offer opportunities for students to interact with artists through classes, workshops, and informal conversations. For example, several local schools hosted a WAC artist-in-residence for six weeks. As a result, WAC mentored seven artists in maintaining valuable educational exchanges with 2,900 young people.

• *JASON Project.* WAC is the only arts-based provider of the JASON Foundation, and for seven years it has been the venue for the Foundation's internationally acclaimed educational program that demonstrates the integration of the arts, science, and technology. The JASON project provides teacher training, school outreach activities, and curriculum-based materials; and it reaches more than 6,900 students by way of performances, exhibitions, camps, and a live satellite broadcast.

• *Professional Development for Classroom Teachers.* The artistic literacy of young people can only be achieved by improving teachers' knowledge, critical acumen, and ability to teach through the arts. WAC is therefore committed to bringing the latest in arts-based professional development opportunities, often provided by nationally recognized experts, to teachers in the region. There are eight workshops

CAITLYN SPAULDING

Young artist creates a "masterpiece" in Bogle Studio at Walton Arts Center, Fayetteville, Arkansas.

months and up. WAC's Young Actor's Training Program, for example, engages community partner Arts Live Theatre to offer instruction and performance experiences in theater arts for students ages 5-18. The program has reached hundreds of young people, and the curriculum has been expanded to meet or exceed national standards for academy-level actor training programs.

• *Community-based Residencies.* Residencies offer a unique opportunity to target underserved groups through master classes, workshops, and discussions. One such residency was developed with the Donald Byrd Group Dance Company, which did a one week community residency based on input from dancers, the University of Arkansas, Alpha Kappa Alpha sorority, and public school teachers. Programs to serve the region's growing Latino community are currently being explored.

WAC's efforts have dramatically changed the landscape of Northwest Arkansas. The region has gone from one with few opportunities in the arts to a wellspring of multiple and diverse arts experiences. WAC's success has been recognized by the Cultural Development Plan Committee—a group of business and community leaders, University of Arkansas representatives, and arts supporters— that requested WAC's involvement in creating a cultural development vision for the region.

Consequently, WAC worked with the Committee to create the "2002-2007 Cultural Development Plan: The Future of the Arts in Northwest Arkansas," which establishes priorities and outlines the goals for stimulating further arts and cultural growth in the region. The very existence of this committee and its plan, in fact, comes in large part from the strong foundation built by WAC's 10-year history of providing quality arts programs and nourishing Northwest Arkansas' vital cultural scene.

each school year—including the five-day Arts With Education (AWE) Institute, where educators learn arts-based strategies for teaching students and measuring their achievement levels. Other opportunities for the region's teaching community, provided by WAC in collaboration with the Northwest Arkansas Education Service Cooperative, include Teacher Training Seminars, Technology Training Seminars, and Professional Development Workshops.

• *Community-Based After School Programs.* WAC provides more than 150 interactive programs, ranging from one-day workshops to ongoing classes in painting, drawing, metals, multi-media, clay, photography, theater, music, and dance for ages 18

Center Theatre Group/Performing for Los Angeles Youth (P.L.A.Y.)

Los Angeles, CA   www.taperahmanson.com

- School districts served per year: 7
- Elementary schools served per year: 66
- High schools served per year: 185
- K-12 students served per year: 50,000

Programs offered:

Performances for K-12 audiences

Short-term in-school residencies (multiple weeks)

Professional development opportunities for teachers

Partnerships with whole schools

Partnerships with whole school districts

Web-based learning opportunities

Programs with parents and/or other adult caregivers

Performances/exhibits by students

PROFILE

P.L.A.Y. (Performing for Los Angeles Youth) has two major goals: to deepen students' understanding and appreciation of the art of theatre; and to use the power of theater to increase students' literacy and collaborative skills, encourage them to think creatively, and enhance their understanding of history, social studies, and the sciences.

The core elements of P.L.A.Y. include:

• Commissioning and producing original plays written specifically for young people. P.L.A.Y. is one of only a small number of theater companies in the United States that actively develops original youth-theater productions.

• Integrating its productions into the school curriculum through teacher guides and student workbooks, P.L.A.Y. works with a team of educators to develop study guides for its touring productions and for every play presented in the regular seasons of the Mark Taper Forum and Ahmanson Theatre.

These materials are available on the Theatres' Web site (www.taperahmanson.com).

• Building long-term relationships with students and their families by providing discounted tickets to regular productions at the Mark Taper Forum and Ahmanson Theatre, together with pre-play and post-play activities designed for children and adults.

• Providing professional development opportunities for teachers, including weekend workshops and symposia on theater's potential role in education. In 2001, P.L.A.Y. was awarded an Exemplary Arts Education grant from the State of California to further enhance this proven program.

• Training theater artists in the special skills needed for successful youth-theater productions. In developing plays for young people, theater artists need to learn new techniques, including particular styles of playwriting, acting, directing, and set design. P.L.A.Y. has already developed a series of workshops on these techniques, with the goal of becoming a national resource for theater artists.

The core strength of P.L.A.Y. is its multi-pronged approach, which offers numerous opportunities for young people and their families to make theater-going a regular part of their lives. This has been demonstrated, for example, by the program's history of creating plays and classroom materials that address significant social and historical themes in a way that is entertaining and relevant to young people.

From its beginnings in 1971 as the Improvisational Theater Project, P.L.A.Y. was one of the first youth-theater programs in the nation founded as an integral part of a professional theater. It remains one of the most innovative and productive. In more than 32 years of operation, the program has reached more than one million young people in schools and community centers throughout the Los Angeles area.

Initially, P.L.A.Y. focused its efforts on a single original production, which toured elementary schools throughout Southern California. But in the last several years, under the direction of producing director Corey Madden and producer Dolores Chavez, P.L.A.Y. has grown significantly, reshaping its programs, renewing its mission, and investigating new

Charles Bodin & David Brouwer in **Legend of Alex** *(P.L.A.Y. Spring tour 2003).*

directions. In 2000, a second touring production specifically directed toward older youth—middle school and high school students—was added. This production, *Black Butterfly, Jaguar Girl, Piñata Woman and Other Superhero Girls, Like Me,* was subsequently selected to be performed at the Kennedy Center and the Smithsonian Institution.

In 2001, P.L.A.Y. inaugurated the Family Performances program, which features discounted subscriptions to four regular season productions at the Mark Taper Forum and Ahmanson Theatre, with workshops led by educators and artists. It also held the first annual P.L.A.Y. Intensive for more than 50 artists working in youth theater, and an Education Workshop for educators.

In the fall of 2002, P.L.A.Y. embarked on the Speak To Me project, a pilot program to expand the reach and increase the depth of the its impact in city schools. Speak To Me is a school-based theater program designed for high school and middle school students. The program seeks to deepen

young people's awareness of the local and global youth community, to teach them a formal dialogue process that promotes respectful interaction, and to use theater to engage them in creative and intellectual communication about the power of art to shape our society.

P.L.A.Y. has formulated a long-range plan with the goal of making the program a national model for arts education. The plan includes strategic partnerships with local educational institutions, pilot residency programs at selected schools, the encouragement of student-created work, a writer-in-residence program in selected schools, and a summer program that brings together several Los Angeles-based arts organizations to offer students a summer course in theater.

In 2004, P.L.A.Y. will acquire a permanent home when the Center Theatre Group creates the new Kirk Douglas Theatre in Culver City as a center for youth-theater and new play development.

Montalvo

Saratoga, CA   www.villamontalvo.org

- School districts served per year: 36
- Elementary schools served per year: 305
- High schools served per year: 73
- K-12 students served per year: 12,000

Programs offered:

Performances for K-12 audiences

Short-term in-school residencies (one week or less)

Long-term in-school residencies (multiple weeks)

After school or weekend programs for K-12 students

Professional development opportunities for teachers

Partnerships with whole schools

Partnerships with whole school districts

Training for school leaders (principals, superintendents, others)

Programs with parents and/or other adult caregivers

Adult education opportunities

Performances/exhibits by students

Evaluation methods

PROFILE

Montalvo maintains a diverse approach to arts education. Programs provide students and teachers with experience in the arts, interaction with professional artists, and adult and community outreach programs.

The core strength of Montalvo is that it not only presents and displays some of the best art of today, it also takes an avid interest in the creative process behind it. The philosophy of the Artist Residency program—the third oldest in the United States—permeates the education programs as well: Art is really about the process more than the product. It is looking at a simple object or the world at large and seeing it in a new way. Montalvo artists are encouraged to explore their creative energies by taking risks and learning from them. The education programs also expect students to step "outside the box" and explore their creative side.

Montalvo inhabits the former estate of Senator James Phelan, who enjoyed and supported virtually all the major creative disciplines during his lifetime. After he died in 1930, his will bequeathed the estate and grounds at Montalvo to the people of California for their deepened appreciation of art, literature, music, and architecture. To that end, Montalvo has structured strong programs in arts education for K-12 students and their teachers.

Programs for students include the Performing Arts Series, which presents some of the best performers from around the world in intimate productions in the Carriage House Theater. More than 12,000 students participate in this program annually, with each class receiving study guides in advance of its visit. The Master Class Series takes further advantage of these great talents' brief stays at Montalvo by bringing them to the schools for direct interaction with students. For example, this past year saw Wynton Marsalis inspiring a local jazz band through careful critique of their work. Noted author Rebecca Walker conducted a memoir-writing workshop for middle school students, and students recently assisted visiting artist Patrick Dougherty in the construction of his outdoor sculpture on Montalvo's grounds.

In a similar spirit, the in-school residency programs allow for artists to work in-depth with students over a period of time. For the past four years Montalvo has supported an artist-in-residence at Trace Elementary School in San Jose. In one project, teachers from Trace trained in the Creating Original Opera program of New York's Metropolitan Opera Guild. Back at school, these teachers worked together with the artist-in-residence to guide their third grade students in the writing, production, and presentation of an original opera, which was then performed on-stage at Montalvo.

Other opportunities for students to create include the Young Writers Competition, now in its 17th year, and regular hands-on art workshops inspired by the exhibiting artists.

"Little Clowns" – elementary level students performing at Montalvo

In 2003, Montalvo instituted a new Teacher Services Initiative, which is expected to greatly elevate the level of its education programs in schools. The first step was to organize a Teacher Advisory Board, whose members include K-12 educators, both from public and private schools, in the South Bay area. Board members will provide professional guidance and expertise in the production, presentation, and evaluation of programs and materials.

Montalvo is also initiating professional development opportunities for educators. Montalvo's first teacher conference, titled "The Arts in Your Classroom," served as an introduction to and training for California's newly adopted Visual and Performing Arts Content Standards. This program, which took place March 7, 2003, at Montalvo, was offered in collaboration with Santa Clara County Office of Education and Cultural Initiatives.

Teaching materials that support the various arts programs at Montalvo will be a regular offering to educators. The spring 2003 teacher guide, for example, was in support of the exhibit "Dwellings." Montalvo has also established a newsletter for teachers, each edition of which will contain lesson-plan inserts, timely articles, and registration information for the Performing Arts Series.

The Artist Residency Program is currently in hiatus, waiting for the completion of construction of 10 new residential villas, each designed by a unique artist/architect team. When the program reopens in the spring of 2004, students will have even greater opportunity to interact with artists. Meanwhile, Montalvo is working to develop ways in which the residency program can train interested artists in teaching methods. Montalvo believes it is this type of collaboration between presenting organization and artist that will produce the highest quality experience for students.

Music Center Education Division (MCED)

Los Angeles, CA   www.musiccenter.org

- **School districts served per year: 100**
- **Elementary schools served per year: 500+**
- **High schools served per year: 60+**
- **K-12 students served per year: 700,000+**

Programs offered:

Performances for K-12 audiences

Short-term in-school residencies (one week or less)

Long-term in-school residencies (multiple weeks)

After school or weekend programs for K-12 students

Professional development opportunities for teachers

Professional development opportunities for teaching artists

Summer institute for K-12 teachers

Summer institute for teaching artists

Partnerships with whole schools

Partnerships with whole school districts

Training for school leaders (principals, superintendents, others)

Programs with parents and/or other adult caregivers

Evaluation methods

PROFILE

The Music Center, the performing arts center of Los Angeles County, gives its Education Division a twofold mission: to support the Music Center's commitment to building audiences by engaging people in the arts at the Center, in schools, and throughout the community; and to advance the quality and scope of arts education as an integral part of the core curriculum in Southern California schools.

The MCED offers some 20 programs, including services for students, schools, teachers, and families as well as the publication of arts-curriculum resource materials, developed in partnership with the school community to address specific learning objectives.

Programming encompasses all types of music, dance, theater (including storytelling, puppetry, and creative writing), and the visual arts; and it reflects not only the full range of styles and traditions, but also the cultural and ethnic diversity of Southern California. The Division has also developed special services to address the needs of underserved populations, including youth-at-risk, physically/mentally/emotionally challenged young people, and preschoolers.

An important programming goal is to provide students with opportunities to experience the work of professional artists in performances and hands-on workshops. Teaching artists must first audition and then participate in the MCED's Artist Training Seminar Series, which focuses on teaching ability, the design of meaningful tasks and projects, and classroom management skills. Novice teaching artists as well as longtime veterans of the MCED roster have found the seminars to be beneficial in increasing their understanding of educational concepts and their effectiveness in the classroom.

Many schools now acknowledge the positive influence of arts education, but they still must overcome serious obstacles to implementing an integrated arts curriculum. With more than two decades of expertise and a continuum of services including introductory programs, in-depth artist-in-residence projects, and teacher training initiatives, the MCED is supporting schools and encouraging them to go beyond the narrow vision of sporadic arts activities to a sequential, standards-based approach. In this spirit, the Education Division has worked in partnership with school districts, including Los Angeles Unified (the nation's second largest), for more than 20 years, and has collaborated as well with other agencies and institutions to create educational-reform initiatives. The Division also works with McGraw-Hill to produce materials for an arts textbook series published for national distribution.

The following are some of the MCED's accomplishments during the 2001-2002 school year. The Division:

- Partnered with 92 school districts and 97 individual private schools to provide arts education programs for students, teachers, and parents

Korean Classical Music and Dance featured at the Music Center Education Division's services for schools

- Presented more than 2,400 assembly performances in music, theater, and dance through Music Center on Tour

- Established 66 long-term artist-in-residence programs for students and their teachers

- Directed 407 professional development activities for teachers at 48 schools

- Set up 54 artist-in-residence projects in preschool facilities, including Head Start centers, through the Southern California Wolf Trap Program

- Presented eight performances by the American Ballet Theatre Studio Company for a total audience of 6,500 fifth graders, who were brought to the Music Center for the 32nd Annual Dorothy B. Chandler Blue Ribbon Children's Festival

- Hosted a five-day intensive Institute for Educators at the Music Center that served 78 teachers

- Installed 65 Arts Care artist-in-residence projects in County-supported mental health and social service agencies

- Recognized 68 nominated teachers and schools through the BRAVO Award for excellence in arts education

- Presented Family Saturdays, an eight-event performance series at the Music Center, which attracted an audience of 3,100 children and adults

- Conducted the 23rd annual Very Special Arts Festival for an estimated audience of 11,000, including young people with disabilities, as well as their parents, their teachers, and members of the general public

- Offered the 2002 Corwin Master Classes, which gave 800 high school and college musicians special opportunities to learn from members of the Los Angeles Philharmonic and distinguished guest artists

- Held the third annual B.E.S.T. Arts Conference (Building Educational Success through the Arts) for preschool teachers in collaboration with Long Beach City College

- Produced the annual Showcase of Artists for an estimated 1,000 visitors, including school administrators, teachers, and parent-group representatives

- Inaugurated a monthly MCED e-mail newsletter

- Distributed *Artsource: The Center Study Guide to the Performing Arts,* the MCED's set of self-published curriculum resource materials for teachers

- Provided nearly $1.6 million in income for the more than 100 individual artists and performing ensembles who participated in MCED services during the year.

San Francisco Performances

San Francisco, CA   www.performances.org

- School districts served per year: 4
- Elementary schools served per year: 3
- High schools served per year: 9
- K-12 students served per year: 3,000

Programs offered:

Performances for K-12 audiences

Performances for K-12 audiences

Short-term in-school residencies (one week or less)

After school or weekend programs for K-12 students

Professional development opportunities for teachers

Partnerships with whole schools

Partnerships with whole school districts

Web-based learning opportunities

Programs with parents and/or other adult caregivers

Adult education opportunities

Mentoring for students with community volunteers

Performances/exhibits by students

Evaluation methods artists

PROFILE

San Francisco Performances' arts education programs seek to increase awareness and participation in the arts. Working with artists, schools, and community organizations, SFP brings internationally acclaimed artists to new settings and audiences of all ages throughout the Bay Area. In partnership with a growing roster of artists-in-residence—including the Alexander String Quartet, jazz percussionist Stefon Harris, classical guitarist Antigoni Goni, and baritone Christopheren Nomura—SFP's school and community programs advance its mission of providing meaningful connections between artists and audiences.

In the Schools

SFP's in-school programs are anchored by multi-year partnerships with artists-in-residence, who add insight and contribute to students' academic and artistic learning. The programs include:

The Story of the String Quartet. This three-part seminar brings the Alexander String Quartet and two younger ensembles into high school classrooms for musical dialogues that introduce motivated English and History students to chamber music. Through performance and discussion, the quartets demonstrate how the evolution of the string quartet reflects Western sociopolitical ideas and events from the 18th to 21st centuries. Study guides, sample CDs, and outlines for classroom activities are an integral part of this program.

Music Mentors. Graduate students and young professional string, jazz, and guitar players provide weekly coaching to music students at two public high schools. Through the Mentors program, high school students improve technique, posture, concentration, and level of performance. Mentors learn and apply techniques for successful outreach to students of all backgrounds.

Dance Mentors. In collaboration with Taylor 2 of the Paul Taylor Dance Company, graduate students in dance teach middle school students basic modern dance technique and choreography. Taylor 2 performs for students and families, and students in turn, perform for peers and the school community.

Jazz Intervention. This four-year program uses jazz, the most democratic of musical forms, to instill leadership skills, effective decision making, communication, and teamwork. Working with an ensemble of local musicians, artist-in-residence Stefon Harris demonstrates how a jazz group must work as a cohesive unit toward the goal of creating a performance.

Performance Poetry. Vocal artist-in-residence Christopheren Nomura addresses issues of music education and literacy with high school students. Working with poet-teachers from California Poets in the Schools, Nomura provides many points of entry into the study of poetry and song through reading, discussion, demonstration, writing, and performing.

Guitar Trek. Artist-in-residence Antigoni Goni's in-school performances and history-based curriculum trace the evolution of the guitar from ancient times

Improvisation session at Eastside College Preparatory School (in East Palo Alto) with the Stefon Harris Quartet

to the present. Advanced placement world history students work with Ms. Goni to learn how to use cultural artifacts such as music and art in research by mining the guitar's rich, mobile history.

In the Community

SFP's artists-in-residence also participate in adult/community education projects. The long-running, free Concerts with Conversation at the San Francisco Community Music Center, for example, bring established and emerging artists to an underserved, appreciative audience. Other programs include:

Delancey Street Foundation. Nationally known for its innovative rehabilitation residency program for ex-convicts and former substance abusers, the Foundation partners with SFP in bringing great artists to their facilities for workshops and performances. Similarly, SFP's programs with Oakland's Allen Temple Baptist Church bring artists on-site to participate in Sunday services, youth music workshops, and the congregation's annual concert series.

Professional Development Workshops for Teachers. SFP offers a series of workshops and lectures, linked to major performances, that sparks new ideas about the performing arts. Teachers in all subject areas are invited, though the workshops and lectures specifi-

cally address SFP's in-school chamber music, jazz, and dance programs.

Family Programs. Now in its eighth season, SFP's Family Matinee series gives families the chance to listen and learn about music and dance in an informal setting. Lively one-hour performances are suitable for children of all ages, and tickets are priced affordably both for children and adults.

Adult Education. SFP presents a series of lectures with noted musicologist/composer Robert Greenberg. In addition, Greenberg joins the Alexander String Quartet for a Saturday morning series that explores specific chamber works through performance and discussion.

Online. SFP's Web site, www.performances.org, makes curriculum materials developed for residency programs in the schools more widely available. Downloadable curriculum guides assist teachers and students not only in music and dance, but also in literature and history classes. The Education page of the Web site is regularly updated with information regarding current activities. Although many in-school events are private performances or sessions with particular classes, public events (such as Concerts with Conversation) are noted, with event information for interested audiences.

Yerba Buena Center for the Arts

San Francisco, CA   www.YerbaBuenaArts.org

- School districts served per year: 1
- Elementary schools served per year: 245
- High schools served per year: 42
- K-12 students served per year: 4,015

Programs offered:

Performances for K-12 audiences

Short-term in-school residencies (one week or less)

Long-term in-school residencies (multiple weeks)

After school or weekend programs for K-12 students

Professional development opportunities for teachers

Professional development opportunities for teaching artists

Partnerships with whole schools

Partnerships with whole school districts

Web-based learning opportunities

Adult education opportunities

Mentoring for students with community volunteers

Performances/exhibits by students

Performances/exhibits by teaching artists

Technical/planning assistance

Evaluation methods

PROFILE

By providing a broad audience with access to exhibitions, films/videos, performing arts, and special community projects, the Education & Community Programs seek to make the Yerba Buena Center for the Arts (YBCA) a living classroom and resource. To ensure that Pre-K-12th grade students, youth, and adult audiences are served alike, the programs are organized into four areas: School Programs, Youth Programs, Public Programs, and Special Community Projects.

School Programs

- *Art Tools for Teachers* is a professional development program that explores the themes and connections in the visual arts; provides ideas for activities at YBCA, the classroom, and after school; and suggests literary and Internet-based resources. Each participant receives a Teacher's Guide on these topics, which is also placed on the Web site, to help serve others' needs and interests.

- *Artful Adventures* are free exhibition tours for school and nonprofit community groups conducted by community volunteers—"Gallery Representatives"—who receive extensive training in exhibition content and touring techniques.

- *Hands-on Activity Workshops* are led by artists-in-residence, as well as by exhibiting and community artists.

- *Discovering Performance* provides Pre-K-12th grade students with access to actors, dancers, and musicians, who explain the artistic process to their young audiences as they perform.

Youth Program

- *Young Artists at Work* is a nationally recognized yearlong art- and job-training youth program, in which 15 ethnically and socioeconomically diverse high school students are paid to learn about visual, performing, and media arts at the Center, and then produce their own original artworks. The program includes three protracted sessions that dovetail with the San Francisco Unified School District's academic calendar, in order to accommodate the young artists' testing dates and other curricular and extracurricular needs. Each session is taught by a noted professional artist-trainer who works with the Education & Community Programs staff to ensure that lessons align with the California State Frameworks in Visual and Performing Arts. In this way, students' out-of-school art and job training enriches their in-school curricula.

Public Programs include tours, lectures, discussions, and events designed for college and adult audiences.

- *First Thursday Tours* for the general public feature YBCA curators, artists, academics, and community scholars who lead focused exhibition tours.

- *In Conversation* programs feature artists, curators, and other professionals whose work colludes or collides with, and illuminates, that of artists presenting or exhibiting at YBCA.

• *Panels and Symposia*

    – **Preparing for Open Studios:** The Artist as Entrepreneur provides information about how to have a successful business. Panelists cover such topics as how to register for Open Studios, photograph and prepare slides of your work, and how to publicize your Open Studio.

    – **Everything You Ever Wanted to Know about the Art World but Were Afraid to Ask, Part 1** provides practical information for young and emerging artists about how to establish oneself in the private sector art world.

    – **Everything You Ever Wanted to Know about the Art World but Were Afraid to Ask, Part 2** explores the topic as it relates to nonprofit arts organizations, such as museums and art centers.

    – **D.E.A.F. Media Salons**, offered in collaboration with D.E.A.F. Media, Inc., to adults who are deaf or hard-of-hearing, are conversations led by artists-in-residence.

Special Community Projects are designed to be responsive to collaborative opportunities and special events, and to continue valuable relationships with health and social service organizations.

• *Thursday Night Live!* series are presented as part of the multidisciplinary CenterFests.

• *Inside the Institution: The Visible Arts Center*, a collaboration between YBCA and the San Francisco Art Institute, is a class aimed at giving students an historical understanding of the motivating factors and origins of Bay Area interdisciplinary art. They also learn about the complexities of curating across disciplines, including social, political, and aesthetic considerations. While the course focuses on the particular strengths of YBCA, students are given a more general context for understanding how curatorial practices are born and how they relate to an institution's mission and role in the community.

• *Milestones Graduation Ceremony* is an annual event honoring graduates of the nonprofit alcohol and drug treatment program for parolees.

• Other programs are produced as well, based on the needs and interests of community partners.

Westport Country Playhouse

Westport, CT   www.westportplayhouse.org

- School districts served per year: 18
- Elementary schools served per year: 26
- High schools served per year: 14
- K-12 students served per year: 5,000

Programs offered:

Performances for K-12 audiences

After school or weekend programs for K-12 students

Professional development opportunities for teachers

Partnerships with whole school districts

Performances/exhibits by students

Evaluation methods

PROFILE

The Westport Country Playhouse provides a wide range of educational programs: internships and apprenticeships for college and high school students; educational theater programs during the academic year, a special children's theater series during the summer; and most recently, the innovative Something of Our Own project that encourages children to create their own works.

The productions selected and their accompanying educational activities are designed to support the objectives of the Language Arts Curriculum Framework set forth by the Connecticut State Department of Education. Programming is also responsive to the needs articulated by teachers and administrators at elementary, middle, and high school levels in a survey conducted by the Playhouse in the spring of 2002. For example, teacher materials and correspondence from the Playhouse apprise educators of how its programming can be incorporated into classes in order to help students meet both content and performance standards for language arts.

For school-age children, excellent educational theater is provided both during the academic year and the summer. The past school year's repertoire included *Romeo and Juliet, The Christmas that*

Almost Wasn't (presented by the Child's Play Touring Theater), Ball in the House (a six-piece a cappella group from Boston, Mass.), and concluded with Something of Our Own, which provides meaningful and collaborative opportunities for educators and students alike.

Westport Country Playhouse joins with Chicago-based Child's Play, the premier U.S. theater company dedicated exclusively to performing works written by children, to offer the Something of Our Own program. Educators can take advantage of workshops on creative and dramatic writing instruction techniques, as well as on methods to encourage children to write. For their part, students are empowered through self-exploration and self-expression, while having the opportunity to submit work (such as a short story, song, poem, or play) to be considered for inclusion in an original Child's Play Touring Theater production commissioned by the Playhouse.

The children's summer series has been introducing youngsters to the wonder of live theater for the past forty years. Traditionally, the series has included children's musical plays, puppets, magicians, and children's music. One programming goal is to combine the best-loved performance groups of previous seasons with new and innovative companies. This variety of work introduces children to the theater's wondrous ability to entertain and inform. Traditional fairy tales and foreign fables, flights of fancy and imagination, classic folk songs and music from other lands, all lead young audience members on a musical, multicultural journey.

Because great socioeconomic disparity exists in Fairfield County, which has wealthy suburbs, as well as cities in great need, the Playhouse's varied programming is designed to appeal to the diverse audiences of its surrounding communities. In that spirit, it has forged a relationship with the Bridgeport Public School system and works with the system's performing arts supervisor to involve educators in projects and encourage them to bring students to the Playhouse. Student matinees provide school groups with unique and entertaining field trips; and study guides titled *Inside Insights* are distributed in advance of the performance to detail themes for discussion, pose study questions, and provide visual images, interesting facts, and activities.

"The Love Bug's Hug by Bugs and Balloons"

The Playhouse's notable educational offerings for young adults are the apprentice and intern programs. The apprentice program is designed to provide local high school students, as well as college and graduate students, with an expansive exposure to theater—for which they can receive academic credit—through practical work with professional actors, designers, and technicians. Apprentices must make an eight-week commitment to the Playhouse, and are expected to be dedicated, hardworking young adults with a passion to learn about the many facets of a professional theater. They rotate through various work assignments while studying the plays of the season with the Apprentice Coordinator and taking workshops with guest artists.

The intern program looks for serious-minded, highly motivated individuals—college students, graduate students, or recent graduates—who have already acquired some theatrical training and experience and are ready for the next step toward a career in professional theater. Internships, offered in various production, administrative, and artistic areas, provide hands-on experience crucial to a professional résumé. Interns must be willing to commit themselves for a period of at least 12 weeks, during which they engage in the creative process and test the limits of their own ingenuity. In turn, they are treated as members of the professional staff.

Broward Center
for the Performing Arts

Fort Lauderdale, FL

www.browardcenter.org

- School districts served per year: one
- Elementary schools served per year: 136
- High schools served per year: 27
- K-12 students served per year: 104,000

Programs offered:

Performances for K-12 audiences

Short-term in-school residencies (one week or less)

Professional development opportunities for teachers

Professional development opportunities for teaching artists

Summer institute for K-12 teachers

Partnerships with whole schools

Partnerships with whole school districts

Training for school leaders (principals, superintendents, others)

Programs with parents and/or other adult caregivers

Adult education opportunities

Performances/exhibits by students

Performances/exhibits by teaching artists

PROFILE

A 40 year partnership with the School Board of Broward County, FL is at the heart of the Broward Center's award-winning educational programs. This collaboration has enabled the Broward Center's 585-seat Amaturo Theater—the site of the Student Enrichment in the Arts (SEAS) program that brings professional-level performances to more than 100,000 public school students each year—to be declared an outside resource classroom for Broward Public Schools. To date, more than 1.2 million students have benefited from the program, at no charge to their families.

Philosophically, the SEAS program goes far beyond arts education per se by encouraging learning through the arts—a result of the very close cooperation between the Broward Center staff and the faculty of Broward Public Schools. For example, a teacher's study guide that accompanies each SEAS performance includes all relevant curriculum ties to Florida's Sunshine State Standards, thereby enabling classroom teachers to use live performances to teach reading, language arts, social studies, and even math and science.

As a member of the John F. Kennedy Center's Partners in Education program, the Broward Center hosts a range of Professional Development Workshops for Educators each year, completely free of charge both to public and arts education teachers. And although the Broward Center is not a visual arts facility, it has also welcomed the visual arts teachers who hold their annual summer institute and other events there.

The Broward Center has also entered into comprehensive partnerships with three performing arts magnet schools: Dillard High School, Parkway Middle School, and Bethune Elementary School. The partnership with Bethune has resulted in two Arts Innovation Awards from the International Network of Visual and Performing Arts Schools, among other accolades. Perhaps the most exceptional aspect of the partnerships with each of these schools is the way they work together. The Broward Center plays a totally different role in each of these partnerships, yet always in response to the needs of the faculty and students.

In fact, a distinguishing feature of all of the educational programs is the Broward Center's desire to work with the schools, on the school's terms, to achieve the school's objectives. Although performing arts centers sometimes bestow arts education programs without fully understanding the goals or needs of the receiving district or individual school, Broward has turned that model completely around. The Broward Center's Department of Education functions primarily as a school resource and believes its most valuable role is to provide opportunities appropriate to the school.

The community enrichment programs are driven by this same philosophy. Classes for senior citizens, pre-concert lectures for adults, and pre-show arts and craft sessions for preschoolers are all presented in response to community requests. In the same way, the college internship programs were custom-designed to satisfy the needs of students and the institutions of higher learning located in the community.

PACT Inc. (Ruth Eckerd Hall)

Clearwater, FL   www.rutheckerdhall.org

- School districts served per year: 50+
- Elementary schools served per year: 100+
- High schools served per year: 30+
- K-12 students served per year: 140,000

Programs offered:

Performances for K-12 audiences

Short-term in-school residencies (one week or less)

Long-term in-school residencies (multiple weeks)

After school or weekend programs for K-12 students

Professional development opportunities for teachers

Professional development opportunities for teaching artists

Summer institute for K-12 teachers

Summer institute for teaching artists

Partnerships with whole schools

Partnerships with whole school districts

Partnerships with public broadcasting

Partnerships with cable media

Web-based learning opportunities

Programs with parents and/or other adult caregivers

Adult education opportunities

Mentoring for students with community volunteers

Performances/exhibits by students

Performances/exhibits by teaching artists

Technical/planning assistance

Evaluation methods

PROFILE

The goals of the Education Program at Ruth Eckerd Hall include: developing new ways of learning and achieving through the arts, based on an arts-integrated learning method; providing enhanced development for students of the arts, as well as professional development opportunities for teachers and artists in the community; designing programs to connect young people and their families through the arts; and utilizing the arts to cross cultural barriers and unify neighborhoods.

These goals have often been realized. The Hall's education program, the largest of its type in the Southeastern United States, directly involves more than 160,000 young people and adults a year, including at-risk youth and residents of low income neighborhoods. The first arts education program in Florida to be honored as a Kennedy Center Arts Partner in Education, it has served more than 1.5 million to date. In addition, a recently completed 17,000 sq. ft. educational institute will increase program impact by 50 percent or more and enable classes drawing upon technology, such as digital learning and digital arts, to be taught. This enhancement will build on the year-round performing arts classes presently offered.

Learning opportunities provided for children and youth, in addition to the classes referenced above, include specialized programs such as the following:

- *Series of performances for school and family audiences*, which include works by the Hall's own producing arm and performances by the Eckerd Theater Company—a professional children's theater group. All productions focus on themes such as friendship, loyalty, courage, and integrity. Teachers are provided with related curriculum materials for their classes.

- The Florida Playwrights' Process offers playwriting workshops in elementary and middle schools and a regional competition for students' original works, winners of which are workshopped and produced professionally at Ruth Eckerd Hall.

- The *Ruth Eckerd Hall Scholarship program* provides four $2,000 scholarships each year for area juniors and seniors excelling in dance, music, or theater. Many of these students have gone on to become nationally recognized artists.

- *Extended residencies for students*. For example, the Chocolate Nutcracker provided 12 weeks of instruction in dance this past year to 200 children from K-12, 85 percent of whom were from multicultural and at-risk backgrounds.

One of the Hall's newest programs is Passport to the Arts, an initiative to bring arts-enrichment experiences to schools and students unable to afford them (high-risk youth). It provides extensive professional development for classroom teachers,

Music Intensive students enjoy a very special guest visit by pianist Chick Corea.

school administrators, and teaching artists to help overcome a general lack of teacher comfort in utilizing the arts to enhance curriculum. An important element of this program is the ongoing assessment and evaluation conducted by outside consultants, which include on-site visits, participant interviews, assessment instruments, and measurement development. The resulting Program Assessment Model, together with program design, materials and lesson plans, and assessment instruments, will be shared nationally in publication form in 2004-2005. At present, the pilot program reaches into three partner schools and 25 classrooms (grades 3, 4, and 5), directly affecting some 800 students.

The core strength of the education program is a committed, knowledgeable, and caring staff that has earned the respect of the entire community and professionals in the national arts and arts education fields. This commitment extends throughout the organization, up to the Board level, thereby enabling the education staff to explore, develop, and implement the newest in programs and technologies as well as the best of existing methodologies and curricula. This serves children and youth not just in Florida, but the whole country.

The program supports in-school residencies by securing renowned national artists for programs, and then supplementing the experiences with teaching artists who provide long-term follow-up. Ruth Eckerd Hall trains these teaching artists by providing them with instruction on state and national educational standards, school and classroom culture, measurement techniques, and curriculum links. The Hall's education department also serves as a clearinghouse for facilitating other local organizations' provision of arts to local school systems.

The Hall supports K-12 classroom teachers through the development of arts-integrated teaching materials based on state and national standards, and the offering of extensive professional development workshops. Teachers are paid stipends, not only to attend, but also to secure substitute teachers to cover their classroom duties. Subsidies are available to cover transportation costs for school programs as well.

Ruth Eckerd Hall's education program has always— and continues—to lead the way in utilizing the arts to secure students' personal and academic achievement. It has served as a model for most education programs presently in place in performing arts centers throughout Florida.

Tampa Bay Performing Arts Center

Tampa, FL   www.tbpac.org

- School districts served per year: 7
- Elementary schools served per year: 41
- High schools served per year: 14
- K-12 students served per year: 100,000

Programs offered:

Performances for K-12 audiences

After school or weekend programs for K-12 students

Professional development opportunities for teachers

Professional development opportunities for teaching artists

Summer institute for teaching artists

Partnerships with whole schools

Partnerships with whole school districts

Partnerships with cable media

Programs with parents and/or other adult caregivers

Adult education opportunities

Performances/exhibits by students

Performances/exhibits by teaching artists

Technical/planning assistance

Evaluation methods

PROFILE

The Center's coordinated efforts allow young people to experience the beauty and importance of the arts. The education and humanities department has initiated numerous and diverse programs since its inception, including the following:

- On School Time

- Partnership in the Schools outreach and master classes

- Outreach to community centers, churches, and neighborhood residential centers

- Outreach to locally based international cultural organizations

- Outreach to smaller community theaters through the Arts in the Community programming

- Kid Time and Wee Folk performances

- Tampa Bay Youth Orchestra

- Classical ballet training program

- Community Arts Ensemble and Community Arts: Winter Institute

The On School Time program provides local schools with exposure to culturally diverse national touring groups. The Wee Folk Series enables preschoolers and kindergarteners to experience close contact with national artists. And the outreach programs offer unique workshop-style interactions in a school environment between artists, hailing from throughout the country and the world, and local children. The commitment to connecting several culturally diverse communities is at the forefront of many of the programs. Last year a Spanish-speaking initiative was implemented to create stronger relationships with local Latin communities. Collaborations with Indian music schools and cultural centers has brought an even wider range of programming.

The Artists as Educators program is designed to connect a specific artist with a local area school and provide students with in-depth learning opportunities in the various fields of performing arts, such as singing, dance, storytelling, theater, and music. The Arts in Action program is designed as a series of extended outreach experiences for advanced arts students in public and private schools. It uses extended artistic residencies to connect the performing arts with other areas of the curriculum, such as literature, language arts, geography, and history.

Artists as Educators is an important initiative that helps performing artists hone their teaching abilities. The goal of the program is twofold: to provide training for local artists who want to develop skills as artist/educators, and to offer high quality performing arts experiences for underserved young people in the Tampa Bay area. The Center has recognized that the greatest moments to inspire often come after the performance, when the artist has the students' attention and can interact with them to great effect. This program also serves as a wonderful vehicle for residencies both in school and at the Center.

The Center is committed to providing K-12 teachers with additional training by extending the outreach artists' efforts to teacher workshops, which help teachers make higher-impact connections with their students in science, literature, language arts, history, and math classes. Also, 10 of the approximately 50 On School Time performances per year are designated as Page to Stage. Designed to improve literacy skills in school-age children, this interactive program demonstrates the link between a work of literature and a corresponding theatrical performance. Using a specially designed study guide, students first read a designated book and then complete related educational activities, including writing an essay. The Summer Teacher Forum supports teachers and also helps teachers support the Center: it is designed to give local educators a way to provide input on Center educational programming. During the summer months, groups of teachers participate in focus groups, give feedback on existing programs, and discuss new curriculum needs.

Several Tampa Bay area public and private schools are designated as "partner schools." The Center provides them with master classes taught by touring artists, helps to design their curricula, and holds practice auditions for their students. These schools are involved, in turn, in educational projects, and they are frequently offered discounted tickets or free admission to many of the Center's presentations, including Broadway shows, plays, concerts, and dance performances.

The Center's reach in the community—currently serving more than 100,000 youth per year—has spread to the point that it has outgrown the current facility, and is now in the process of building a School for the Performing Arts. This expansion will enhance the Center's ability to broaden that reach and provide the space to offer year-round classes in all phases of the performing arts from beginner to pre-professional level.

Van Wezel Performing Arts Hall

Sarasota, FL   www.vanwezel.org

- **School districts served per year:** 4
- **Elementary schools served per year:** 75
- **High schools served per year:** 57
- **K-12 students served per year:** 30,000

Programs offered:

Performances for K-12 audiences

Short-term in-school residencies (one week or less)

Long-term in-school residencies (multiple weeks)

Professional development opportunities for teachers

Professional development opportunities for teaching artists

Partnerships with whole schools

Partnerships with whole school districts

Partnerships with cable media

Training for school leaders (principals, superintendents, others)

Programs with parents and/or other adult caregivers

Adult education opportunities

Mentoring for students with community volunteers

Performances/exhibits by students

Technical/planning assistance

Evaluation methods

PROFILE

The Van Wezel Performing Arts Hall, designed by Frank Lloyd Wright's Taliesin firm, is a purple seashell-shaped building that sits on the edge of the Gulf of Mexico. Owned and operated by the City of Sarasota, the Hall has an active education department that puts on more than 130 events per season aimed at providing meaningful arts experiences for all members of the community. These arts education programs are delivered in a variety of ways to actively engage all learning styles.

The Schooltime Performance series presents 26 performances featuring national and international artists—including such main-stage groups as the Alvin Ailey American Dance Theatre,

The Acting Company, and the Moiseyev Dance Company—to K-12 students and their teachers. Many of these performances include a question-and-answer session afterward; and the performing artists often go into the schools to provide master classes for dance/drama/music students or lead workshops in the classrooms.

More than 30,000 students are brought to the Hall performances from four surrounding counties. Ticket prices are an affordable six dollars, and teacher and student study materials are provided in advance. These programs and education materials are carefully selected to reinforce the local curriculum and the Florida State curriculum. The Hall has even committed to printing study guides for every student, when appropriate, if schools' printing budgets have been cut; and it provides bus-fare reimbursement in cases where the students would be charged. The youngest audiences are welcomed to the Saturday Morning For Kids series with performances such as *The Little Engine That Could, Alice In Wonderland,* and *Franklin.*

The Van Wezel is partnered with the Sarasota County School District in the Partners in Education program of the John F. Kennedy Center for the Performing Arts. This program offers professional development workshops that help teachers to teach in, through, and about the arts. Nationally renowned educators are brought to Sarasota to lead these dynamic three-hour workshops, for which the school district gives in-service credit. The educators continue their work the next day by coaching and modeling in the classroom with participating teachers, who report that their mastery of the techniques increases through these classroom/workshop extensions. Evaluations on in-classroom activities following the workshops are collected for use in assessment. Participating teachers are later invited to a Teacher Recognition Evening with dinner, an artist talk, and a performance; and they receive discounts on selected performances designed to improve their own arts literacy.

The Kennedy Center has also selected the Van Wezel/Sarasota County School District partnership for two other projects involving national evaluation and research. The first two-year effort involved the assessment of the professional development programs and the effectiveness of teaching science through movement. The second project investigates the value of arts integration for improving literacy skills and instructing teachers to collect, analyze, and interpret research data to better advocate for the arts. The Hall also works intensively with individual schools on specifically designed yearlong projects that support achievement goals such as math and interdisciplinary learning.

The Hall's Education Department plans long-term artist residencies each season to engage a larger fraction of the community, bring new audiences to the Hall, and further explore a particular art form. Past residencies have included The Tibetan Monks, Urban Tap, Urban Bush Women, and WOFA!, as well as local drumming circles, senior citizen centers, gospel choirs, and martial arts/dance studios. Evening audiences participate in pre- and post-performance discussions with the artists, and have spent an hour with Paul Stokey (of Peter, Paul and Mary), Bobby McFerrin, Yo-Yo Ma, Awadagin Pratt, and Pilobolus, among others.

The Hall's innovative programs include unexpected collaborations. Van Wezel is partners with the Ringling School of Art and Design to provide live performing arts experiences to its visual arts college students, working with 300 freshmen who attend six selected evening programs at the Hall. Afterward the artists come to the campus for an exchange of art-making. For example, Parsons Dance Company choreographed and video-recorded dance sculptures with the students, and Aquila Theatre Company worked with welding students in the studio to create mythological characters through drama and metal. Another collaboration involves Sarasota's New College, whose ethnomusicology classes use the main-stage performances as their syllabus each semester.

Spivey Hall
Clayton College &
State University

Morrow, GA   www.spiveyhall.org

- School districts served per year: 18
- Elementary schools served per year: 74
- High schools served per year: 92
- K-12 students served per year: 18,937

Programs offered:

Performances for K-12 audiences

Short-term in-school residencies (one week or less)

After school or weekend programs for K-12 students

Professional development opportunities for teachers

Adult education opportunities

Performances/exhibits by students

Performances/exhibits by school-based teachers

Performances/exhibits by teaching artists

Technical/planning assistance

Evaluation methods

PROFILE

Spivey Hall's eight music education programs build bridges between individuals and the world of music by reaching area school students and their parents, some of whom have never heard quality music in a world-class facility before. Through these experiences, accessibility to the arts is established. Spivey Hall's programs expand the community's appreciation for music and help create a future audience for the arts:

• The Spivey Hall Choral Workshop has served more than 1,600 of Georgia's students in just eight years. It provides metro area middle and high school vocalists with the finest in choral training. These week-long interactive learning experiences culminate in a final performance for friends, family, teachers, administrators, and the choral community.

• Teachers earn staff-development credit while observing some of the nation's leading conductors at work—for example, 2002 Choral Workshop conductors were Janet Galvan and Eph Ehly.

• The Children's Concert Series, for students Pre-K through 12, provides performances by some of today's renowned musicians. The series covers a variety of musical genres and is designed to complement the public-school curriculum. With 60 concerts to choose from, teachers are certain to find programs to meet their own curricular needs.

• In March 2001, Spivey Hall created a new educational program to help train orchestra students. The Spivey Hall Chamber Orchestra Workshop, structured much like the Choral Workshop, provides selected metro-Atlanta high school students with instruction of the highest quality. Dr. William LaRue Jones conducted the first performance. Subsequent workshops were conducted in March 2002 featuring Louis Bergonzi and in November 2002 with Kathleen DeBerry Brungard.

• The Spivey Hall Children's Choir Program consists of 150 gifted singers between the ages of 10 and 18 who perform in three choirs: the Spivey Hall Tour Choir, Spivey Hall Children's Choir, and the Spivey Hall Young Artists. Formed in the Fall 2002, Young Artists is a training choir for children ages 10-13. The program offers its members professional-level music training in vocal pedagogy, music theory, sight singing, ear training, and presentation, as well as exposure to a variety of choral styles.

• Another of Spivey Hall's distinguished education-outreach programs is its master classes. World-renowned performers at Spivey Hall work with local and regional performing artists, as well as high school and college students, giving insight into their craft in one-on-one coaching sessions while others observe. Master classes have included soprano Sylvia McNair, harpist Nancy Allen, saxophonist Harvey Pittel, organist Richard Morris, and flautist Jean-Pierre Rampal. These classes have gained recognition across the southeast as students from neighboring states travel to Spivey Hall to participate.

• Throughout the year, teachers gain additional training and maintain teaching certification through various staff-development opportunities.

For example, concentrated summer courses are provided to keep Atlanta area educators up to date, and encourage collaboration with colleagues in the region. Summer 2002 courses included Teaching Methods for General Music Educators, Choral Techniques, Introduction to Finale, and Web page Design.

• In April 2002 Spivey Jam! was introduced—a program in which middle school bands perform for professional jazz musicians/analysts, who offer expert advice and mentoring. This is not a competition, but rather a celebration of young talent and music in the schools. The 2002 event culminated with a private dinner with international jazz-singing star, Grammy nominee and Atlanta resident Freddy Cole.

SPIVEY HALL

This set of education outreach programs, one of the largest in Georgia, imparts vital skills to many of the Atlanta area's students. Members of the Spivey Hall Children's Choir learn the importance of discipline and hard work, while sharpening social and artistic skills. The Choral and Chamber Workshops hone students' innate abilities, build self-esteem, and create a sense of the value of teamwork. The Children's Concert Series nurtures an appreciation of music, while igniting students' own creative impulses. Master classes allow young players to learn from masters of their craft and develop confidence in their own capabilities.

Hancher Auditorium
The University of Iowa

Iowa City, IA

www.uiowa.edu/hancher

- School districts served per year: 36
- Elementary schools served per year: 50
- High schools served per year: 28
- K-12 students served per year: 12,500

Programs offered:

Performances for K-12 audiences

Short-term in-school residencies (one week or less)

Long-term in-school residencies (multiple weeks)

Professional development opportunities for teachers

Partnerships with whole schools

Partnerships with whole school districts

Partnerships with public broadcasting

Programs with parents and/or other adult caregivers
Adult education opportunities

Performances/exhibits by students

Evaluation methods

PROFILE

Hancher Auditorium offers a wide range of educational programs both for adults and children. Every year, it presents master classes, lectures, free family concerts, a school matinee series, networked learning programs, and in-school residencies. During the 2001-2002 season, the education programs reached more than 17,000 people in the region.

Hancher Auditorium presents a Stage Door series every season, which includes five matinees for K-12 students. Tickets for this series, which began in 1980, are only $4. During the 2001-2002 season, more than 7,200 students attended the Stage Door performances. During the past year, they saw artists such as Preservation Hall Jazz Band, Ballet Folklorico de Mexico, Shaolin Warriors, and Sweet Honey in the Rock.

Pilobolus Dance Theatre Workshop with elementary school students

In 1996, Hancher began to broadcast educational programs on the Iowa Communications Network (ICN), a fiber-optic system that permits interactive communication in real time. For example, four times a year hosting free ICN workshops with visiting artists, students in classrooms throughout Iowa can watch the artists on the Hancher stage and ask them questions. Since 2000, schools in more than 50 (mostly rural) communities have participated in this process. Artists have included jazz pianist Marcus Roberts, the Ying Quartet, and the cast of Blast!, among others.

Hancher Auditorium also emphasizes educational programming for families and adults, with several free family concerts a year. In 2001, Hancher finished a three-year partners project that specifically targeted the 25 to 45 year-old segment of the potential audience; free concerts were held in the workplace, libraries, museums, and other locations in the general community.

As a university presenter, it is also important that educational programming be brought to the immediate community. Every year, university students attend open rehearsals in the auditorium; in the past year, they were able to see the Jazz at Lincoln Center Orchestra, Academy of Ancient Music, and Compania Nacional de Danza. Master classes last season for university students were given by opera singer Frederica Von Stade and members of the Philadelphia Orchestra and Houston Ballet. Visiting artists in university classrooms present lectures and discussions, and they are often highlighted in university media and radio shows.

Each season, Hancher sponsors residencies that bring artists into the K-12 classroom. A three-year project, called Arts Across the Curriculum, involved 12 elementary and middle schools in eastern Iowa and 6 visiting artists . This multi-layered project—which included teacher workshops, creation of new units of study, in-school workshops by visiting artists, Hancher performances, ICN workshops, and free evening family events in every community—was designed to encourage the integration of the performing arts into all areas of school curricula. Educators learned how to incorporate music, dance, and theater into subjects such as math, social studies, and reading.

Urban Gateways:
Center for Arts Education

Chicago, IL   www.urbangatetways.org

- School districts served per year: 89
- Elementary schools served per year: 393
- High schools served per year: 35
- K-12 students served per year: 320,000

Programs offered:

Performances for K-12 audiences

Short-term in-school residencies (one week or less)

Long-term in-school residencies (multiple weeks)

After school or weekend programs for K-12 students

Professional development opportunities for teachers

Professional development opportunities for teaching artists

Summer institute for K-12 teachers

Partnerships with whole schools

Training for school leaders (principals, superintendents, others)

Programs with parents and/or other adult caregivers

Performances/exhibits by students

Evaluation methods

PROFILE

Urban Gateways holds that the arts constitute basic learning experiences for all people, and that, when taught effectively, they can provide valuable skills applicable to other subjects. The arts are a means to discovering and developing new and creative ways of thinking, learning, and expressing oneself. When children study an art form in-depth to discover its historical and cultural significance, they strengthen their abilities to comprehend, conceptualize, and problem-solve. Through the sustained efforts of adults, parents and teachers alike, these skills can be reinforced and further developed in children, producing positive effects on their performance in other subject areas and a long-term impact on their lives.

These objectives are persued through in-school and out-of-school performances, classroom residencies, specially designed programs, and professional development for educators and artists. Using Urban Gateways' methodology of "Encounter, Engage, and Reflect," teachers and students first encounter the professional work of an artist, then engage in the making of art, and lastly reflect upon the process.

Core programs include:

- *Artist-in-Residence.* Urban Gateways' professional artists work with teachers to design and achieve arts instruction that incorporates and complements science, math, history, and literature. The artists visit classrooms weekly for up to four months, helping children to use art and their imagination to expand their learning possibilities. More than 95,000 students, teachers, and parents in more than 60 schools participate in this program each year.

- *Touring Performances.* Educators may choose from a list of 50 programs in dance, music, and theater that will then travel to their schools. Urban Gateways also provides educational materials that teachers use to prepare students for the performance they will see and to help them discuss the programs after the touring artists have departed. Immediately following performances, companion workshops bring greater understanding of the art form to the audiences. More than 800 performances are scheduled each year, reaching 230,000 students.

- *Student Matinee Program.* Students attend performances of national and international touring companies in some of Chicago's historic theatrical sites. Here, too, Urban Gateways provides educational materials that teachers use to prepare students for the performance they will see and to help them discuss the programs after they return to school. Fourteen to nineteen titles are presented annually, reaching 25,000 students.

• *Customized Programs.* Urban Gateways designs customized programs to meet specific themes or special needs for a variety of educational, community, and professional settings. For example, it collaborates with the Elgin Symphony Orchestra and Hamilton Wings (an Elgin, Ill.-based not-for-profit organization) on "SCORE!" In that program, which stands for "Students Creating Opera to Reinforce Education! " Urban Gateways assists in the conception, development, and production of an original opera.

• *Professional Development Programs.* Urban Gateways emphasizes child-centered education— using the arts as a generative force through which a holistically healthy child may be developed. To adequately equip teachers, the professional development programs for teachers—the Summer Institute—also trains teachers in aesthetic education and its integration into the curriculum. Twenty to twenty-five teachers participate each summer. Educator-artists themselves must be similarly prepared. Urban Gateways' artists are required to participate in training seminars conducted by staff and master artists prior to beginning their work in schools each year. Topics include creative teaching techniques, relating art forms to societal and historical contexts, engaging students in the learning process, and general classroom management. Each artist is taught how to present a performance or workshop within the classroom. Special attention is paid to ensuring that each contact with students and teachers reflects diverse classical and cultural forms, is age appropriate, and has a high educational and artistic value. New and emerging artists receive adddtional training through working with master artists, serving as mentors.

Clowes Memorial Hall of Butler University

Indianapolis, IN   www.cloweshall.org

• **School districts served per year: 100+**
• **Elementary schools served per year: 75+**
• **High schools served per year: 25+**
• **K-12 students served per year: 60,000+**

Programs offered:

Performances for K-12 audiences

Short-term in-school residencies (one week or less)

Professional development opportunities for teachers

Partnerships with whole schools

Partnerships with whole school districts

Adult education opportunities

Evaluation methods

PROFILE

The goal of the Clowes Memorial Hall education program is to educate, enrich, and entertain students and adults of all ages through a broad range of arts offerings—performances, teacher workshops, interactive distance-learning sessions, clinics with artist-educators, in-school residencies, open rehearsals, and facility tours—that will meet the needs and interests of virtually all learners. The growth over the last 12 years of the Pre-K-12 program in particular has led to an emphasis on integrated programming that helps students and educators from across the state to value, connect with, and engage in the arts. All Pre-K-12 events and programs are designed to enhance the Indiana Academic Standards in language, science, history, social studies, character education, and the fine arts. They also help teachers address issue-based curricula on topics such as human rights, self-confidence, cooperation, and careers.

The School Matinee Series serves as the foundation on which other Clowes educational activities are built. Diverse programs and presentations in instrumental and choral music, opera, theater, and ballet not only connect with the school curriculum, but also provide students and educators with new appreciation of the arts and the role of the artist. To prepare students for a matinee program, the Clowes Education Department publishes student study guides, called *Clowes Sheets*, that are sent to every student three weeks prior to attending a performance. The Clowes Sheet can include a synopsis of the story, pertinent vocabulary, discussion of the art form, historical or geographic information, or interesting facts about the production. In addition, students are challenged to interpret lines from the play, solve problems relating to the story, or evaluate the adaptation of a book into a stage production.

As a charter member of the John F. Kennedy Center's Partners in Education program, Clowes Hall has embraced teacher training as an integral part of its mission. Through teacher workshops that model arts-integrated teaching methods, the Partners in Education program helps the Hall reach teachers and their students with innovative learning techniques and materials. Workshop leaders are trained artist-educators who work with teachers to develop their understanding of an art form, connect the content of a production to the school curriculum, and demonstrate arts-in-education teaching strategies that can be implemented immediately in the classroom. Teachers have the option of earning Indiana license-renewal credit or Butler University academic credit for participating in these workshops.

Clowes works with partnering schools to develop artist residencies that meet specific curricular needs and goals. Artists, principals, teachers, and Clowes education staff participate in the planning and implementation of the residencies, which often

Students participating from their classroom in a "distance learning" (teleconferencing) education session – "Dancers Are Athletes"

CLOWES MEMORIAL HALL OF BUTLER UNIVERSITY

include both teacher workshops and student sessions that model effective arts-integration strategies.

Another aspect of the education program involves the use of distance-learning technology. Made possible by the "magic" of fiber optics, distance learning utilizes two-way teleconferencing to connect students in the classroom or adults in retirement homes and learning centers with educators at Clowes Memorial Hall; this technology is particularly valuable for groups with accessibility needs or those located in remote areas. Distance-learning sessions are designed by the Clowes Education Department to complement various aspects of the education program, and they can include: behind-the-scenes looks at performances, informal conversations with artists, opportunities to observe master classes, explorations of the playwriting process, or in-depth looks at careers in the arts.

Clinics with artists are open both to student and adult learners and are held in informal settings where patrons can hear guest artists talk about their art form and personal performance history. Question-and-answer sessions usually follow. In addition, master classes are offered at Butler's Jordan College of Fine Art. Students can participate in these classes led by leaders in the fields of dance, music, and theater, where they can perform and be critiqued.

Events and activities of the Clowes education program are rigorously evaluated on a continual basis. Response forms and surveys, requesting both qualitative and quantitative data, are collected from all participants and staff. Surveys solicit responses to the overall quality of the presentation, access, seating, student study guides, and specific issues relative to each presentation. Results of evaluations are tabulated and compiled for each educational event, and reports are presented to to Clowes's Advisory Council and staff. The Education Department also compiles an annual report summarizing the year's programming with statistics and evaluation results, which is then used as the basis of a year-end report given to the Advisory Council for its assistance in evaluating operational procedures and planning future programs.

The Lied Center of Kansas
University of Kansas

Lawrence, KS   www.lied.ku.edu

- School Districts served per year: 1
- Elementary schools served per year: 18
- High schools served per year: 3
- K-12 students served per year: 9,000

Programs offered:

Performances for K-12 audiences

Short-term in-school residencies (one week or less)

Professional development opportunities for teachers

Partnerships with whole school districts

Training for school leaders (principals, superintendents, others)

Programs with parents and/or other adult caregivers

Adult education opportunities

Performances/exhibits by school-based teachers

Evaluation methods

PROFILE

The Lied Center of Kansas offers a comprehensive set of educational programs that serve not only K-12 learners but also adults in the community.

The K-12 Adventures in Imagination (AiI) program includes school performances and workshops that support classroom curriculum; they are accompanied by student study guides and teacher lesson plans. Formed as a Business/Education Partnership among the Lied Center, U.S. Bank, and the Lawrence Public Schools, AiI creates opportunities through the arts that enhance reading, writing, critical thinking, and creative expression for students and teachers.

The Lied Center and the Lawrence Public Schools are founding members of the Partners in Education program of the John F. Kennedy Center for the Performing Arts. Curriculum-based arts-integration workshops for teachers are the foundation of the Partners in Education Program.

The Lied Center also pursues its mission through Pre-Performance Lectures and Post-Performance Discussions, Artists' Talk-Backs, and extended residencies in the community of Lawrence and throughout Kansas. Residencies include opportunities to engage artists in master classes, workshops, lectures, demonstrations, and imaginative activities that are as varied as the artists themselves.

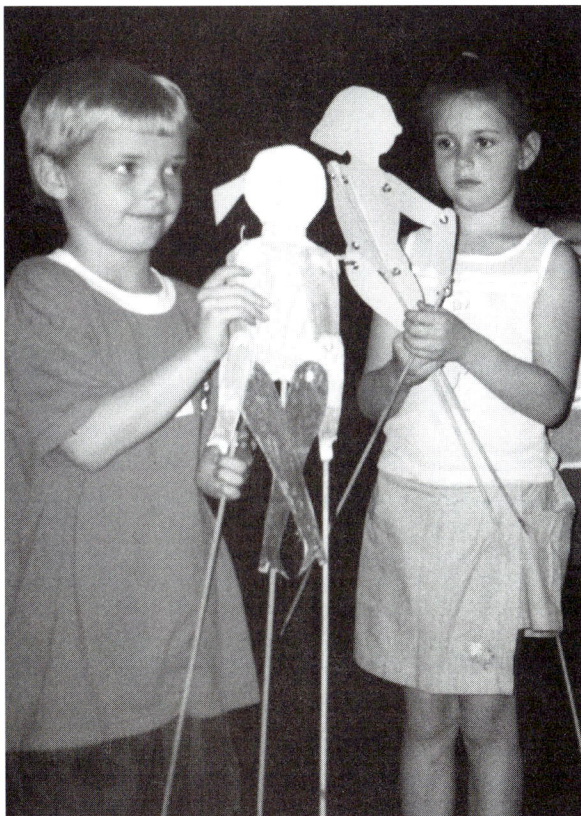

THE LIED CENTER OF KANSAS

Puppet–building workshop with students, conducted by members of DRAK Puppet Theatre from the Czech Republic

Glema Mahr Center for the Arts

Madisonville, KY   http://www.glemacenter.org

- School districts served per year: 17
- Elementary schools served per year: 102
- High schools served per year: 26
- K-12 students served per year: 16,498

Programs offered:

Performances for K-12 audiences

Short-term in-school residencies (one week or less)

Professional development opportunities for teachers

Partnerships with whole schools

Web-based learning opportunities

Programs with parents and/or other adult caregivers

Adult education opportunities

Performances/exhibits by students

Performances/exhibits by teaching artists

Technical/planning assistance

Evaluation methods

PROFILE

The full potential of the comprehensive arts education programming of the Glema Mahr Center for the Arts could not be realized without the commitment and shared vision of local, regional, and national organizations. These partners bring financial and technical resources, as well as unique expertise, to Center programs. During 2001-2002, these partnerships included:

• *Partners in Education Program of the John F. Kennedy Center for the Performing Arts (Washington D.C.)*
Since 1992, the Glema Mahr Center for the Arts has been involved with this national program committed to teacher training in making the arts integral to education. All professional development activities sponsored by the Center, in partnership specifically with the Badgett Cooperative for Educational Enhancement, fall under the umbrella of this comprehensive program.

• *Binney & Smith, makers of Crayola Products*
In 1994, the Glema Mahr Center for the Arts became one of only seven arts centers in the nation to be selected for the Crayola Dream-Makers program, a cross-curriculum approach to the visual arts implemented by classroom teachers. The Center has continued to expand the Dream-Makers program each year, and has now successfully completed a seventh year in this collaborative project. This past season, six Hopkins County elementary schools participated in the program. Crayola Workshops were conducted for students, parents, and administrators. Of the more than 2,500 students who created artwork, 234 were chosen to exhibit in the Anne P. Baker Gallery of the Madisonville Community College's Fine Arts Center.

• *The GE Fund*
Enriching the lives of young elementary school children by engaging them with the arts is what the GE Creative Connections program is about. Originating as a three-year partnership among the Glema Center, the Kentucky Center for the Arts, the GE Fund, and two elementary schools, GE extended this successful program last season for another three years and invited two more schools to participate. Each school develops an individual program addressing its needs, with equal emphasis given to student, teacher, and community learning. With the help of Creative Connections, all participating schools have been able to host several week-long residencies.

• *Numerous contributors to the STAR PASS Program*
This program, developed to encourage low-income families and individuals to attend the cultural and educational events offered by the Glema Mahr Center for the Arts, is an example of how a community partnership can be very effective through a dignified process. In 2001-2002, its successful fourth season, more than 400 STAR PASSES were redeemed, with broad community support. Contributors included the Mayor's Fund of the City of Madisonville, Mrs. Glema Mahr, the Madisonville BPW (Kentucky Federation of Business and Professional Women), and the Madisonville Rotary Club.

• *The Woman's Club of Madisonville*
The Woman's Club sponsored an annual exhibit of works by students from Hopkins County

JIM PEARSON

"Trust us." Students learn the trust fall, and then implement it for an afternoon rehearsal of the Summer Arts Academy production of Once Upon a Mattress.

Central High School and Madisonville North Hopkins High School as part of the season's offerings at the Anne P. Baker Gallery. The exhibit was juried and awards were given to the winning entries in several categories.

The third annual Summer Arts Academy (2002), an intensive 10-day drama day camp, was met with enthusiasm by students, parents, and community members; and for the first time, a one-week Academy was offered for elementary school students. A total of 130 students participated in the two academies. From June 3-7, the younger students learned to sing, dance, and design scenery for the performance of *Stinky Cheese Man*. Middle and high school students then attended the traditional Academy from June 10 - 21. Working with professional actor/director F. Reed Brown, they learned about the various aspects of producing and performing in a play. The culmination of the two weeks was a wonderful performance of *Once Upon a Mattress*.

The Glema Mahr Center for the Arts housed several community events again this past year, but for the first time it presented a community musical, *The Music Man*. Local talent was used onstage and off to mount this American classic; several of the cast members were former participants in the Summer Arts Academy. Sponsored by the J. B. and Kiel Moore Community Program Endowment, three performances were presented.

The Center has become the home for area dance-school recitals, Hopkins County Schools band and choral concerts and plays, and KMEA (Kentucky Music Educators Association) Band and Choral Festivals. Every December, the local police band Street Heat performs twice on the stage before hundreds of middle school students, providing them with an anti-drug message.

All of these events bring students into the Center, educate them, and excite them about the arts.

RiverPark Center
Owensboro, KY

- School districts served per year: 33-KY and IN
- Elementary schools served per year: 114
- High schools served per year: 46 middle and high
- K-12 students served per year: 50,000

Programs offered:

Performances for K-12 audiences

Short-term in-school residencies (one week or less)

After school or weekend programs for K-12 students

Professional development opportunities for teachers

Professional development opportunities for teaching artists

Partnerships with whole schools

Partnerships with whole school districts

Partnerships with public broadcasting

Mentoring for students with community volunteers

Performances/exhibits by students

Technical/planning assistance

Evaluation methods

PROFILE

RiverPark Center offers the following learning opportunities for children and youth:

• *Arts Teach Kids*. School-day performance series (K-12) that is related to core content and academic-performance standards (approximately 70 shows per year).

• *Arts in the A.M.* A three-hour program, normally held in the morning, that utilizes professional artists to involve students in activities related to the core content in arts and humanities on which they are tested later in the school year. Between 4,000 and 5,000 children participate in this program, and it is growing by approximately 1,000 children per year.

• *Missoula Children's Theatre*. This company gives workshops for children and produces shows in which local children can star.

• *Kentucky Shakespeare Festival.* Brings its educational outreach workshops to the Center.

• *Creative Connections.* General Electric enables schools to work in partnership with arts centers to improve student learning in arts education program funded by Gen the arts.

• *Summer Arts Camp.* A weeklong camp for children (K-12) in which they are actively involved in the arts. One hundred ten young people participated in the camp in 2002.

• *Partnerships.* Many other learning opportunities are offered through the partnerships with local school systems. The Center sponsors the Daviess County Public School Class of 2013 and plans activities every year for this class.

• *Grants.* RiverPark Center has provided local children with a variety of opportunities through financial support.

• *Performances.* Students at many schools are given the opportunity to perform on the RiverPark Center stage.

• *Back-Stage Tours.* Normally led by the technical director.

The basic strengths of the education programs are the partnerships with the schools, the connection of the RiverPark Center's education programs to core content of curriculum, outstanding programming, close communication with teachers and arts coordinators, and continual evaluation.

In-school residencies are supported in large part through the Creative Connections program. The program helps to prepare teaching artists by sharing information with them (for example, on core content), connecting them with school arts coordinators and seasoned teaching artists, and forwarding feedback from teachers and staff.

RiverPark Center also supports K-12 classroom teachers through:

• Partnerships with their schools

• Receptions for teachers

• Reduced rates to performances, when possible

• High-quality professional development, assisted by the partnership with the Kennedy Center Partners in Education Program

• Reading to students on "I Love to Read" Day

• Study guides for all performances

• Arts in the Afternoon—an after school workshop for an entire faculty, led by a professional artist, that focuses on one area of the arts

• Arts Education Showcase. Artists come to the Center, give mini-performances, and talk with teachers who may want to bring them to their schools

• Technical assistance for teachers in schools who present their performances at RiverPark.

The RiverPark Center has more school-day performances than most other centers its size. Yet, it also supports an after school theater program for at-risk children in the schools with Neblett Center, an inner city community center, and other arts partnerships funded by Kentucky Arts Council.

RIVERPARK CENTER

Workshop in "Summer Arts Camp"

Jefferson Performing Arts Society

Metairie, LA   www.jpas.org

- School districts served per year: 6
- Elementary schools served per year: 21
- High schools served per year: 7
- K-12 students served per year: 10,800

Programs offered:

Performances for K-12 audiences

Short-term in-school residencies (one week or less)

Long-term in-school residencies (multiple weeks)

After school or weekend programs for K-12 students

Professional development opportunities for teaching artists

Partnerships with whole schools

Partnerships with whole school districts

Partnerships with public broadcasting

Partnerships with cable media

Adult education opportunities

Performances/exhibits by students

Performances/exhibits by teaching artists

PROFILE

The Jefferson Performing Arts Society (JPAS) offers four types of outreach programs dedicated to the artistic enrichment of students of all ages: the Arts Adventure Series, which presents full-length ballets, musicals, and ethnic programs during the school day in a "field trip" format; Cultural Crossroads, which brings artists of diverse disciplines into residencies at alternative schools for at-risk students; Stage Without a Theater, which takes artistic programs, including jazz, storytelling, and musical theater, into area schools; and the Children's Chorus and Youth Chorale, which offer after school, summer study, and performance programs for student musicians from Pre-K through 12th grade.

- *The Arts Adventure Series* makes full-length performances, from ballets to musicals to grand opera, available to school groups at greatly discounted prices. This program allows schools to integrate the classic works that JPAS presents into their curriculum, and it gives students the opportunity to experience performances in a real theater environment.

- *Cultural Crossroads*, a residency-based program, integrates arts and cultural activities with core curriculum at alternative schools in the Greater New Orleans region. The goal of this outreach is to improve student achievement through in-school arts activities for students who have not succeeded in the traditional education environment. Throughout the school year, the program focuses on math, language arts, Louisiana and world history, and social skills (including conflict management and self-esteem).

- *Stage Without A Theater* brings artists and productions into local schools during the school day.

- *The Children's Chorus and Youth Chorale* have provided high quality choral training to the children of the greater New Orleans area for 19 years. The choirs are comprised of more than 95 children, ages 4-18. While participating in weekly chorus rehearsals they study music, poetry, and movement. Chorus members perform in a variety of settings throughout the community and on the concert stage. In 2003, JPAS began offering a Summer Show Choir Workshop, a one-week activity for boys and girls in grades 3-8 that helps them develop the fundamental singing and dancing skills of show-choir performance.

JPAS develops study-guide materials for teachers and students to relate the arts to other areas of core-education curriculum. It also offers a Summer Musical Theatre Program that provides a challenging and high-quality education in musical theater. Through workshops, classes, and public performances, students focus on the preparation of musical-theater productions; they receive training in acting, singing, dancing, staging, costuming, and technical production.

In March 2002 JPAS received the Gambit Weekly Newspaper's "Tribute to Classical Arts" Arts Education Award.

FleetBoston Celebrity Series

Boston, MA   www.celebrityseries.org

- School districts served per year: 20
- Elementary Schools served per year: See profile
- High Schools served per year: See profile
- K-12 students served per year: 20,000

Programs offered:

Performances for K-12 audiences

Short-term in-school residencies (one week or less)

Long-term in-school residencies (multiple weeks)

After school or weekend programs for K-12 students

Partnerships with whole schools

Partnerships with whole school districts

Partnerships with public broadcasting

Adult education opportunities

Performances/exhibits by students

Evaluation methods

PROFILE

Project Discovery is a citywide arts-in-education initiative designed to make the arts available to all Boston area residents. It uses the FleetBoston Celebrity Series' distinction as a leading performing arts presenter by accessing nationally and internationally recognized artists in classical music, dance, jazz, world music, and theater. Since 1984, a key part of the Celebrity Series' mission has been to introduce these artists, and the performing arts, to new and diverse audiences through engaging, entertaining, and enriching artistic experiences. Each year approximately 25,000 people, many of whom might not otherwise have the opportunity to enjoy the performing arts, participate in more than 110 Project Discovery activities that include master classes, lecture-demonstrations, residencies, workshops, a summer camp, interactive concerts, premieres of newly commissioned works, and discount ticket distribution programs.

In the 2002-2003 season, Project Discovery was comprised of the following:

Programs for Students (K-12)

- *Artists-in-Residence.* In-school residencies at Boston public and charter schools, featuring visiting Celebrity Series artists in dance and music, are intended to supplement the dance and music curricula of these schools. The goal of the dance residencies is to introduce students to dance and choreography as creative art forms, while the music residencies' aim is for participants to acquire a better understanding of composition, performance, and instrumentation. Students interact with visiting artists through master classes, lecture-demonstrations, open rehearsals, and advanced workshops. These in-school residencies have included artists such as Yo-Yo Ma, Marvin Hamlisch, Wynton Marsalis, Bobby McFerrin, and dancers from the Paul Taylor Dance Company and American Ballet Theatre.

- *Community Arts Link.* Project Discovery's discount ticket program involves more than 300 schools, community groups, and social service organizations throughout Massachusetts. The Celebrity Series offers $9 tickets to more than 90 percent of each season's Celebrity Series performances, and more than 12,000 students, special interest groups, and special needs individuals participate in this program each year.

- *AileyCamp Boston.* Established in partnership with the Alvin Ailey American Dance Theater, AileyCamp Boston is a six-week, full-scholarship summer program that combines dance instruction with personal-development workshops, creative-communications classes, and field trips for 80 Boston area middle school students. The program's mission is not to train students to be professional dancers but to challenge them, strengthen their self-esteem, and provide an inspirational summer alternative within a structured setting.

- *Act 2* is a free after school program that uses dance, music, theater, and visual arts to help develop confidence and creative expression among inner city Boston middle school students. Inspired by the success of AileyCamp Boston and held at the Boston

AileyCamp Boston campers in modern class

Arts Academy, ACT 2 offers dance, introductory music, theater, and visual art classes to AileyCamp alumni. The program also engages guest speakers from the community to promote the personal and civic growth of the students, and it offers workshops in volunteerism, academic support, and goal-setting.

Programs for Families

• Family Musik. Celebrating its eighth season in 2002-2003, Family Musik was created to spark family-wide interest in music through a series of fun-filled interactive concerts and workshops that incorporate music, words, and movement. Past Family Musik concerts have included The Polar Express, Elijah's Angel, Many Moons, Carnival of the Animals, A Soldier's Tale, Everybody Dance Now!, April Fools! and MozartBridge.

Programs for Community

• *Dance Across the City* is a collaboration between FleetBoston Celebrity Series and the Wang Center for the Performing Arts that aspires to showcase dance in the Boston community as a vital and enriching experience. Through a series of free,

creative, and interactive events, this community-dance initiative provides the rare opportunity to experience the artistry and energy—outside of staged performances—of some of the world's most innovative dance companies. In its inaugural season last year, Dance Across the City invited adults to participate in master classes, panel discussions, and conversations with some of today's leaders in modern dance, including Bill T. Jones, Mark Morris, and Jonathan Wolken of Pilobolus.

• *What Makes It Great?* is both a formal concert and an educational workshop. Composer/conductor/ commentator Robert Kapilow introduces new audiences to classical music composition and dance and gives already knowledgeable audiences new ways to understand them. Mr. Kapilow and guest artists deconstruct well-known works into manageable sections, explain the works' structure, highlight important motifs, and encourage the audience to think like the composer or choreographer. When the workshop component is followed by a formal performance of the entire piece by the guest artists, the audience experiences it with a new depth of understanding and familiarity.

The Wang Center for the Performing Arts

Boston, MA   www.wangcenter.org

- **School districts served per year: 43 towns (not districts)**
- **Elementary schools served per year: 56, varies each year**
- **High schools served per year: 88, varies each year**
- **K-12 students served per year: 770 (plus 100 educators)**

Programs offered:

Performances for K-12 audiences

After school or weekend programs for K-12 students

Professional development opportunities for teachers

Professional development opportunities for teaching artists

Partnerships with whole school districts

Performances/exhibits by students

PROFILE

The core strength of the education program, called Suskind Young at Arts, is its commitment to the arts as an essential part of daily life. Numerous opportunities are offered through student programs, which include a variety of art forms and accommodate a range of schedules. Programs involve participants in the literary, visual, and performing arts (e.g., BroadWays, Songwriting, Writers in Residence, Arts by Kids). No experience is necessary to participate and acceptance is based on enthusiasm and commitment. All programs are free and are offered throughout the year, including the summer. They can be short-term (from a one-day workshop to several after school sessions) or long-term (from 3 to 6 months in length, meeting once or twice a week). Programs are both in-school and out-of-school.

Arts Can Teach (ACT) is a partnership—among Suskind Young at Arts, LynnArts, Inc., and the Lynn [Mass.] Public Schools—that gives Lynn middle school teachers the opportunity of working with local professional artists to learn elements of an art form and to develop, implement, and assess arts-integrated projects in their classrooms throughout the school year. Art forms include the literary, visual, and performing arts. ACT begins in the spring, with the selection of artists and teachers, who then work together for 28 hours during a Summer Institute. They plan a 10-day residency project for the fall, followed by an independent project (facilitated by the teacher) in the spring. Exhibits take place at each school and at LynnArts during the month of March, and the evaluation component finishes the year in April. Residency work is a large part of the learning process in this program, but the teacher is more actively involved in the planning and implementation process than in most traditional residencies.

Every other year a seminar is offered, developed by the John F. Kennedy Center for the Performing Arts, called "Artists as Educators: Planning Effective Workshops for Teachers." This seminar, which details a process for planning, presenting, and evaluating workshops for teachers, helps artists identify components of their work with students that teachers will find valuable in their own teaching; the seminar also assists artists in developing proposals for teacher workshops.

The Artists' Project is another program that offers development opportunities for Boston area artists who present workshops and other educational events. Meetings throughout the year provide additional occasions for area artists to network and collaborate with each other.

Meanwhile, the Suskind Young at Arts staff continually shares resources and professional development information, hosts events that enable artists to introduce their work to, and make connections with, area educators, and notifies artists of openings for instructors and presenters at a variety of organizations.

The Arts for Teachers program offers free professional development workshops for K-12 educators. Prominent local and national presenters lead this series of interactive workshops, which explore different ways for teachers to integrate the arts into their curriculum while meeting Massachusetts Department of Education standards. Participants who complete all sessions in a workshop series are eligible for a minimum of 10 professional development points.

The Wang Center for the Performing Arts and the Boston Public Schools, both members of the Kennedy Center's Partners in Education program, have partnered in collaborative efforts to make the arts integral to education. The Kennedy Center's annual Partners in Education meeting, helps the Wang Center keep on top of national education trends and issues, and throughout the year provides excellent workshop presenters from around the country.

Through a partnership with the Boston Public Schools, an Arts Symposium is offered each season that is focused on the specific needs of BPS teachers. The Arts Can Teach program in Lynn, MA, enables teachers to work with local professional artists for integrating arts projects into their curriculum.

On a more executive level, Teacher Liaisons is Suskind Young at Arts' connection to the Boston area's school community. Established in 1995, this group of 30 K-12 educators serves as an advisory panel, as volunteers for Suskind Young at Arts (for which they help recruit participants), and as liaisons between the Wang Center and their partner schools.

Suskind Young at Arts is committed to growth and expansion—not just through numbers, but through creative thinking about innovative practices in arts language.

Clarice Smith Performing Arts Center University of Maryland

College Park, MD

www.claricesmithcenter.umd.edu

- School districts served per year: 4
- Elementary schools served per year: 24
- High schools served per year: 21
- K-12 students served per year: 6,000

Programs offered:

Performances/exhibits by students

Partnerships with whole schools

Summer institute for K-12 teachers

Professional development opportunities for teachers

Long-term in-school residencies (multiple weeks)

Short-term in-school residencies (one week or less)

Performances for K-12 audiences

Adult education opportunities

PROFILE

As a new organization, the Clarice Smith Center is just beginning to shape learning programs both for adults and youth. The primary goals of the Center's programs generally are to:

- Offer programming that is reflective of the diverse communities within and around the university

- Establish a context for performances in order to engage the audience more deeply

- Contribute to the repertoire of new work

- Provide resources for artists from the Center's communities and around the world to pursue their art forms.

Learning is at the heart of all Center programming. In some cases, courses and ongoing humanities activities are offered; in others, one-time lectures, panel discussions, or artist talk-back opportunities enhance a performance experience. Either way, programs presented by the Center are usually framed by occasions intended to inform, engage, and ultimately build new audiences (of all ages) for a wider range of performing arts.

A primary emphasis at this time is the engagement of adults from the diverse communities within and around the University.

But the Center does work in the K-12 environment as well, with an aim of increasing students' interest, understanding, and participation in the performing arts. The Center's initiatives involve the building of partnerships with community organizations, youth groups, and local schools. In 2002-2003, Northwestern High School and Hyattsville Middle School, located near the University, were the Center's primary school partners. Interactions included:

• Local artists in residence throughout the year, both for music composition and playwrighting projects

• Workshops with visiting artists from the Maryland Presents season, both in the school and at the Center

• Opportunities for student performers to visit the Center to rehearse or perform in the Center's venues.

In 2003-2004, the Center plans to continue deepening these school partnerships, and to establish models and best practices for building others.

For the past three years, the Center has also sponsored teacher training institutes during the summer. While teacher training is not a primary focus at this stage of development, the Center expects to host institutes of this nature again during the summer of 2003.

Emery Community Arts Center & Foothills Arts

Farmington, ME   www.emeryartscenter.org

• School districts served per year: 5
• Elementary schools served per year: 7
• High schools served per year: 4
• K-12 students served per year: 1,012

Programs offered:

Short-term in-school residencies (one week or less)

After school or weekend programs for K-12 students

Professional development opportunities for teachers

Professional development opportunities for teaching artists

Partnerships with whole schools

Partnerships with whole school districts

Programs with parents and/or other adult caregivers

Adult education opportunities

Evaluation methods

PROFILE

Foothills Arts (founded in 1989) and the Emery Community Arts Center (founded in 2002) have allied to form an education program with the following objectives:

• Empower classroom teachers to use the arts as a vehicle for teaching their curricula, and foster collaborations among teaching artists, classroom teachers, and students

• Nurture the creative voices of youth, of all backgrounds and levels of experience, by providing after school and summer enrichment programs in which they experiment in partnership with Maine teaching artists.

Found Story Theater combines hands-on professional development workshops for K-8 teachers with in-school artist residencies; the classroom teachers and teaching artist together design curricular units involving theater games and improvisation. For each of the past three years, 12 teachers have participated, working with actor-playwright Jeri Pitcher. For the units, whose objectives match the Maine Learning Results, teachers have chosen subjects such as language arts, math, health, German, history, and the district's bullying-and-teasing prevention initiative.

Participating teachers report that they have changed many of their teaching strategies and that they see children more fully engaged in learning and, consequently, better understanding content. The program accommodates children with diverse intellectual and social-emotional needs, from those who need new challenges to those in special education programs. Another bonus of Found Story Theater is that teachers and students are both energized about learning. One teacher sums it up: "We're so lucky to have this [program]. The kids come to school excited. They come to the door asking, 'What are we doing today?' "

The Gear-Up Arts Residency is a five-day integrated arts residency in a rural paper-mill-town school in which arts programs have traditionally taken a back seat. Music, creative movement, theater, and poetry teaching artists come into all six of the school's 5th- and 6th-grade classrooms. Students interact with the artists on a first-name basis, discovering how accessible these art forms really are. Similarly, the expectation is to encourage classroom teachers to start using these arts in their own teaching, just as is done so successfully with the Found Story Program.

Theater for Peace brings together actor-playwright Jeri Pitcher and 12 high school students of diverse backgrounds. They meet after school for 10 weeks, to explore teen-relevant social issues through intense and lively discussions and theater improvisations. Products of this program include an original theater piece and discussion questions that the teen actors share with 7th and 8th graders in individual classrooms in three rural school districts. Classroom teachers conduct additional follow-up

discussions and writing assignments on the topics raised. In the four years of this program, 35 high school students have participated, and they have presented to a total of 400 middle school students, whose teachers praised the quality and impact of the performances and discussions. These teachers' students have reported that the program makes them think in new ways about topics like suicide, disrespectful behavior, and alcohol abuse. The Theater for Peace actors, for their part, say that they have made new friends and increased their own self-confidence.

Foothills Arts Day Camp (sliding fee scale subsidized by local businesses and individuals, and Emery Center endowment) exhilarates and inspires 4th through 12th graders to explore, make new friends, and be themselves through theater, poetry, music, art, and movement. Students improvise, choreograph, and create with teaching artists who renew their own creative spirits as they work with their youthful counterparts. Highly acclaimed since its founding in 1991, this camp—with an interdisciplinary curriculum unified by a theme—was the vision of community members who wanted to provide enrichment for rural adolescents.

In order to encourage risk-taking and experimentation, the camp's curriculum focuses on process rather than product. Youth of all abilities and socioeconomic backgrounds from 35 Maine towns attend, with more than half of the total 150-camper enrollment qualifying for and receiving scholarships based solely on financial need. When asked on evaluation forms, "What did you like best about camp?" the most common replies over the camp's 12 years have been much like these from the 2002 campers: "I was able to express myself any way I wanted in a safe place." "It makes you stretch yourself." "I loved the way it let me be myself and be creative."

L/A Arts

Lewiston, ME   www.laarts.org

- School districts served per year: 3
- Elementary schools served per year: 17
- High schools served per year: 2
- K-12 students served per year: 9,300

Programs offered:

Performances for K-12 audiences

Short-term in-school residencies (one week or less)

Long-term in-school residencies (multiple weeks)

After school or weekend programs for K-12 students

Professional development opportunities for teachers

Professional development opportunities for teaching artists

Summer institute for K-12 teachers

Summer institute for teaching artists

Partnerships with whole schools

Partnerships with whole school districts

Training for school leaders (principals, superintendents, others)

Programs with parents and/or other adult caregivers

Mentoring for students with community volunteers

Performances/exhibits by students

Performances/exhibits by teaching artists

Technical/planning assistance

Evaluation methods

PROFILE

For the past 30 years, L/A Arts has been offering continuous programming in all of Lewiston/Auburn's public schools. This past year outreach grew to include neighboring communities as well as parochial institutions, for a total of 21 schools. At the heart of each arts-in-education activity is the desire to build a community of lifelong learners who realize the potential of the arts to understand, express, teach, and enlighten.

L/A Arts's education programs include the following:

- *Artist-in-Residence.* Every school year, L/A Arts sponsors a long-term artist residency in each K-8 school. Artists work with the classroom teacher in planning thematic connections and interdisciplinary approaches to teaching subject matter and social issues. Media such as dance, theater, singing, painting, poetry, and puppetry help engage students of all learning abilities and styles. Residencies often include presentations by the visiting artist and a culminating student performance This program typically reaches more than 5,000 students and 350 teachers.

- *Visual Literacy* is a way of understanding what an artist is trying to communicate in a piece of art. As children begin learning language skills, they are taught not only how to read and write, but also about the reading and writing process; the process of looking at, analyzing, and reacting to artwork can be learned in a similar way. In fact, for some students who struggle with reading and writing, the arts can provide a new way of encouraging literacy. The Visual Literacy project is a collaborative effort among L/A Arts, Bates College Museum of Art (in Lewiston), and local elementary schools. Art that visually represents or enhances curricular themes is selected from the museum's collection; students then visit the museum and work with a museum educator on "reading" the art and articulating what they see. Of equal value, educators are introduced to a new and accessible resource within their community.

- *Newspapers in Education* (NIE) developed out of a partnership between L/A Arts and the local newspaper. The Breakfast Serials program commissions children's book authors to write serialized stories to be printed on the Backpage section of Friday's paper. Supplementing each installation is an educational sidebar, which provides discussion topics, extension activities, and writing prompts. The L/A Arts/NIE partnership provides funding for each author to visit local schools to conduct assemblies and writing workshops.

- *21st Century Community Learning Center.* Community Learning Centers were established by Congress to help schools expand their academic and social outreach. In partnership with Auburn's CLC, L/A Arts has developed an after school dance

CHERI DONAHUE, L/A ARTS

Two young actors gear up for L/A Arts' Summer Theatre production of Alice in Wonderland.

cabaret setting or on a more formal concert-hall stage. Through this program students have the opportunity to become familiar with a variety of performing arts and develop the habit of attending live performances.

• *Professional Development.* As partners in the Performing Arts Centers and Schools program of the John F. Kennedy Center for the Performing Arts, L/A Arts sponsors professional development workshops for all Lewiston, Auburn, and Mechanic Falls public school educators and administrators. The program helps train those educators interested in exploring different ways to interpret, understand, and teach their areas of specialization through an arts perspective. These workshops intend not only to encourage participants to continue the integration conversation back in their schools, but also to bring the philosophy of teaching in and through the arts into their classroom and to become advocates for art education within their school community.

program at the middle school that culminates in an evening performance and reception for dancers and their families and friends. This program not only teaches students how to dance, but also increases self-awareness and provides a safe environment for personal expression.

• *ArtsPass* is an L/A Arts initiative that provides every high school student at the local high schools with a voucher entitling him or her to a free ticket to each L/A Arts live performance. An event may consist of dance, music, theater, or comedy; it may be in a

• *Special Performances.* In addition to the annual educational programming, L/A Arts also offers special programs throughout the year. The fall of 2002 brought the Looking Glass Theatre out of Providence, RI. Committed to promoting reading, the series, There's Nothing to Read!, presented excerpts from children's novels spanning a host of different topics and authors' styles. Using minimal props and sets, and letting the power of language speak for itself, the Looking Glass Theatre presented twelve shows in elementary and middle schools throughout the community.

University Musical Society

Ann Arbor, MI   www.ums.org

- School districts served per year: 35
- Elementary schools served per year: 55
- High schools served per year: 20
- K-12 students served per year: 16,500

Programs offered:

Performances for K-12 audiences

Short-term in-school residencies (one week or less)

Long-term in-school residencies (multiple weeks)

Professional development opportunities for teachers

Professional development opportunities for teaching artists

Partnerships with whole school districts

Programs with parents and/or other adult caregivers

Adult education opportunities

Performances/exhibits by students

Performances/exhibits by teaching artists

Technical/planning assistance

Evaluation methods

PROFILE

The main elements of the University Musical Society's Youth, Teen, and Family Education program are as follows:

• *Youth Performance Series*. Features daytime and evening performances of diverse world-class artists. Fifteen thousand to twenty-five thousand K-12 tickets are offered each season. UMS develops all curriculum, CDs, and videos to be used in conjunction with these performances. Emphasis is on teacher/school customer service, the elimination of barriers to participation, and transformative experiences for students.

• *Teacher Workshops*. UMS presents five to eight teacher workshops each season for two different series: Kennedy Center teacher workshops, and performing arts teacher workshops. The former focus on incorporating arts education into classroom instruction, while the latter give teachers solid information and experience in teaching about specific artists and art forms.

• *First Acts Series*. Seen as an extension of the Youth Performance Series, this is a sequence of events drawn from public performances that offer special student access and rates; it is primarily geared toward high school students.

UMS also provides in-classroom visits by artists, special projects for teachers and schools, pre- and post-event activities for students who attend performances, and general consultation for arts education in the schools.

UMS engages a Teacher Advisory Committee that counsels UMS on all aspects of its youth-education program. USM is also considered an official partner with the Ann Arbor Public Schools, and has a special relationship with many other school districts.

CLAIRE MOLLOY, UNIVERSITY MUSICAL SOCIETY

"Dinosaur Detectives," a Kennedy Center Workshop for Teachers led by Michele Valeri, held in partnership with the University of Michigan Exhibit Museum of Natural History.

Ordway Center for the Performing Arts

St. Paul, MN

http://www.ordway.org

- School districts served per year: 27
- Elementary schools served per year: 99
- High schools served per year: 25
- K-12 students served per year: 69,750

Programs offered:

Performances for K-12 audiences

Short-term in-school residencies (one week or less)

Long-term in-school residencies (multiple weeks)

Professional development opportunities for teaching artists

Summer institute for K-12 teachers

Partnerships with public broadcasting

Adult education opportunities

PROFILE

In response to teacher needs and changing community demographics, the Ordway Center has partnered with artists and educators since 1991 to provide education programs for students, teachers, and the general public. These programs include:

• *Performing Arts Classroom series*. Each year, more than 35,000 public and private school students (grades 1-12) from throughout Minnesota attend these weekday matinee performances by the world music, dance, and theater groups that often appear in the "Planet Ordway" series. Accessibility to these performances is enhanced by the Center's commitment to offer tickets at low cost (with free busing) for area schools. The Ordway Center is proud to have been the number one cultural destination—both for Minneapolis and St. Paul public schools—for five consecutive years.

• *Flint Hills International Children's Festival*. This annual spring event offers world-class performers from around the globe who perform for young and family audiences. The festival includes puppetry, theater, music, dance, and performance art; it is presented during the week for school groups and on the weekend for families. Several schools are involved in workshops and in-school residencies that lead up to art installations of children's work at the festival. On the two weekend days, a large World Party is staged in Rice Park that features performances of local artists, as well as a myriad of free activities and events for families.

• *Living Study Guides: Arts Workshops for Teachers*. Hands-on workshops explore the art forms presented on stage and connect performances to curriculum. Continuing education unit (CEU) credit is available.

• *Putting It Together: Responding Collaboratively and Creatively to a Musical Theater Production* is a 20-hour course for teachers and students to explore the world of musical theater.

• *Ordway/COMPAS Residencies* are two week, in-depth explorations of an Ordway Center production and its art form, in conjunction with a trip to the Center. COMPAS teaching artists visit classrooms and engage students in the creative processes used by the performing artists. (COMPAS, which stands for Community Programs in the Arts, is a Minnesota-based nonprofit organization.)

• *Ordway Center Critics Circle* offers high school students an opportunity to engage in critical thinking and writing.

• *Study Guides*. Curriculum materials (including resources, cultural information, and suggestions for classroom activities tied to graduation standards) are written to accompany each Performing Arts Classroom presentation. The guides are reviewed by curriculum specialists from the St. Paul School District, edited by Ordway Center staff, and printed by the school district as part of its contribution to Education at Ordway Center.

• *Insights* allows the audience to gain a deeper understanding of the artists and art forms presented during the Planet Ordway and U.S. Bank

Children in Ordway Center's Main Hall

Theater seasons. Led by artists, community leaders, and educators, these pre-performance discussions/workshops are free and open to all ticket holders. Teachers may be eligible for CEU and in-service credits for their attendance at Insights.

• *Discussion and Dessert* are play discussion groups that offer the audiences an opportunity, in an informal gathering, to talk about performances they have seen on Ordway Center stages.

• *Workshops for Artists* provide area artistic communities with developmental opportunities, such as open forums, chances for dialogue, and networking.

• *The Honors Concert & Art Exhibit*, presented by Ordway Center and St. Paul Public Schools, celebrates the talents of 400 of the most gifted visual arts, orchestra, chorus, and band students from high schools in the St. Paul Public School District.

• *Education Advisory Committee and Cultural Advisory Committees*. In order to meet the needs of the entire community—persons of all cultures, backgrounds, ages, and experiences—Education at Ordway Center works closely with its advisory committee members, who are involved in the planning and development of the educational and outreach programs.

• *Leadership*. Ordway Center was integral to the writing of St. Paul's Capital City Education Initiative. Also, Ordway Center and St. Paul Public Schools are team members of the nationally recognized Partners in Education program of the John F. Kennedy Center for the Performing Arts.

• *2002 Arts Advocacy Leadership Award: Arts Organization Excellence in Educational Programming*. The Ordway Center for the Performing Arts was selected to receive this award from the Minnesota Alliance for Arts in Education for its strong vision and commitment to education consistent with its mission to "entertain and educate diverse audiences," according to the Alliance's Debra Hunt. The programming of the 2001 Koch International Children's Festival (now called the Flint Hills International Children's Festival) was specifically cited.

St. John's University/ College of St. Benedict

Collegeville, MN   www.csbsju.edu/finearts

- School districts served per year: 10-15
- Elementary schools served per year: 35-40
- High schools served per year: 3-5
- K-12 students served per year: 13,000

Programs offered:

Performances for K-12 audiences

Short-term in-school residencies (one week or less)

Long-term in-school residencies (multiple weeks)

After school or weekend programs for K-12 students

Professional development opportunities for teachers

Professional development opportunities for teaching artists

Partnerships with whole school districts

Web-based learning opportunities

Training for school leaders (principals, superintendents, others)

Adult education opportunities

Mentoring for students with community volunteers

Evaluation methods

PROFILE

Saint John's University and the College of Saint Benedict seek the finest artists to perform on the stage, present exhibitions in the galleries, and teach in-residence on campus and in the communities it serves.

Fine arts programming:

- Provides opportunities for growth in the arts by making the artists available through lectures and demonstrations, master classes, and pre- and post-performance discussions

- Offers presentations in all four artistic disciplines during the season (visual, theater, music, and dance)

- Enables "point of entry" experiences for the novice audience member

- Challenges audiences through innovative programming

Artworks program with artist–in–residence, DuJun, teaching Chinese paper cutting, October, 2000, Saint John's University.

- Brings artists of all ethnic and religious backgrounds into a homogenous community to promote cultural diversity

- Creates future audiences for the arts through an extensive Partners in Education program modeled by the John F. Kennedy Center for the Performing Arts.

The education program includes:

- The only professional educational outreach program in the Central Minnesota region

- A nationally recognized formal partnership with District 742 of St. Cloud, as part of the Kennedy Center's Performing Arts Center and Schools Program, offering workshops to educators on arts integration in the curriculum led by nationally recognized master artist/educators

- In-school residencies with professional touring artists, providing hands-on classroom experiences in dance, music, visual arts, and theater at no charge to local schools

- Exploratory and interactive experiences for adult audience members, in support of lifelong learning in and through the arts

- Year-round after school arts programs in partnership with the Boys & Girls Clubs of Central Minnesota

- Relationships with local social service agencies to facilitate outreach to new audiences of all ages through education programs.

COCA
(Center of Contemporary Arts)

St. Louis, MO   www.cocastl.org

- School districts served per year: 4
- Elementary schools served per year: 30
- High schools served per year: 2
- K-12 students served per year: 14,500

Programs offered:

Performances for K-12 audiences

Short-term in-school residencies (one week or less)

Long-term in-school residencies (multiple weeks)

After school or weekend programs for K-12 students

Professional development opportunities for teachers

Professional development opportunities for teaching artists

Partnerships with whole schools

Partnerships with whole school districts

Partnerships with cable media

Adult education opportunities

Performances/exhibits by students

Performances/exhibits by teaching artists

Evaluation methods

PROFILE

COCA's mission in general is to provide an integrated forum for fostering the appreciation of the arts in the greater St. Louis community by producing and presenting performances, exhibitions, and educational programs. The mission of COCA's Education Department in particular is to provide high quality arts education in drama, dance, music, and the visual arts for the widest possible audience. The program serves students from 18 months old to senior adults, from all areas in metropolitan St. Louis, and—thanks to generous scholarship programs—from all socioeconomic levels.

Among the core strengths are:

- Education programs that relate across arts disciplines

- Programs that reach economically and racially diverse segments of the public

- Community partners who work cooperatively to further COCA's values.

COCA's Education Department offers 500 tuition-based classes a year, and employs more than 100 artist-instructors, all highly trained professionals and practicing artists in their fields. The Scholarship Fund administers more than $100,000 in financial assistance to approximately 300 students-in-need for classes and camps at COCA's main campus in University City. That campus currently serves a total of more than 6,000 students of all ages, participating in dance, music, theater, and visual arts classes and camps. In addition, COCA On-site serves more than 2,000 students at numerous schools and community centers in St. Louis County and Illinois. Students work with COCA faculty in after school, weekend, and summer camp programs as well as in in-school residencies, all of which develop the students' artistic skills, confidence, and cultural awareness.

COCA's Pre-Professional Dance Program, one of its most innovative activities, is a long-term, individualized curriculum to encourage the development of talented young dancers toward their professional goals, regardless of income, race, or ethnicity. The Program, designed to nurture the unique talents and interests of each future performer, offers training in ballet, modern, jazz, tap, acting, and voice, along with master classes with nationally known teachers and workshops on related topics such as anatomy and health. Students receive academic counseling, guidance in their dance training, and assistance in pursuing further training and career opportunities after high school.

COCA's grant-funded Urban Arts Program provides a range of in-school and after school arts education each year for approximately 9,000 children in low-income areas, helping to make the arts a basic part of their learning experience. It includes:

- *After School Arts Classes* at city schools that provide art experiences not only to teach students about a particular art form, but also provide discipline, stability, and self-esteem through participation in the arts

- *Summer Arts Camp* for teaching arts disciplines to students in grades K-5. Camps conclude with a student demonstration/display of learned skills

- *Art and Technology Program*, which offers elementary school students well-structured and closely supervised computer-based art classes that foster literacy, creativity, and modern technical skills

- *SchoolTime Arts Education Program* that provides short-term in-school residencies with national performers and long-term in-school residencies with local artist/instructors to children throughout the City of St. Louis. These residencies also provide a learning opportunity for K-12 classroom teachers, who observe and participate with COCA artist/instructors. Nine in-school residencies were offered through Urban Arts this past year. The artist/instructors are highly trained professionals who come to COCA with extensive teaching experience and, in most cases, advanced degrees in their arts disciplines.

Biannual faculty meetings, visits with guest artists, and a faculty policy manual offer additional support and preparation information. Artist/instructors receive periodic observations and feedback from education staff and lead teachers in their disciplines. In the summer of 2002, for example, COCA began a program of biweekly in-service workshops with an art therapist/trainer for its summer camp instructors at all locations.

DANCE St. Louis

Saint Louis, MO

www.dancestlouis.org

- **School districts served per year: 25**
- **Elementary schools served per year: 100**
- **High schools served per year: 85**
- **K-12 students served per year: 6,000**

Programs offered:

Performances for K-12 audiences

Short-term in-school residencies (one week or less)

Long-term in-school residencies (multiple weeks)

After school or weekend programs for K-12 students

Professional development opportunities for teachers

Partnerships with whole schools

Partnerships with whole school districts

Adult education opportunities

Performances/exhibits by students

Performances/exhibits by teaching artists

Technical/planning assistance

Evaluation methods

PROFILE

Dance St. Louis's commitment to facilitating strong programs has produced multiyear relationships with community arts councils, a prison arts program, corporate education programs, and especially the regional school districts. Since 1977, some 50 to 100 in-school activities per year have introduced a total of more than 250,000 students to all styles of dance; the Dance St. Louis Education Impact Program instructs students in dance as an art form, a physical sport, and even a career while offering them a rare opportunity to work with professional dancers in intensive in-school workshops.

Dance St. Louis supports in-school residencies by selecting top-quality artists, helping raise money for programs, organizing artist logistics, conducting

GIGI WEAVER

Parkway North High School dancers performing ShemoVes, *the original work they created with Pilobolus dancers, Adam Battelstein and Becky Jung, during Dance St. Louis' spring 2002 Pilobolus Too Institute.*

on-site observations to ensure program quality, developing study guides, and conducting follow-up surveys. The strength of these activities lies in the quality of the artists and a goal to balance the number of students served with a lasting educational impact. The roster of artists who have particpated includes dancers from the Miami City Ballet, Paul Taylor Dance Company with Taylor 2, Alvin Ailey American Dance Theatre, Ballet Folklorico de Mexico, Dayton Contemporary Dance Company, David Dorfman Dance, David Parsons Company, Pilobolus, and the Pilobolus Too Institute.

Dance St. Louis supports K-12 teachers in this enterprise by providing study guides that include background on dancers, dance history, classroom activities, dance bibliographies, Internet links, and news articles so that teachers can prepare their students for the visiting artists.

Dance St. Louis looks for projects that can make an impact over a long period on a variety of audiences—from dance students to youths from a juvenile detention center. Two examples of innovative programming are the following:

• With major help from Southeast Missouri State University, Dance St. Louis undertook the major project of bringing the internationally renowned Miami City Ballet to Cape Girardeau and Sikeston, Missouri, during April 2002. It took four years of planning and a significant grant from the Wallace-Reader's Digest Funds to get the Ballet to Cape Girardeau, but when they finally arrived they took the river town by storm. Dance St. Louis' crew moved a 10-ton sprung floor into Blanchard Elementary in Cape Girardeau for a lecture demonstration at which 160 fifth graders heard Edward Villella narrate an in-school lecture demonstration with members from his renowned company. The following day, the Ballet moved its lecture/demonstration to Sikeston, Missouri, and performed for 800 middle and high school students.

• *The Pilobolus Too* residency, founded in 1998 with support from the Missouri Arts Council, has been Dance St. Louis's largest Education Impact Program to date. In the 2001-2002 season, Dance St. Louis recruited Pilobolus Too—often called the "little luxury edition" of the acclaimed Pilobolus dance company—for nine weeks of residency activities culminating in a performance of an original work titled *ShemoVes,* which was created and performed by Parkway North High School students in collaboration with Pilobolus Too dancers. Lorilee Richardson, dance educator in the Parkway School District, had this to say about the program in general and the performance in particular: "*ShemoVes* reflected the discipline, the skill with improvisation, and the ability to work collaboratively, which many of the Parkway dancers learned through work with Dance St. Louis. Lessons learned from [Pilobolus Too artists] have also been integrated into the Parkway curriculum, and shared with other dance educators through the National Dance Education Organization and the Missouri Dance Education Organization. This was an authentic experience for the kids: creating, learning, and performing a dance in just three weeks, something they could [only] experience working in a dance company."

Juanita K. Hammons Hall for the Performing Arts Southwest Missouri State University

Springfield, MO   www.hammonshall.com

• School districts served per year: 50+
• Elementary schools served per year: 60+
• High schools served per year: 40+
• K-12 students served per year: 7,000+

Programs offered:

Performances for K-12 audiences

Short-term in-school residencies (one week or less)

Professional development opportunities for teachers

Partnerships with whole schools

Partnerships with whole school districts

Adult education opportunities

Performances/exhibits by students

Evaluation methods

PROFILE

The Center for Arts in the Schools began as a partnership among Hammons Hall, the Southwest Missouri State University's College of Arts and Letters, and the Springfield Public Schools. Other partners have since joined, both as individual schools and entire districts. This past year's partner schools included 44 elementary schools, 17 secondary schools, a K-12 lab school, and a variety of alternative education programs. A much broader area is served, with student and teacher participants also coming from public, private, and home schools from across the 24-county region served by SMSU.

The Center presents an annual series of matinee performances for K-12 students. These live, professional performances incorporate other educational aspects, such as study guides, supplemental materials for teachers, Q&A sessions, and workshops or clinics. The Center has helped more than 60,000

K-12 students experience the thrill of seeing a live performance, many for the very first time.

An annual series of professional development workshops for teachers allows educators from all disciplines—especially non-arts teachers—to gain the skills and confidence they need to use the arts as an effective teaching tool in the classroom. By training and encouraging teachers to use the arts in their teaching, the Center believes the impact will be far greater and longer lasting than merely exposing a student to a one-time arts experience.

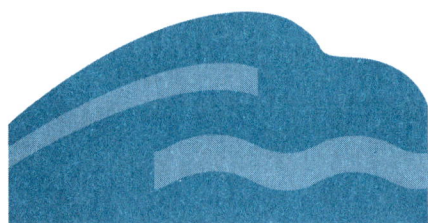

Juanita K. Hammons Hall for the Performing Arts

The Center also provides in-school mini-residencies, bringing professional performing artists directly to students in their classrooms. The education program works closely with a variety of artists who perform during the Hall's season to present master classes, clinics, open rehearsals, and panel discussions for students of all ages.

The Hall's Introduction to the Performance series coordinates with university professors and local arts professionals, as well as touring artists and artistic/management staffs, to arrange pre-performance lectures that provide patrons with additional insights into the season's performances.

The education program is based on the John F. Kennedy Center's Partners in Education model, pairing arts organizations with local school districts. Through its affiliation with the Kennedy Center, there is access to a wealth of educational materials, touring productions, classroom and Internet resources, a nationwide network of arts education specialists, and the finest teacher workshops available. This partnership is able to bring these assets to teachers and students, and adults, throughout the predominantly rural region of southwest Missouri, where they would not otherwise have access to such programs.

Alberta Bair Theater
Billings, MT   www.albertabairtheater.org

- School districts served per year: 72
- Elementary schools served per year: 140
- High schools served per year: 20
- K-12 students served per year: 27,000

Programs offered:

Performances for K-12 audiences

Short-term in-school residencies (one week or less)

Long-term in-school residencies (multiple weeks)

After school or weekend programs for K-12 students

Professional development opportunities for teachers

Professional development opportunities for teaching artists

Partnerships with whole schools

Partnerships with whole school districts

Partnerships with public broadcasting

Partnerships with cable media

Web-based learning opportunities

Training for school leaders (principals, superintendents, others)

Programs with parents and/or other adult caregivers

Adult education opportunities

Mentoring for students with community volunteers

Performances/exhibits by students

Technical/planning assistance

Evaluation methods

PROFILE

The Alberta Bair Theater provides opportunities for learning about the performing arts through the following core programs:

• School performances

• Professional development workshops for educators

• Outreach

• Access to the Arts

ALBERTA BAIR THEATER
FOR THE PERFORMING ARTS

These activities are guided by a strong mentor relationship with the Partners in Education program of the John F. Kennedy Center for the Performing Arts. Established in 1991, the partnership—involving the collaboration with the local Billings School District #2 (12,000 students) and the rural neighbor to the south, Laurel Public Schools (1800 students)—enables almost every student in the Billings and Laurel public schools to come to the theater at least once a year.

Every school in these two districts (total number of schools: 36) has a teacher representative who meets with the Education Director of the Alberta Bair Theater three times a year to provide feedback about the Theater's education programs. These teachers also offer invaluable information about curriculum connections and other school-related issues. In addition, they act as "communication/marketing ambassadors," taking program information back to their schools and presenting it to their colleagues.

School performances

Each year, the Alberta Bair Theater offers specially designed matinees for students (in grades Pre-K through 12), at discounted prices ($3 - $5), which are held during school hours at the theater. Performances have included *The Mouse and the Motorcycle,* Pilobolus Dance Theatre, *Carmen,* Eric Carle's *The Very Hungry Caterpillar* and The Acting Company's *Taming of the Shrew.* In the 1998-1999 season, ten performances for approximately 12,000 students were presented. In 2001-2002, more than 22,300 students were brought to the theater from 135 public, private, and home schools from Billings and the surrounding communities for a total of 18 performances. The school performances are each recommended for specific grade levels, and study guides are sent to the schools prior to each show with program information, history, curriculum connections, discussion questions, and activities to help enhance the student's educational experience at the theater.

Professional development workshops for educators

Teacher workshops are presented in conjunction with the Billings and Laurel School Districts as part of the partnership with the John F. Kennedy Center. These are all hands-on workshops, presented in a safe and nonthreatening environment, designed to help educators better understand and integrate the arts into their classrooms. In 1998-99, 6 workshops were offered with 92 educators participating. In 2001-02, 14 workshops were held with 260 teachers participating.

Outreach programs

Each year, the Alberta Bair Theater offers school residencies, from one day's to ten weeks' duration, featuring touring and local artists. Community master classes, workshops, lecture demonstrations, panel discussions, and informal performances are also offered, featuring artists who are appearing at the Alberta Bair Theater.

The primary outreach program is called the Stories Project. Now in its fifth year, at-risk teens are selected by the school faculty and staff for classes in and about the arts and field trips to local theaters, museums, and businesses during and after school. In cooperation with Billings School District #2, local and nationally known artists work with the students in the middle and high schools in theater, creative writing, visual art, music, video, collage, and photojournalism. Each series of classes culminates with a performance or exhibition of the students' work both at the school and at the local art museum.

The goals of the Stories Project include giving the students skills, self-awareness, and self-esteem to help them stay in school and find positive pathways of development. The project uses the arts as a way to help young people channel their energy toward creativity, healing, and expression. The 268 students who have participated in the 20 different workshops in the first four years of the project report that they also feel more connected with the arts and cultural institutions in the community through their involvement in the classes and field trips.

ToursFree offers tours of the theater for groups of 15 or more students (age 7 and older). The average tour is 60 minutes in length and includes the history of the theater and a view of backstage. Students from local and rural classrooms, theater classes, summer camps, and civic groups get a behind-the-scenes look at the theater.

Access to the Arts

This program offers complimentary tickets to evening performances at the Alberta Bair Theater to hundreds of children and their families in the community, distributed through 39 local social service agencies.

Myrna Loy Center

Helena, MT   www.myrnaloycenter.com

- School districts served per year: 8
- Elementary schools served per year: 27
- High schools served per year: 3
- K-12 students served per year: 3,600

Programs offered:

Performances for K-12 audiences

Short-term in-school residencies (one week or less)

Long-term in-school residencies (multiple weeks)

After school or weekend programs for K-12 students

Professional development opportunities for teachers

Professional development opportunities for teaching artists

Partnerships with whole school districts

Web-based learning opportunities

Programs with parents and/or other adult caregivers

Adult education opportunities

Performances/exhibits by students

Performances/exhibits by teaching artists

Technical/planning assistance

Evaluation methods

PROFILE

Bringing artists into the schools has been one of the major programs of the Myrna Loy Center for more than 10 years. The MLC has a long and vital relationship with the Helena School District through the John F. Kennedy Center's Partners in Education program. In past years, artists have gone several times a year to schools in East Helena, Montana City, Lincoln, and Boulder; and students from Augusta, Wolf Creek, Whitehall, and White Sulphur Springs have attended performances and workshops in Helena. This past year the MLC has renewed relationships with Helena-area preschools such as Rocky Mountain Development, Rocky Mountain East, St. Pete's Place, and Head Start for hands-on art activities, performances, and residency programs. Carroll

CLAIRE BROWNELL

Lost Journals of Lewis and Clark *at 4 Georgians Elementary in Helena, MT*

College education, music, and performance majors participate in the workshop opportunities and classroom visits.

During the past two years, the Myrna Loy Center has provided residency opportunities to schools involving such artists as the Ying Quartet, the Fry Street Quartet, Obo Addy, the Scott Wells Dance Company, Il Teatro Calimari, Todd Green, Melissa Kwasney, Jack Gladstone, Rob Quist, and Katherine Kramer's Rhythms of Helena.

Over the next five years, the Center will be managing and organizing a host of dance, music, storytelling, performance art, video, and visual-arts events and activities related to the Lewis and Clark Bicentennial; the MLC will in fact be the official umbrella arts organization of the Bicentennial, an activity that will also bring many more artists and arts organizations to its doorstep. Under this project, an expanded series of arts residency activities in Helena and surrounding schools will be created, enabling Montana's rural students to work with national-level poets, musicians, dancers, Native American storytellers and performers, and video artists.

Recently, using the Surdna Foundation's residency-evaluation tool, the following strengths of the Myrna Loy Center program were identified:

• Its continuing commitment to providing rural Montana communities, schools, teachers, and youth with the opportunity to work with professional artists both from the region and elsewhere in the nation

• The commitment of the MLC to providing artistic experiences to youth that they would not normally be able to access in Montana, including innovative and challenging arts and approaches to arts education

• The commitment of a qualified staff to keep arts residency opportunities a central part of the organization's work

• The ability of the MLC to maintain funding over 12 years that has continued to bring artists and programs back to rural communities and schools, giving youth a continuous arts experience and education

• The willingness of strong national artists to work with the MLC in providing unique opportunities to rural Montana communities and schools.

Lied Center for Performing Arts

Lincoln, NE   www.liedcenter.org

- School districts served per year: 2
- Elementary schools served per year: 1
- High schools served per year: 15
- K-12 students served per year: 4,500

Programs offered:

Performances for K-12 audiences

Short-term in-school residencies (one week or less)

Long-term in-school residencies (multiple weeks)

Professional development opportunities for teachers

Partnerships with whole schools

Partnerships with whole school districts

Partnerships with cable media

Adult education opportunities

Performances/exhibits by students

Evaluation methods

PROFILE

"AdventureLIED" programs, which facilitate learning and interaction between the community and artists who perform at the Lied Center, are as follows:

• *Education and Community Residencies.* Lied Center artists offer master classes and other residency activities—for schools, colleges and universities, senior and community centers, and businesses throughout Nebraska—where students and teachers interact directly with performing artists. Residencies in this statewide outreach program, called Arts Across Nebraska, are developed with the participation of community leaders and community-based artists.

• *The Partners in Education program of the John F. Kennedy Center for the Performing Arts.* The Lied Center, Omaha Nation School District (in Macy, NE), and University of Nebraska-Lincoln Teachers College are partnering to provide professional development experiences in the performing arts to teachers and staff of the Omaha Nation School District (ONSD). In one recent activity, for example, 27 teachers, administrators, and school-board members from ONSD attended the Kennedy Center's production of *A Light in the Storm*, after which they talked with cast members. On the following day, the group participated in a day-long professional development workshop in the visual and theater arts. The Lied Center is also working with the Lincoln Public School District to provide professional development experiences for high school theater teachers.

• *Lincoln Puppetry Cooperative.* The Lied Center collaborates with local artists and arts and community organizations to bring the diverse cultures of puppets to area children, youth, and families. Participating organizations include: Arts Are Basic, Lincoln Community Playhouse, Lincoln Children's Museum, Magic Penny Puppeteers, Brian Henning Marionettes, Urban-Prairie Puppet Company, First Plymouth Preschool, the Council of Ethnic, Family, and Community Centers, and puppetry artists and enthusiasts throughout Nebraska.

• *New Voices for Hope* is an initiative devoted to expanding awareness about human-rights issues, using performing arts and personal experience wherever possible as vehicles for creating dialogue. During the 2003-2004 season, the In the Heart of the Beast Puppet and Mask Theatre will bring *Befriended by the Enemy* (based on the true story of a grand dragon in the Ku Klux Klan and a Jewish family that transformed his life) to the Lied Center stage.

• *Student Matinee Series.* The Lied Center provides, for nominal cost, opportunities for elementary, middle, and high school students to experience a performance on its stage. Teachers receive support material in advance that is designed to enhance the students' learning experience.

• *Studio for Students.* The Lied Center displays the visual artwork of public and private school students in the balcony lobby throughout the performance season.

Students from Lincoln, NE, area Community Centers work with puppeteer Trish Place to research, rewrite, and produce a shadow puppet performance of **Persian Cinderella** *at the Indian Center.*

• *VIP (Ventures in Partnership) Program.* The Lied Center is a VIP partner with the Lincoln Public Schools to enhance education and build a stronger community. At this past year's VIP Kickoff, the Center's 2001/2002 "Riverdance Immersion Project" received a VIP "Pioneer Award" for blazing a new trail in partnerships. For the Center's 2002/2003 season, the "STOMP Immersion Project" involved curriculum planning among sponsors, teachers, and Lied staff; *STOMP* competitions at two middle schools; a workshop with STOMPers; pre- and post-performance discussions with artists; the *STOMP* performance itself; and a dinner reception for the local community and artist VIPs. According to Playbill, the Broadway show "*STOMP* is a high-energy, percussive symphony, coupled with dance, played entirely on nontraditional instruments such as garbage can lids, buckets, brooms, and sticks."

• *Curriculum Development.* This is a new educational project whose objective is to create a curriculum that relates a Lied Center performance to middle or high school objectives. This past year, six teachers from Lincoln and Omaha high schools attended four workshops as part of the "Noise/Funk Curriculum Development Project." (Noise/Funk refers to the national touring company of the Broadway show *Bring in 'Da Noise, Bring in 'Da Funk*.) Participants gained information about the Noise/Funk performance and production, for example, the relevance of "da beat" to African-American history. They had opportunities to write supplementary curriculum-development materials that will be shared with teaching colleagues at their schools.

Capitol Center for the Arts

Concord, NH   www.ccanh.com

- School districts served per year: 55
- Elementary schools served per year: 110
- High schools served per year: 8
- K-12 students served per year: 25,000

Programs offered:

Performances for K-12 audiences

Short-term in-school residencies (one week or less)

Professional development opportunities for teachers

Partnerships with whole schools

Partnerships with whole school districts

Web-based learning opportunities

Training for school leaders (principals, superintendents, others)

Adult education opportunities

Mentoring for students with community volunteers

PROFILE

The Capitol Center for the Arts operates a number of programs that enhance arts appreciation for learners of all ages from throughout northern New England:

• In its *School Series*, the CCA offers an expansive array of school-time curriculum-based performances, symposia, and outreach activities that have involved every school district in the state. Many of these presentations offer theatrical interpretations of award-winning children's literature and historic events, while others introduce students to internationally recognized dancers and musicians. The series also offers a variety of workshops for students and teachers held both at the Center and in the classroom, which deepen the theatergoing experience and introduce new teaching techniques.

• *Achieving Literacy Through the Arts* is a partnership between the Capitol Center and the Concord School District to promote reading skills and provide early intervention for at-risk learners. The program recognizes the opportunities afforded by a diverse learning environment that utilizes a variety of means, especially the arts, for meeting core achievements. The Center and Concord School District work closely to present performances in the School Series, geared specifically to grade 1-3 students, that are taught by four District literacy arts specialists in the classroom. These specialists work with classroom teachers to promote literacy achievement through integration of the arts, and the Capitol Center's performances in particular, in all subject areas.

• The partnership with the Concord School District also engages in special projects in the areas of advocacy and community development. In 2001-2002, the partnership produced a video for use in elementary school classrooms to prepare students for their first visit to the Capitol Center. The video, shot and edited by high school students under the mentorship of a professional photographer, features the theater as a workplace (depicting staff preparing for the students' visit) as well as curriculum tie-ins and theater etiquette.

• During the 2002-2003 season, the Center is spearheading an oral-history project with elementary school students and senior citizens in conjunction with a School Series performance. The project includes training by a commissioned historian on the oral-history process to extend the District's writing curriculum. The interaction between these two age groups is an inspiring and effective way to build community through linking generations and cultures; collecting oral histories and making artworks intensifies the exchange of personal history and culture, reduces age-related stereotypes, and empowers both young and old alike.

• The Capitol Center, in partnership with the Integrated Arts M.Ed. program at Plymouth State College, also offers graduate-level credit to teachers for workshop participation and follow-up curriculum-development projects in its graduate course, Integrated Arts at the Capitol Center.

• The Center has experienced tremendous success with its pre-show outreach program, Behind-the-Scenes. Inaugurated in the 2000-2001 season, Behind-the-Scenes offers patrons dialogues that feature directors, performers, and expert scholars. These discussions deepen the audience's appreciation of the historical, cultural, and structural contexts of the performance, and provide an inside perspective on the performing arts.

New Jersey Performing Arts Center

Newark, NJ   www.njpac.org

- School districts served per year: 20
- Elementary schools served per year: 125
- High schools served per year: 72
- K-12 students served per year: 200,000

Programs offered:

Performances for K-12 audiences

Long-term in-school residencies (multiple weeks)

Professional development opportunities for teachers

Professional development opportunities for teaching artists

Partnerships with whole schools

Partnerships with whole school districts

Training for school leaders (principals, superintendents, others)

Programs with parents and/or other adult caregivers

Performances/exhibits by students

Performances/exhibits by teaching artists

Evaluation methods

PROFILE

Arts education is a central part of New Jersey Performing Arts Center's (NJPAC) mission. Even before the Center opened its doors in 1997, the department had been reaching thousands of young people through its in-school and community-based programs and performances. Six years later, NJPAC boasts one of the largest and most highly regarded programs of its kind in the nation. The department's arts education programs serve the entire state of New Jersey, with more than 200,000 children, families, and educators participating each season. In the spirit of continually exploring new and innovative ways to use its resources to serve the community, the department has formed partnerships with school districts, educational institutions, social service agencies, and arts organizations statewide.

The department focuses on the following:

• *Performances:*

 –SchoolTime Series (performances for school-based audiences held from September-May)

 –FamilyTime Series (performances for the entire family held from September-May)

 –Parent/Child Workshops (pre-performance workshops for adults and children)

• NJPAC Long-Term (10-12 weeks) *Residency Programs*:

 –Dance Academy (grades 3-6)

 –Theater Academy (grades 5-12)

 –Early Learning Through the Arts - NJ Wolf Trap program (ages 3-5)

• *SchoolTime Professional Development Workshops for Educators*: Arts Basic to the Curriculum (ABC) Conference

• *School District Partnerships* enable schools to incorporate art and cultural performances, arts education, and curriculum-based activities into daily classroom experiences. NJPAC has established partnerships with five school districts throughout New Jersey, which involve the participation of more than 48 schools and approximately 120 residency programs in dance, theater, and Early Learning Through the Arts. Additionally, more than 24,000 students within partnership districts will attend SchoolTime performances during the 2002-2003 academic year.

• *Arts Training Programs*:

 –Summer Youth Performance workshops

 –Summer Musical Theater productions

 –NJPAC/ WBGO Jazz for Teens

 –NJPAC/ NJSO Youth Orchestra Festival

 –NJPAC/ NCSA Jeffrey Carollo Music Scholarship

 –*Star-Ledger* Scholarship for the Performing Arts

Within all program areas, the department provides ancillary curriculum materials and services to further support classroom instruction and educational experiences in the arts.

• *Innovative Curriculum Materials*, integral parts of every program of the NJPAC department, are created with the intention of guiding educators through a learning process in the arts that enhance the value and experience of the residency activities and reinforce the New Jersey Core Curriculum Content Standards for the Visual and Performing Arts. NJPAC's Teacher Resource Guides for the SchoolTime Performance Series also highlight activities and resources for teaching across the curriculum, with specific links to science.

• *Professional Development.* NJPAC is registered with the New Jersey State Department of Education as a professional development provider. Educators who attend NJPAC's workshops are thus eligible to receive continuing education credits.

The Lucent Technologies Center for Arts Education is a state of the art facility that houses the multitude of programs undertaken by NJPAC's arts education department. Located at 24 Rector Street in Newark, the Lucent building has an area of 30,000 square feet, including some 24,000 square feet of recently renovated space. It contains a 100 seat theater, two dance studios, a recital hall, seven classrooms, nine music practice rooms, and office space for NJPAC's staff.

Bardavon 1869 Opera House

Poughkeepsie, NY   www.bardavon.org

• School districts served per year: 8
• Elementary schools served per year: 35
• High schools served per year: 8
• K-12 students served per year: 40,000

Programs offered:

Short-term in-school residencies (one week or less)

Performances for K-12 audiences

Performances/exhibits by teaching artists

Performances/exhibits by students

Training for school leaders (principals, superintendents, others)

Partnerships with whole school districts

Partnerships with whole schools

Professional development opportunities for teaching artists

Professional development opportunities for teachers

Long-term in-school residencies (multiple weeks)

Evaluation methods

PROFILE

Since its construction in 1869 as the Collingwood Opera House, the Bardavon has existed not only as a superb performing arts venue, but also as a cultural and educational mentor and advocate for the community's youth. Today, out of an overall audience of 120,000, the Bardavon serves some 25,000-30,000 children and teens annually with two special school-day performance series and a broad-based arts-in-education residency program.

The Bardavon's education program, formally established in 1985, has grown to encompass a wide age-range of students (pre-school through college), and corporate and foundation supporters have helped the program offer them in-depth artist residencies of several days, weeks, or months. Content of the programming for young audiences also ranges widely, from swing music for jazz-band members in local high schools, to playwriting with middle school students, to circus arts with elementary school students.

In 1999, the Bardavon assumed management of the region's symphony orchestra, the Hudson Valley Philharmonic (HVP), and one of the first priorities was to redesign its education program with the consultation of Lincoln Center Institute and New York Philharmonic arts-in-education specialists. The result was a dynamic new format that provides students with the opportunity to hear fine music played by a full orchestra while relating the listening experience to academic and personal learning.

The concept behind the Bardavon's Daytime Performances series and related artist residency activities is that art is not a product. Rather, it's a process that evolves from what the artist brings to the stage to what can be enjoyed by youthful senses, minds, and imaginations. In and of itself, the experience of attending a live performance is tremendously valuable. But, the artist-in-residence workshops that bring series performers directly into the classroom enable educators to take the process even further, making vital connections to curriculum as well as to students' other academic and social needs.

The Bardavon routinely reaches nearly 2,000 students with these residencies:

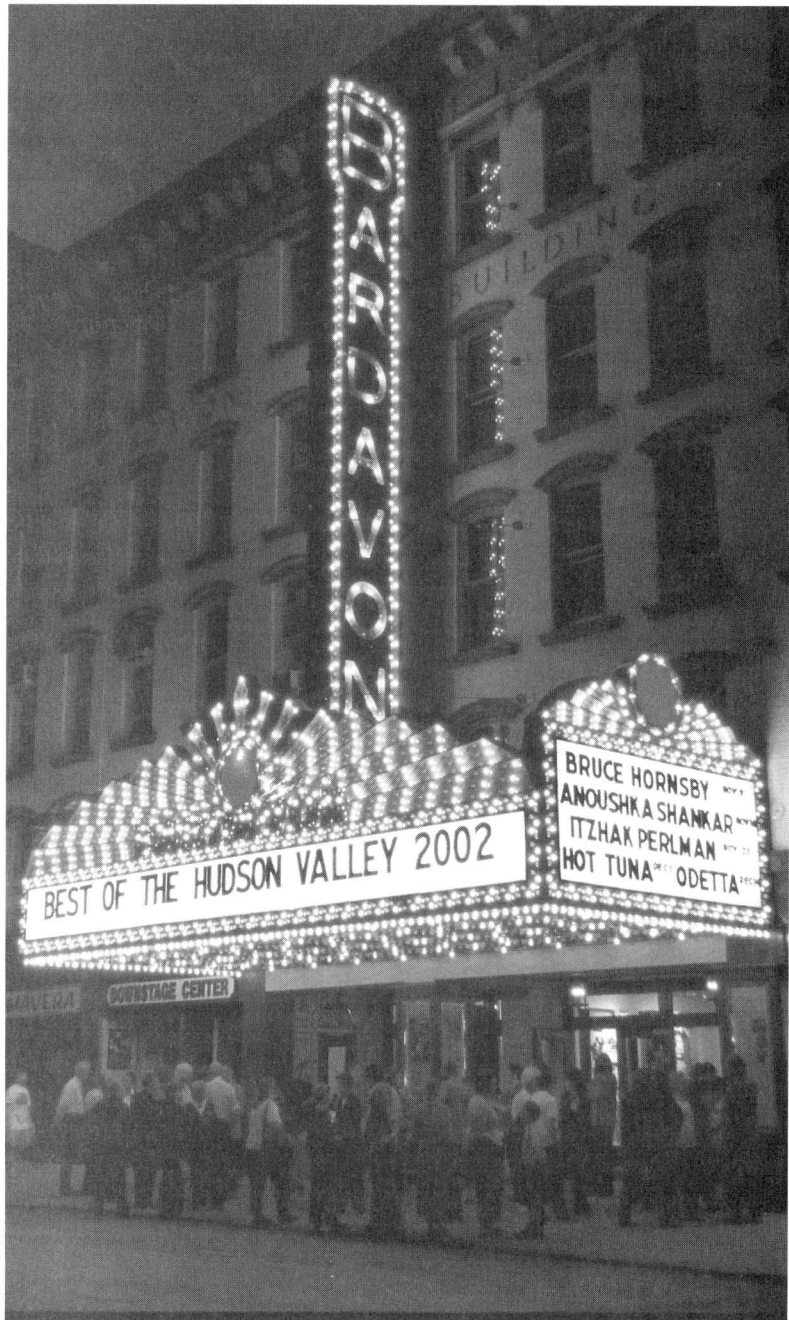

KATHY TORIS

Showtime under the renovated marquee at the Bardavon 1869 Opera House in Poughkeepsie, NY

• *The Young Playwrights Festival* introduces up to 50 students to every part of the theatrical creative process by teaming them with professionals in writing, directing, lighting, and costumes.

• An intensive *20-week Writer-in-Residency* program with Emmy nominated writer Casey Kurtti culminates in a performance.

• *Night of the Big Bands* brings two high school jazz ensembles to the Bardavon stage after six weeks of master classes with professional musicians. At an earlier phase, three big bands perform together, creating the big-band sound. A residency then begins with students attending a concert that features Tony Corbiscello's Big Band, which highlights the style of the Swing Era. Following the concert, four musicians from the Big Band visit each school six times. Working closely with students, they choose a repertoire, and the Night of the Big Bands is one result.

- *IABAS Traditional Brazilian Band* offers an uplifting introduction to Brazilian instruments and music. Two members of this all-female ensemble share the art of instrument-making, movement, and traditional Brazilian music with 100 students. The students then bring their newly learned skills and instruments to the annual kickoff of the holiday season in downtown Poughkeepsie, marching and performing in the Celebration of Lights Parade.

- *Arm of the Sea Theatre* brings the magic of puppetry to 100 fifth graders. The company is renowned for its giant puppets and commitment to putting environmental issues into focus. Patrick Wadden, the founder of Arm of the Sea Theatre, works with students to create puppets. The students bring their own puppets that then lend a touch of fantasy to the Celebration of Lights Parade.

- *Basically Blues* by Kenneth Jackson came to Poughkeepsie briefly in 1999, and again for an entire week in 2002, to visit classrooms and perform at the Bardavon. Among other things, students learned that the blues is not just a mood but an art form; they analyzed the music, its history, and its impact on virtually all other types of music.

- *The Acting Company Teaching Artists* spend up to five days working in schools, teaching a hands-on curriculum related to *The Taming of the Shrew*.

- *Circus Minimus*, a circus that kids create, brings 100 students to the Bardavon to present it. After a two-week in-school residency, students acquire skills in the circus arts that range from clowning to acrobatics to walking the tight rope, culminating in a fun-filled show that enchants audience members of all ages.

Brooklyn Academy of Music (BAM)

Brooklyn, NY   www.bam.org

- **School districts served per year: 27**
- **Elementary schools served per year: 21**
- **High schools served per year: 69 HS, 21 JHS**
- **K-12 students served per year: 11,000**

Programs offered:

Performances for K-12 audiences

Short-term in-school residencies (one week or less)

Long-term in-school residencies (multiple weeks)

After school or weekend programs for K-12 students

Professional development opportunities for teachers

Professional development opportunities for teaching artists

Partnerships with whole schools

Programs with parents and/or other adult caregivers

Adult education opportunities

Performances/exhibits by students

Technical/planning assistance

Evaluation methods

PROFILE

Brooklyn Academy of Music's (BAM) Department of Education and Humanities is dedicated to bringing an exceptional and innovative series of performances, films, residencies, and workshops to students, teachers, and families. The focus is on challenging work that has social and cultural as well as high artistic merit. In the 2002-2003 season, for example, students saw *Medea*, directed by Deborah Warner and starring Fiona Shaw; *Twelfth Night*, directed by Sam Mendes and starring Simon Russell Beale and Emily Watson; the South African apartheid drama, *The Island*; and an in-school tour with David Dorfman Dance. Students engaged in panel discussions with leading scholars, artists, and critics, published an anthology of theater criticism, and participated in residencies in Shakespeare, music, and dance.

RICHARD TERMINE

Children from the Bedford Stuyvesant Restoration Corporation perform with the BAM/Restoration DanceAfrica ensemble.

Programs include:

• *Performance Programs.* Performances comprise student matinees of main-stage BAM programs as well as presentations given exclusively for young audiences, both in the schools and at BAM (at greatly reduced prices). All students who attend performances and films at BAM are given appropriate background through pre-show in-school visits from a BAM teaching artist, post-performance/film discussions with the artists involved, post-show workshops, and extensive study guides for teachers. BAM teaching artists are experienced educators as well as professional artists. They must have extensive experience before joining the roster, and they work closely with curriculum consultants and BAM staff to continue developing their teaching skills.

• *Film Programs*

–**The Screening Series** (a high school film-literacy program) is designed to teach students how to analyze and appreciate the art of film and to understand the social issues addressed in the films, which are chosen for curricular connections, artistic excellence, and role in film history. Films are thematically linked, covering topics such as: prejudice, immigration, cultural diversity, civil rights, technology, labor relations and the work environment, war and international relations, socioeconomic class, and corporate identity vs. individualism. They have included such classics as *The Grapes of Wrath, To Kill a Mockingbird, Casablanca, Citizen Kane, Do the Right Thing, Daughters of the Dust,* and *Twelve Angry Men.* After each screening, well-known speakers lead challenging student discussions about the film.

–**kaBAM films** deal with curriculum issues relevant to elementary and junior high school students. Examples include an animated version of *The Diary of Anne Frank* , and films about Vincent Van Gogh and the Inuit people. Each screening is followed by a question-and-answer session.

• *Residency Programs*

–**Shakespeare Teaches Students** is a multi-session in-school program of study and performance for intermediate and high school students.

–**Shakespeare Teaches Teachers** is a professional development program at BAM in which intermediate- and high school teachers develop a Shakespeare curriculum. Taught by a university professor, the course also features leading scholars and artists as guests.

–**Dancing into the Future** is a series of master classes, led by highly acclaimed dance companies and choreographers, designed to immerse students in the many forms of contemporary dance.

–**Arts residencies.** BAM also offers residencies in dance, theater, and music that provide in-depth participatory experiences in making and appreciating the art form. Residencies culminate in attendance at related performances at BAM.

–**Young Critics Institute.** Selected high school students work with a master teacher to learn more about theater and to hone their critical thinking and literacy skills. Participants review BAM performances and meet with critics and theater artists.

• *Professional Development for Teachers.* In addition to the Shakespeare Teaches Teachers program, BAM periodically offers workshops and other professional development opportunities for teachers.

• *BAMfamily* programs include weekend matinee performances and the BAMkids Film Festival, an annual weekend film marathon of features and shorts from around the world.

• *Adult Humanities programs* enrich audience members' understanding of the work on stage by engaging them in discussion with artists, scholars, critics, and community members. Programs include BAMdialogues, which are interviews with artists; BAMtalks, or informal discussions about ideas affecting art and society; and symposia/panel discussions.

• *African Arts.* BAM's Department of Education and Humanities also collaborates with the Bedford-Stuyvesant Restoration Corporation to provide an arts and humanities curriculum to students who perform on stage in BAM's DanceAfrica program and create an African Sculpture Garden at BAM.

Carnegie Hall
New York, NY   www.carnegiehall.org

- School districts served per year: 70
- Elementary schools served per year: 200
- High schools served per year: 80
- K-12 students served per year: 27,000

Programs offered:

Performances for K-12 audiences

Long-term in-school residencies (multiple weeks)

Professional development opportunities for teachers

Professional development opportunities for teaching artists

Web-based learning opportunities

Performances/exhibits by students

PROFILE

The Carnegie Hall Education Department seeks to offer programs in which students not only attend concerts but also participate in the music-making process, thus becoming a part of each performance:

• *CarnegieKids*, the program for children 3 to 6, features a storyteller and a small group of musicians who engage the children through stories, music, and movement. Students are exposed to a variety of musical styles and instruments in a 45 minute presentation specifically designed for pre-schoolers.

• *LinkUP!*, Carnegie Hall's music education program for children in grades 4-6, introduces a particular musical concept each year through a comprehensive curriculum that includes lessons in music (with recorder instruction in particular), language arts, social studies, and visual arts. Teachers attend a workshop at which they receive curriculum materials and instructions on how to use them in their classrooms to prepare students for the concert experience. At the end of the year, these students attend a concert at Carnegie Hall and participate in the performance by singing or playing the recorder with the orchestra. This past year's LinkUP! curriculum, "Music Under Construction:

Professional Training Workshop with Christa Ludwig and student

Imitation," featured the Orchestra of St. Luke's and performers aged 11 to 13 performing J.S. Bach's *Concerto for Two Violins* and Bach's *Concerto for Two Pianos in C minor*. The concert also included Juan Bautista Plaza's *Fuga Criolla*.

• *Global Encounters* is Carnegie Hall's world-music program for high school social studies and music classes. It allows teachers to integrate music from different areas of the world into their curricula. This year, "Global Encounters: South African Sounds" highlighted the music and cultures of South Africa, featuring legendary trumpeter, band-leader, composer, singer, and lyricist Hugh Masekela and friends in a culminating concert. Before bringing students to the concert, teachers attend a workshop at Carnegie Hall, where they receive a Teacher's Guide and supporting materials for classroom use. A guest instructor also visits each school.

• *Carnegie Hall High School Choral Festivals* encourage excellence in performing at the pre-college level. For each festival, four choirs of high school-age singers are chosen through a taped audition to perform in a concert at Carnegie Hall. Throughout the year, the conductor of the Choral Festival rehearses each choir four times; it performs on its own there, and then all choirs at the Festival join

forces with a professional orchestra to present a major choral work. This year the New York City Area High School Choral Festival featured J.S. Bach's Magnificat. The New York State High School Choral Festival culminated in a performance of Poulenc's Gloria.

• *Musical Explorers*, a new music education program that teaches children in grades 2-3 about the instruments of the orchestra through musical activities, listening games, and singing, is scheduled for Fall 2003. Teachers first attend a workshop at Carnegie Hall, where they receive materials for classroom use and instructions on how to prepare students for two concerts that their children will attend at Carnegie Hall in the fall and in the spring. Each concert features the family of instruments (strings, woodwind, brass, or percussion) studied in that unit.

• In addition to its onsite presentations, Carnegie Hall offers an *online Listening Adventure* at www.listeningadventures.org. Here students can explore Dvorak's *New World Symphony* through visual animation, composing activities, theme-recognition games, and other interactive features. A teacher tutorial and online lesson plans to accompany the Listening Adventure are planned for Fall 2003.

The Chamber Music Society of Lincoln Center

New York, NY   www.chambermusicsociety.org

- School districts served per year: 24
- Elementary schools served per year: 19
- High schools served per year: 21
- K-12 students served per year: 10,700

Programs offered:

Performances for K-12 audiences

Short-term in-school residencies (one week or less)

After school or weekend programs for K-12 students

Professional development opportunities for teachers

Professional development opportunities for teaching artists

Partnerships with whole schools

Programs with parents and/or other adult caregivers

Adult education opportunities

Performances/exhibits by students

Performances/exhibits by teaching artists

Technical/planning assistance

Evaluation methods

PROFILE

As one of America's leading cultural institutions, the Chamber Music Society of Lincoln Center strongly believes in the importance of a complete arts education. Nearly 16,000 children and adults from the New York metropolitan area participate in a variety of educational programs each year that offer points of entry into the world of live music making, as well as opportunities for deeper engagement. They are captivated by the work of world-class musicians whose superb artistry communicates ideas in ways that words never could.

Programs for Students and Children

- *Chamber Music Beginnings* introduces students ages 7 to 14 to chamber music through preparatory classroom materials, in-school teaching-artist visits, and a culminating live-concert experience. Scheduled throughout the year, the curriculum lays the groundwork for the development of aesthetic awareness by teaching the vocabulary, concepts (form, rhythm, expression, timbre), and rudimentary skills of music making, thereby enhancing children's ability to appreciate and reflect on any music they hear and on other art forms they encounter. Praised by a number of participating music educators, the classroom materials tackle even the most complex musical concepts by employing metaphor, real-life experiences, and related art forms through activities both reflective (such as guided listening) and active (including student created musical compositions). More than 6,000 students from 19 schools participate in Chamber Music Beginnings.

- Designed for families with children ages 6 to 12, *Meet the Music!* is a series of four concerts that combine performances of the highest artistic caliber with narration, scripted dialogue, props, costumes, performances by children, and audience interaction with artists. Sophisticated musical concepts such as counterpoint, fugue, and sonata form are explained in a humorous and delightful manner to an often sold-out audience of children and parents. Approximately 4,000 children and parents attend each season.

- *The Young Musicians Program* provides an annual opportunity for up to 10 ensembles of talented high school musicians to receive coaching from Chamber Music Society artists. They then perform in a professionally produced concert at Lincoln Center's Alice Tully Hall before an audience of more than 1,000 student peers.

- *The Young Ensembles Program* offers junior high school ensembles a similar experience of coaching, followed by a performance in the Daniel and Joanna S. Rose Rehearsal Studio. Approximately 60 students from the metropolitan area perform in the Young Musicians and Young Ensembles programs each year.

Bruce Adolphe, the host and creator of Meet the Music!, invites a few brave audience members on stage to help him demonstrate a rhythm.

- Developed as a means of attracting more high school students to the art of chamber music, the *Student Advisory Committee* is a group of highly motivated and multi-talented high school music students who meet with Chamber Music Society staff every other week to plan and program events for their peers. Programs include concerts, ticket giveaways, social gatherings, and a CMS teen Web page.

- The Chamber Music Society also provides a variety of programs for high schools specifically tailored to meet the needs of an individual school's music curriculum. These programs include master classes, coaching sessions, teacher workshops, concert/demonstrations, open rehearsals, and free tickets to subscription concerts.

The Chamber Music Society Two program is a two-year professional development residency that identifies young talented musicians who show great promise in the area of chamber music. Through main-stage performances and educational programming, CMS Two offers participants mentoring and coaching in the art of chamber music; opportunities for performance with other first class musicians; and opportunities to engage in educational-outreach programs and activities.

The Chamber Music Society's education enterprises are nationally recognized as a model of quality programming—the result of a successful combination of world-class artists and a staff of creative and innovative educators. Now in its 21st year, this collaboration continues to offer an impressive range of presentations that are meaningful for a variety of ages and all levels of experience.

Jazz at Lincoln Center

New York, NY   www.jazzatlincolncenter.org

- School districts served per year: 1,500
- Elementary schools served per year: 1,300
- High schools served per year: 1,300
- K-12 students served per year: 110,000

Programs offered:

Performances for K-12 audiences

Short-term in-school residencies (one week or less)

After school or weekend programs for K-12 students

Professional development opportunities for teachers

Summer institute for K-12 teachers

Partnerships with whole school districts

Partnerships with public broadcasting

Partnerships with cable media

Web-based learning opportunities

Training for school leaders (principals, superintendents, others)

Adult education opportunities

Performances/exhibits by students

Performances/exhibits by teaching artists

Evaluation methods

PROFILE

To ensure that the appreciation and practice of jazz flourish among future generations, Jazz at Lincoln Center (J@LC), under the visionary leadership of Artistic Director Wynton Marsalis, is committed to educating audiences around the world about this distinctly American heritage. Carefully coordinated with the New York City concert season and Lincoln Center Jazz Orchestra tours, J@LC Education directly reaches more than 110,000 people annually, plus another 100,000 who use the Jazz for Young People Curriculum—the first-ever comprehensive jazz appreciation curriculum for middle school students and teachers.

These programs and publications are designed to raise awareness and understanding of the richness and diversity of jazz, foster the skills of young musicians, and promote the instruction of jazz in schools. J@LC Education serves students, educators, families, and the general public. Its programs, available on a broad geographic basis, include high-quality materials (print music and publications for student-musicians and educators), instruction, performances, professional development, and advocacy.

"Essentially Ellington" High School Jazz Band Competition and Festival Winners; 315 All–Stars of Greater Syracuse, NY, on stage with Wynton Marsalis, Artistic Director of Jazz at Lincoln Center, May 2001

Programs range from the innovative Essentially Ellington High School Jazz Band Competition and Festival (which reaches 1,200 schools in the U.S. and Canada annually) to the Jazz for Young People Curriculum. Jazz at Lincoln Center serves teachers by offering professional development in a summer band-director academy and dozens of shorter sessions throughout the year, and provides other opportunities through Jazz Talk (a lecture-demonstration series), Jazz 101 courses, Jazz in the Schools performances, Jazz for Young People family concerts, master clinics and classes, and an array of other activities involving the Lincoln Center Jazz Orchestra's national and international tours.

The Joyce Theater

New York, NY   www.joyce.org

- School districts served per year: 15
- Elementary schools served per year: 8
- High schools served per year: 7
- K-12 students served per year: 2,000

Programs offered:

Performances for K-12 audiences

Short-term in-school residencies (one week or less)

After school or weekend programs for K-12 students

Professional development opportunities for teachers

Professional development opportunities for teaching artists

Partnerships with whole schools

Partnerships with whole school districts

Training for school leaders (principals, superintendents, others)

Programs with parents and/or other adult caregivers

Adult education opportunities

Mentoring for students with community volunteers

Performances/exhibits by students

Performances/exhibits by school-based teachers

Performances/exhibits by teaching artists

Technical/planning assistance

Evaluation methods

PROFILE

Since its founding in 1982, the Joyce Theater Foundation has had a strong commitment to education in and through the art of dance, offering a comprehensive education program for New York City public school children as well as activities for adults and community organizations.

The Joyce Theater Dance Education Program for schools is an innovative collaboration among dance companies from around the world, schools, and the Theater. The program is specifically designed to foster an understanding of dance for students in K-12th grade, encourage the development of students' perceptions and imaginations, and integrate the arts into classroom learning.

The Dance Education Program operates during the academic year and includes live dance Performances for Study, continuing education workshops for teachers, and planning sessions for classroom work with Joyce teaching artists (TAs), its education staff, and mentoring schools.

Performances for Study are presented at the Theater by leading national and international dance companies, reflecting the cultural, ethnic, and stylistic diversity of the Joyce season. Dance TAs and classroom teachers collaborate throughout the academic year to develop study units around these performances, with classes attending two to four performances a season.

Professional development workshops for teachers create opportunities for continuing learning in order to effectively integrate the various aspects of the education program into school curriculum; these workshops constitute a year-long sequentially designed series and another ongoing partnership between TAs and classroom teachers. The Joyce Theater's education program for schools was in fact selected as an Arts Education Professional Development Services Provider for the New York City public schools, but the strength of its work draws education professionals from throughout the metropolitan area as well.

Additionally, extended dance residencies in two different schools are conducted by dance artists from companies performing at the Joyce during the fall and spring semesters. These residencies provide students and the schools with valuable opportunities for in-depth explorations of choreography and movement in classroom settings.

Family Matinee series and Joyce Junior Membership programs are offered by the Joyce as part of its commitment to make dance performances accessible to families and cultivate new and younger audiences. Six to eight family-oriented performances, followed by Meet-the-Artists gatherings, are offered each year. The Joyce Junior Membership program, which is modeled after the Theater's successful adult membership program, provides children

(ages 6-14) with backstage tours of the Theater and special participatory Family Matinee Events at Joyce SoHo.

Outreach activities for adult audiences include the Joyce's popular Humanities series that offers post-performance discussions with artists, including choreographers, artistic directors, designers, and dancers from the featured dance companies. The new Dance Talks is a series of conversations with artists, scholars, dance writers, and audiences that is illustrated with dance videos and movement demonstrations. The series, held at Joyce SoHo, provides an informal but in-depth examination of issues shaping dance today.

The Joyce's outreach efforts, both alone and in partnership with other arts institutions, schools, and community or social service organizations, take place continuously throughout the year in order to reach and serve diverse constituencies. Recent collaborators include the New School, New York University, the Hudson Guild, the Children's Aid Society, Career Transitions for Dancers, and the American Dance Legacy Institute.

PS 56Q 5th graders participate in a Joyce Theater movement workshop.

The New Victory Theater

New York, NY   www.newvictory.org

- School districts served per year: 30
- Elementary schools served per year: 25
- High schools served per year: 29
- K-12 students served per year: 18,000

Programs offered:

Performances for K-12 audiences

Short-term in-school residencies (one week or less)

After school or weekend programs for K-12 students

Professional development opportunities for teachers

Summer institute for K-12 teachers

Partnerships with whole schools

Programs with parents and/or other adult caregivers

Technical/planning assistance

PROFILE

The New Victory Theater, a "New 42nd Street project," is New York City's first and only theater for kids and families. The first historic theater to reopen on 42nd Street (December 11, 1995), the New Victory has become one of the city's most respected cultural institutions, "credited with having pioneered a new, sophisticated vision of children's entertainment" (*Time Out New York*).

Underscoring the New Victory's commitment to presenting an innovative and diverse range of performing arts experiences (in theater, dance, music, circus, puppetry, and more) to the next generation of theatergoers, the New Victory School Membership Program enables schoolchildren and educators to see the same acclaimed productions presented to the public on evenings and weekends. In addition, the Theater provides comprehensive resources designed to augment the theater experience, such as Talk Back sessions with the artists. The students' detailed and imaginative questions posed to the artists in these sessions, which follow each performance, beautifully illustrate the connection occurring between the work of the classroom and their experiences at the New Victory.

Free study guide materials complement each of the season's nine productions. Free Teacher Institutes are available in which educators participate in hands-on, interactive workshops that demonstrate how the New Victory's programming can be incorporated as a component of the curriculum. A sign-interpreted performance of each of the season's productions is offered, enabling hearing-impaired schoolchildren to attend.

In all, the New Victory's 7th season last year included 42 weekday-morning performances reserved specifically for school audiences of grades pre-K-12, reaching some 18,000 schoolchildren and teachers from 75 schools throughout New York City's five boroughs.

This past year saw several enhancements to the School Membership program that were designed to deepen the relationship with member teachers and students, and to make more concrete and individualized curricular connections to the Theater's programming. For example, the Summer Teacher Institute, held in July 2002, featured a residency with The Abbey, Ireland's national theater, whose exemplary outreach programs serve as international models for excellence in arts education. In three full-day sessions, The Abbey's education director led workshops on how to use theater as a resource in the classroom. In September 2002, the Back-to-School Institute presented an overview of the season and program procedures, and teachers had the opportunity to meet the Theater's front-of-house staff.

In addition to the Summer and Back-to-School Institutes, teachers attended free Mini-Institutes, led by New Victory education staff and guest teaching artists, that were held a few weeks prior to each of the season's presentations; these two-hour workshops focused on creating lesson plans to link the production with the particular needs of each teacher and his or her classroom.

Finally, to further enrich the students' experience, the Theater offers the option of on-site classroom visits both before and after attending a performance. Also, an upgraded New Victory Theater Web site now features articles and video clips about each show, along with background on the companies and related activities, and online ticket ordering for schools.

An excerpt from **Fuerza y Compas,** *a two-act suite that traces Cuban flamenco tradition*

The activities of the New Victory's education department also include a paid Apprenticeship Program for high school through graduate-school students, and a Weekend Workshop series for families, who are given the opportunity to explore various elements of the performing arts together while working with professional teaching artists. This past year the workshops, informed by the work on the stage, included storytelling, creative drama, puppetry, juggling and physical comedy, improvisation and ensemble-building, hip-hop dance and culture, creative movement, playwriting, and an intensive Studio Week for teens inspired by the season's closing production, *A Midsummer Night's Dream.*

The work presented on stage is the central force in the educational planning. Its dynamic nature constantly challenges the New Victory to explore and develop complementary and parallel programming for students, educators, and families, in order to enhance and extend their engagement with the performance experience.

New York State Theatre Institute
Troy, NY   www.nysti.org

- School districts served per year: 126
- Elementary schools served per year: 160
- High schools served per year: 50
- K-12 students served per year: 35,000

Programs offered:

Performances for K-12 audiences

Short-term in-school residencies (one week or less)

Long-term in-school residencies (multiple weeks)

After school or weekend programs for K-12 students

Professional development opportunities for teachers

Professional development opportunities for teaching artists

Partnerships with schools

Partnerships with school districts

Partnerships with public broadcasting

Partnerships with cable media

Web-based learning opportunities

Programs with parents and/or other adult caregivers

Adult education opportunities

Mentoring for students with community volunteers

Performances/exhibits by students

Performances/exhibits by teaching artists

Technical/planning assistance

Evaluation methods

PROFILE

New York State Theater Institute's (NYSTI) entire program—its productions, study guides, pre-show introductions, and residency classes—all provide learning opportunities. Tens of thousands of students attend performances, and more than 25 percent of the student audience participates in extensive education programs. This enhancement of the theatrical experience uses the production as a catalyst for teaching curriculum-based lessons.

The residency, for example, is a series of classes taught by Institute teacher/actors and teacher/technicians using the play as a vehicle for making connections between what has happened on stage and what the students are studying. Lessons are planned to meet New York State (NYS) Learning Standards, and each program is customized to serve specific grade levels and curricular concentrations. For example, after seeing *American Enterprise*, a teacher/actor involves social-studies students in role-playing through a situation in which labor and management must work together to solve a problem. Similarly, *A Wonderful Life* becomes the springboard for activities exploring the economics of the 1930s. In a language arts class, *The Miracle Worker* allows students to explore various modes of communications, and *The Wizard of Oz* becomes an opportunity to write travel brochures for an exotic place.

During the course of the season, almost 50 percent of students attending the morning performances participate in the Classroom Preparations and Pre-Show Intros program. Audience appreciation, comprehension, and behavior are elevated by providing behind-the-scenes information prior to a performance. A member of the NYSTI education department travels to the school and, using a slide presentation, introduces characters and setting while tracing the technical development of the production from conceptual design stage to completed product. These sessions are interactive and grade-level-specific.

Teachers, meanwhile, are provided with a variety of learning experiences and teaching tools to link the production with the classroom curriculum; for example, study guides suggest activities and specific connections to the NYS Learning Standards across the disciplines. Also, some 25 percent of teachers making ticket reservations attend the Teacher Inservice program. Designed to aid them in student preparation for the performance by revealing the creative processes and concepts involved in the production, this two-hour symposium includes presentations by the director and members of the creative team, observation of a rehearsal segment, and additional classroom materials.

Other educational outreach programs serve approximately 2,500 children and their teachers during the course of a season. These activities include career days, shadowing experiences, teacher professional development, technical theater workshops, and worksops using theater as a teaching tool.

The Theatre Arts School, Summer Stage, and Summer Theatre programs, for example, provide young people with a short-term opportunity to gain the skills and experiences necessary for participating in theater in their schools and communities. In a more professional vein, the Intern Program provides high school seniors and college students, as well as educators, the opportunity to work full-time within a professional theater and gain an understanding of, and perspective on, the possible career opportunities in theater. Each intern is guided by a mentor from NYSTI's professional staff, and earns academic credit from his or her home campus.

TIMOTHY H. RAAB

Lynnie Godfrey performs the title role in NYSTI's original musical The Snow Queen *with Ashton Holmes as Kai, the young lad she puts under a spell.*

NYSTI's education and internship programs have been in place since its inception, long before the concept of using the arts to teach across the curriculum became popular. The NYSTI continues to develop programs that meet the needs of students and teachers while maintaining the highest standards of professional theater.

Symphony Space

New York, NY   www.symphonyspace.org

- School districts served per year: 9
- Elementary schools served per year: 5
- High schools served per year: 7
- K-12 students served per year: 5,880

Programs offered:

Performances for K-12 audiences

Long-term in-school residencies (multiple weeks)

Professional development opportunities for teachers

Professional development opportunities for teaching artists

Web-based learning opportunities

Programs with parents and/or other adult caregivers

Adult education opportunities

Performances/exhibits by students

Performances/exhibits by teaching artists

Technical/planning assistance

Evaluation methods

PROFILE

For 22 years, Symphony Space has offered the Curriculum Arts Project (CAP)—workshops and activities across the arts, including music, dance, drama, and the visual arts, that mirror the diversity of programming at Symphony Space—to New York City public-school teachers and students. CAP brings professional artists to the students at participating schools, many of which have few or no arts specialists; provides artist-guided tours of major New York City museums; and presents special concerts for students at Symphony Space.

The project is instrumental in helping schools meet New York State and New York City learning standards in several key areas, particularly social studies. By imparting curriculum-related information through stimulating projects that use a variety of

different art forms, CAP develops students' abilities to use art works to illuminate concepts and themes; and it actively cultivates their critical viewing, listening, and reading skills. Meanwhile, the project offers increased access to the arts for a traditionally underserved population.

CAP is available to students in the second through twelfth grades, and is centered on a semester-long series of five to eight workshops taught by professional artists. It provides specific instruction in three subject areas—American history, African studies, and Asian studies—with activities that are thematically linked to the class's social studies curriculum.

Each program includes the following components:

- *Creative Arts Projects.* In a series of workshops in their schools, students work with artists and teachers on creative assignments. For example, they write and perform plays or rap songs, create musical instruments, or execute visual arts projects.

- *Museum tours to the Metropolitan Museum of Art or other museums.* Artist-led tours of exhibits connected to the current social studies curriculum give students an opportunity to examine works of art in a cultural context. At the same time, the experience enables them to interpret and appreciate artworks, helps them develop insights into the creative process, and ultimately leads to a broader understanding of the potential of the arts to communicate on multiple levels.

- *Culminating Concerts at Symphony Space* provide students with an opportunity to experience a professional performance of the dance, drama, or music of the culture they have been studying.

- *Staff Development Workshops for Teachers.* Annual all-day staff development sessions, held early in the semester, provide teachers with the tools to expand upon lessons taught by participating artists. These training workshops also supply teachers with a CAP study guide, audiocassettes with musical selections, and slides of works of art. Using these and other resource materials, the teachers can prepare students in advance of each CAP session. Classroom teachers also reinforce the artist-led visits through suggested follow-up activities. In this way, even after the sessions end, teachers and students can continue to study and discuss art from the period or culture under investigation.

In 2001-02, CAP served approximately 4,770 students. In 2002-03, enrollment increased by 23 percent to some 5,880 students from 29 schools in Brooklyn, Manhattan, the Bronx, and Queens. Innovations this past year included the pilot implementation of a new CAP in Native-American studies, an expanded CAP Web presence as part of the newly redesigned institutional Web site; and the start of a two year analysis of the project by an independent education evaluator.

CARNEY HABERMAN

Madeleine Yayodele Nelson and Marsha Perry Starkes, members of the performing ensemble Women of the Calabash, teach a class at I.S. 259 in Brooklyn as part of the CAP in Africa unit of the Curriculum Arts Project.

Tilles Center for the Performing Arts CW Post Campus/ Long Island University

Greenvale, NY   www.tillescenter.org

- School districts served per year: 43
- Elementary schools served per year: 45
- High schools served per year: 17
- K-12 students served per year: 13,500

Programs offered:

Performances for K-12 audiences

Short-term in-school residencies (one week or less)

Long-term in-school residencies (multiple weeks)

Professional development opportunities for teachers

Professional development opportunities for teaching artists

Summer institute for K-12 teachers

Summer institute for teaching artists

Partnerships with whole schools

Partnerships with whole school districts

Partnerships with public broadcasting

Training for school leaders (principals, superintendents, others)

Performances/exhibits by students

Evaluation methods

PROFILE

The Tilles Center's arts education program has grown tremendously in a very short time. Beginning with a modest series of four performances for school audiences in 1992, the Center now involves more than 13,000 students each year from schools across Long Island. More than a dozen professional performances form the centerpiece of a range of complementary educational activities, including artist residencies in schools, workshops for educators, and intensive school partnerships. All of the programs share a common purpose: to allow each student to encounter performing and visual arts first-hand and to develop greater awareness of how the arts relate to their lives. By challenging preconceptions and stimulating fresh insights, students gain a more informed and thoughtful appreciation of works of art, artists, and the creative process.

The focus of current efforts is the School Partnership program, which involves educational collaborations among schools, the Tilles Center, and other arts institutions. The program provides teachers, students, and parents with an intensive and structured series of arts experiences. At the heart of the program are encounters by students with great works of art from many cultures—performances of dance, theater, and music, as well as exposure to paintings, sculpture and architecture. Attendance at professional performances at the Tilles Center, or museum visits, are combined with artistic explorations in the school led by teaching artists, classroom teachers, and arts specialists. This approach prompts students to ask questions about works of art and grapple with problems that artists faced in the creative process. Through active engagement with artistic materials, students gain insight into the works they see and hear.

The school partnership program is unusual in its close relationship between a leading presenter of performing arts—the Tilles Center—and a major institution of higher learning, Long Island University (C. W. Post Campus). Companies and artists being presented in public concerts by Tilles—companies such as the New York Philharmonic, Alvin Ailey American Dance Theater, and Pilobolus, as well as artists such as Bobby McFerrin, Twyla Tharp, and Yo-Yo Ma—are directly involved in the education program. The Center also employs the resources of the C.W. Post School of Education by drawing on its faculty and students for assistance in developing the program and providing training opportunities for teachers and teaching artists.

The program's partnerships combine intensive teacher training and multiple encounters by students with artists. Each teacher attends a two-week seminar in July as an introduction to the program, during which time he or she takes workshops led by Tilles Center teaching artists, sees performances, visits museums, learns about the philosophy and approach of the program, and begins to consider plans for incorporating specific arts experiences into the classroom.

Teachers then have one or more teaching artists assigned to them.. These artists will work with them and their students during the year, which begins with extensive collaboration between the artists and teachers in developing goals and activities. The result is that each class participates in two projects, which focus on attendance at a performance or a visit to a museum. Complementing the actual performance or visit are a series of six to eight class sessions, half of which involve the teaching artist working in the classroom; the other sessions are led by the teacher independently. All of them, however, have been jointly derived.

Students meet the cast after a performance at Tilles Center of Lisa Loomer's play Bocon.

Prospective teaching artists engage in a week-long series of workshops designed to introduce them to the approach as well as determine their suitability for the program. Subsequently, each artist goes through a mentoring process during which he or she works as an apprentice alongside experienced teaching artists in classrooms, much as a student-teacher would. This is supplemented by semi-annual training workshops, led by education professionals, on lesson planning, partnering with teachers, classroom management, child development, and other basic pedagogical matters.

The program is innovative in allowing teachers (together with artists) to develop their own curriculum connections and teaching approaches throughout the year, depending on the needs of their individual classes. Teachers may choose from a wide variety of arts experiences in dance, theater, music, and visual arts. In some cases, when schools have chosen to tie the Partnership to school-wide goals in literacy and language arts, specialists from the C.W. Post School of Education have been asked to consult on the development of the projects.

North Carolina Blumenthal Performing Arts Center

Charlotte, NC   www.blumenthalcenter.org

- School districts served per year: 13
- Elementary schools served per year: 1,100
- High schools served per year: 200
- K-12 students served per year: 125,000

Programs offered:

Performances for K-12 audiences

After school or weekend programs for K-12 students

Professional development opportunities for teachers

Professional development opportunities for teaching artists

Summer institute for K-12 teachers

Summer institute for teaching artists

Partnerships with whole schools

Partnerships with whole school districts

Partnerships with cable media

Web-based learning opportunities

Adult education opportunities

Performances/exhibits by students

Performances/exhibits by teaching artists

Technical/planning assistance

Evaluation methods

PROFILE

In 1999, following an extensive assessment of local arts education needs, the North Carolina Blumenthal Performing Arts Center launched the Education Institute to provide educational programs and services—including the best in local, state, and national performing and visual artists—to thousands of students, teachers, artists, adults, and families. In the past year alone, the Institute reached 125,000 students and pre-school children.

In-School Partnerships

The Education Institute's signature programs are its K-5 arts-integrated curriculum partnerships, which operate in two county school systems on a year-round basis. Artists and teachers work together to create arts-integrated units of study that motivate students to learn through active participation. Last year, the Institute directly served 525 teachers and students at the two systems with 1,068 contact hours. Once the model process and curriculum are fully established in the pilot schools, they will serve as "lab schools" to help the Institute replicate the programs in others.

Educational Quality through Arts for Lifelong Learning (EQUALL). University Park Creative Arts School (Mecklenburg County's arts magnet school) is the site of a partnership that is now in its fifth year. Grades K-3 are currently included, and plans are in place for expansion into grades 4 and 5. The Institute has partnered with the Charlotte Symphony, Opera Carolina, the Light Factory (Charlotte's contemporary visual arts center), and individual teaching artists to help classroom teachers make a positive impact on student learning in and through the arts.

Gaston Arts Integration Nurtures Success (GAINS). The Institute partners with Gaston County Schools, specifically the Ida Rankin Elementary School, the United Arts Council of Gaston County, and the Gaston County Public Library to create this model arts-integrated curriculum program in a traditional school. GAINS is in its fourth year of operation with grades K-3, and will shortly expand into grades 4 and 5. The Kennedy Center selected the GAINS partnership to become an affiliate of its national Partners in Education Program.

Northwest School of the Arts (NWSA). In its eighth successful year, the Theater Arts Education Partnership between the Institute and this Mecklenburg County arts magnet school gives middle and high school students the opportunity to work alongside the Center's professional staff on their annual musical-theater production. Students play an integral role in every part of the process from set design and construction, lighting and sound, and ticket sales to marketing and public relations, budgeting, and event management. The more advanced students now help teach those who are new to the school or partnership. Last year's performance of *Sweeney Todd* engaged 86 students and 20 teachers and advisors in more than 11,000 hours of activity.

Performance-Based Programs

The Education Institute provides unique programs for Charlotte-area schools and communities in conjunction with the highly acclaimed presentations at the Performing Arts Center. Participants enjoy high quality arts and learning experiences through performances, master classes, lectures, skills workshops, exhibitions, and other innovative activities with visiting artists.

Community-Building Partnerships. With input from advisory groups and individuals, these partnerships may include children's arts programs within community festivals, working with elders, conducting classes, showcasing local artists from culturally diverse communities, providing arts for after school programs, or audience development.

The MetLife Family Arts Experience provides opportunities for underserved families to attend performances of the Center's Broadway Lights and Special Attractions series by making tickets available to them at reduced rates. Last year more than 1,000 people benefited from this program.

Services

Professional development training for teachers. Specialists conduct workshops that focus on curriculum planning and development, arts-integration methods, effective program evaluation and assessment, and building and sustaining effective arts education partnerships.

Professional development training for artists. The Education Institute, with major funding from the North Carolina Arts Council, recently offered the Kennedy Center's professional development seminar for artists throughout North Carolina. These sessions are designed to help them plan workshops to train teachers to use the arts more effectively in their classrooms.

SUZANNE DANE, NCBPAC EDUCATION INSTITUTE STAFF

Children perform cultural dances as part of the "Passport to Latin America" program at Charlotte's annual Latin American Festival.

Curriculum resources and materials. The Institute's specialists in arts-integrated teaching identify or develop relevant resources and materials to use as "tools for teaching," which are made available to participating schools. These tools include curriculum-aligned study guides for performance-based programs in schools and communities, arts-integrated lesson plans, online resources, and trained teaching artists.

Assessment and evaluation tools and procedures have been developed by the Institute specifically for evaluating arts education programs.

Technical support services are available for artists, schools, and communities that wish to employ the arts as an effective tool for teaching and learning.

Audience development support is provided through the Institute's ongoing community partnerships, advisory groups, contacts, and tested strategies.

Cincinnati Arts Association

Cincinnati, OH   http://www.cincinnatiarts.org

- **School districts served per year:** 400
- **Elementary schools served per year:** 400
- **High schools served per year:** 80
- **K-12 students served per year:** 100,000

Programs offered:

Performances for K-12 audiences

Short-term in-school residencies (one week or less)

Professional development opportunities for teachers

Professional development opportunities for teaching artists

Partnerships with schools

Performances/exhibits by students

Performances/exhibits by teaching artists

Evaluation methods

PROFILE

The Cincinnati Arts Association (CAA) employs a multidisciplinary, multicultural approach to arts education through its three distinct programs to schools in a 22-county region of Southwest Ohio, Northern Kentucky, and Southeast Indiana. These programs are as follows:

• *SchoolTime* presents a variety of performances to student audiences while offering high-quality study-guide materials to support the classroom teacher and prepare the student for each performance. CAA also provides ticket and transportation subsidies so that no child will be turned away; last year more than 9,000 children received subsidy support. Featured artists offer several teacher workshops as part of the School Time series. These supply additional training to help teachers in the classroom, and also give them an opportunity to experience artists as people.

• *Artists on Tour* sends 23 local and regional artists into the schools to conduct assemblies and workshops, do short-term residencies, and support teachers' academic instruction through integration of their art into the curriculum. CAA also conducts Education 101 workshops so that the artists may be better informed on schools, classroom management, and a host of other topics relevant to placing artists in a classroom setting.

• *CAA's Overture Awards* program offers 400-plus local high school students, representing 85 schools, the opportunity to compete for $39,000 in scholarships and to be recognized for their excellence in any of six artistic disciplines. In addition, the program periodically provides workshops, career planning guidance, and master classes to these students throughout the year.

RICH SOFRANKO

Brian Malone of the Bacchanal Steel Band conducts a percussion workshop with area children.

Franciscan Center of Lourdes College

Sylvania, OH   www.franciscancenter.org

- School districts served per year: 52
- Elementary schools served per year: 400
- High schools served per year: 25
- K-12 students served per year: 28,000

Programs offered:

Performances for K-12 audiences

Short-term in-school residencies (one week or less)

Professional development opportunities for teachers

Professional development opportunities for teaching artists

Partnerships with whole schools

Partnerships with whole school districts

Partnerships with public broadcasting

Partnerships with cable media

Adult education opportunities

Performances/exhibits by teaching artists

Technical/planning assistance

Evaluation methods

PROFILE

The Franciscan Center of Lourdes College was founded by the Sisters of St. Francis in support of their mission to bring the arts to the local community. In 1985, the Center initiated its Theater Vision series, which for 18 years has presented quality educational-theater performances by professional touring companies for student audiences in pre-kindergarten through grade 12.

Theater Vision presentations are designed to introduce and enhance understanding and appreciation of drama and acting, dance and movement, music and singing, language and literature, and history and culture. Performances are linked to *Ohio's Model Competency-Based Program for Comprehensive Arts Education,* published by the Ohio Department of Education.

Through the years, the Theater Vision program has grown in size and scope. The first season featured 12 performances of 4 shows; season 18 featured 46 performances of 15 shows.

As Theater Vision has grown, the Franciscan Center has added complementary theater arts education programs. Theater Vision Days, which combine performances with interactive workshops, allow students to explore behind the scenes with members of performing companies or work with local artist/educators to deepen their knowledge of subjects related to particular performances. Complementary educational materials include teaching manuals provided by performing companies and original "Prompt Pages" that are written for student audiences and distributed to them in advance of each performance.

The Franciscan Center has built partnerships with local schools and school systems. Particularly strong is its long-standing partnership with Sylvania Schools, enabled by the John F. Kennedy Center's Partners in Education program, to provide arts education opportunities. For example, Kennedy Center artist/presenters have trained local artists to give workshops and fulfill residencies. In the 11-year history of the Franciscan Center/Sylvania Schools partnership, more than 100 arts education workshops at the Franciscan Center have involved hundreds of teachers.

The Franciscan Center continues to enhance its innovative arts education programming, particularly in the area of creating partnerships:

- During the 2002-2003 season, a partnership with the Lourdes College Life Lab Program for Natural and Environmental Sciences offered Theater Vision presentations and Simply Science Theater Vision

Days based on performances of *The Very Hungry Caterpillar* and *The Very Quiet Cricket* and *Sarah Plain and Tall*. In addition, students were able to do hands-on explorations of some of the flora and fauna portrayed in these presentations.

• A partnership with WGTE-TV (the local public broadcasting station) presented literature- and history-based professional development workshops for teachers.

• The Franciscan Center plans to partner with other local organizations as well, in order to present a wide range of professional development opportunities for educators.

All in all, the Franciscan Center's education department has so far brought 18 seasons of theater performances and a growing number of related arts education activities to more than 360,000 students, educators, and parents in 11 Ohio and Michigan counties. The core strengths of the Center's educational programs are:

• The trust that exists between the Center and its audiences, resulting in continued strong support of the program

• The Center's dedication to building new partnerships with other community organizations

• Positive relationships with artists, both local and national

Playhouse Square Foundation
Cleveland, OH   www.playhousesquare.com

• School districts served per year: 73
• Elementary schools served per year: 187
• High schools served per year: 29
• K-12 students served per year: 50,000

Programs offered:

Performances for K-12 audiences

Short-term in-school residencies (one week or less)

After-school or weekend programs for K-12 students

Professional development opportunities for teachers

Professional development opportunities for teaching artists

Summer institute for K-12 teachers

Summer institute for teaching artists

Partnerships with whole schools

Partnerships with public broadcasting

Programs with parents and/or other adult caregivers

Adult education opportunities

Performances/exhibits by students

Performances/exhibits by teaching artists

PROFILE

The Playhouse Square Foundation education department was created four years ago to address the growing need to enhance the performing arts experience for local teachers, students, community members, families, and artists. Today, Playhouse Square offers two children's theater series and educational-support materials for elementary school children; extensive high school programs including a teen volunteer program and weekends of workshops and performances; and professional development to help teachers integrate the arts into their classrooms. Family audiences are offered pre- and post-show activities and educational newsletters to enhance their experience of the Broadway shows. Local arts organizations are supported by creating partnerships that infuse the arts with educational programs in the region's schools.

Grades K-8

• Two series for young audiences: *The Huntington Children's Theatre Series* for ages 3 to 8 and the *Discovery Theatre Series* for ages 8 to 12. More than 50,000 school children attend one or more of these performances each year, and an additional 20,000 children attend weekend matinees with their families.

PLAYHOUSE SQUARE STAFF

Giselle *Master Class – American Ballet Theater*

• Newsletters for children's shows that complement the theater experience for students; and study guides that assist educators in developing curriculum connections with performances.

Grades 9-12

• *The eXtreme Theatre Festival*, an annual event during which 100 high school students participate in workshops on topics ranging from auditioning to dance techniques. Students also see and critique performances during the weekend-long festival.

• Opportunities for high school students to serve as ushers for children's theater and Broadway performances as part of the *Students Take a Role at the Square* (STARS) volunteer team.

• *Career Day* is an annual event that brings 250 students to the Center to spend the morning meeting with a panel of touring and local artists and arts administrators and engaging in hands-on workshops.

• *Master Classes*, presented by touring artists from the national Broadway series, are open to high school and college students interested in the performing arts. These classes are free of charge and attract approximately 100-150 students each season.

• *Special projects*, including a workshop this past season that brought local students into contact with professional theater critics and administrators to discuss musical theater on stage and on screen.

Professional Development

Central to the education department's efforts is the creation of high quality professional development workshops that equip Cleveland-area educators with the tools they need to implement arts education in their curriculums. Programs include:

• *Graduate-level courses*, in partnership with Cleveland State University, taught by national teaching artists. The past year's courses included "Literacy through Storytelling and Movement" and "Teaching to Multiple Intelligences through the Arts."

• An annual field-trip expo called *Fair on the Square*, during which more than 900 teachers meet with local organizations to book cultural and other field-trip opportunities for the coming school year.

• *Teacher Tuesday workshops*, which enable teachers to come to the Center monthly to work with professional teaching artists and learn hands-on methods of integrating the arts into classroom lessons.

• *An arts-in-education advocacy Web site* (www. playhousesquare. com/culturalconnections) that offers resources to Ohio teachers and gives them insight into legislative developments affecting arts education.

Adult Education/Families

A variety of pre- and post-show opportunities are available for adult and family audiences of Broadway performances. These events, which comprise the Broadway Buzz program, include:

• *Pre-Show Talks*, during which a local performing arts professional speaks with audiences about the history of a particular Broadway show before curtain

• *Post-Show Chats* with the cast, enabling artists from touring Broadway shows to speak with audience members and answer questions after a specific performance

• *A Broadway Buzz newsletter*, distributed to 23,000-plus Broadway subscribers, that gives insights into each upcoming show by providing information on actors, the history of the show, and related themes

• *Broadway Bound*, a series of lobby exhibits and educational events presented before the matinee performances of specific Broadway shows

• *CenterFest*, an annual open house arts festival that attracts nearly 9,000 families, community members, and others to the Center for a free day of activities, performances, exhibits, and more.

The Center also sponsors community-focused events such as Teatro Popular, a two-year project that united local Latinos with Playhouse Square to encourage their creative expression. In 2004 a new Arts Education Center will link the education department with Cleveland's two public broadcasting organizations and provide much needed space for the constantly growing educational programs. This partnership also gives the Center the opportunity to serve as a content provider for community-based distance-learning initiatives.

Annenberg Center for the Performing Arts

Philadelphia, PA   www.pennpresents.org

• School districts served per year: 7
• Elementary schools served per year: 134
• High schools served per year: 20
• K-12 students served per year: 30,000

Programs offered:

Performances for K-12 audiences

Short-term in-school residencies (one week or less)

Long-term in-school residencies (multiple weeks)

Professional development opportunities for teaching artists

Partnerships with public broadcasting

Adult education opportunities

PROFILE

The strength of the Annenberg Center's education programs is the ability to provide young people in the West Philadelphia region, many from disadvantaged schools and neighborhoods, access to some of the most innovative and provocative artists. As an arts presenter affiliated with the University of Pennsylvania, the Center has access to Penn's extensive resources, and helps make connections and create relationships within the community. These assets help to harness the talent and time of the artists presented, thereby creating innovative and meaningful education and outreach programs that really affect the community. The Center's education programs include:

• *Philadelphia International Children's Festival.* Since 1985, the Children's Festival has brought together young people and families of all ethnicities and socioeconomic backgrounds to experience the magic of children's entertainment. Through high-quality presentations by imaginative young people's artists, the Festival provides the opportunity to explore many different art forms from all over the world. During the past three years, the Festival has featured acrobats from China; music and dance from Uganda, Canada, the United States, and South Africa; clown theater from the United States and Canada; storytelling from Japan; dramatic theater from Belgium and Canada; puppet theater from Japan, Vietnam, the Netherlands, and Canada; mask theater from Canada; and object theater (which uses ordinary objects in place of crafted puppets) from Italy and France.

Each year the Festival draws approximately 20,000 young people and families, with deeply discounted tickets provided to schools and organizations in disadvantaged communities. In addition, partnerships began last year with the Philadelphia Cultural Fund to provide free tickets to 500 children involved in the City's Department of Recreation programs. The Center worked last year with WHYY's Caring Community Coalition, Penn's Center for Bioethics, and Peter's Place (a center for grieving children and families) to present a symposium to teachers and parents on working with children coping with loss; the symposium was driven by two plays that addressed death and grieving. Brian Joyce, the director of the Festival, is internationally recognized for his work as a presenter for young people.

• *Artists in schools.* The Center has been working with the University's Center for Community Partnerships (CCP) for the past three years to build relationships with the community's schools, largely in the disadvantaged neighborhoods of West Philadelphia. Outreach activities have ranged from artists conducting one-day workshops and master classes in schools to multi-week artist residencies. David Parker was sent to Drew Elementary School to conduct a workshop on tolerance and the Lula Washington Dance Theatre to the Lea School to help students create an original piece that was then performed by students before the Dance Theatre's own performance at the Center.

Also with CCP, artists were sent into schools to conduct master classes; for example, Pinchas Zukerman (classical violin) went to West Philadelphia High School, and the Mingus Big Band, Herbie Hancock, Jane Monheit, and Wynton Marsalis visited University City High School. Of the Marsalis event, the principal of UCHS wrote: "Our students are still talking about the experience. I continue to feel thankful that the University City High School/ University of Pennsylvania partnership gets better every year."

During 2001-2002, a 10-week residency was implemented featuring South African drummer and educator Mogauwane Mahloele with two fourth-grade classes of Drew Elementary School. The residency culminated in the students creating, producing, and performing an adaptation of a Zulu tale for Home-School Night in April 2002. They plan to repeat this multi-week residency model in 2004 with two semester-long residencies tied to a new gospel-music series.

• *The Student Discovery Series* provides school groups with discounted tickets to matinee performances of regular presentations (such as Dance Celebration, World Music, and Jazz), as well as to theater and music programs created specifically for young people. In 2002, attendance in the series increased nearly 40 percent, thanks in large part to a new partnership with the *Philadelphia Inquirer's* Newspaper in Education program, which produced 40,000 tabloid educational inserts for the 16-performance season. More than 21,000 school children, many from low-income backgrounds, have benefited from this series over the past two years.

The Kimmel Center
for the Performing Arts

Philadelphia, PA   www.kimmelcenter.org

- **School districts served per year: 20**
- **Elementary schools served per year: 90**
- **High schools served per year: 10**
- **K-12 students served per year: 7,000**

Programs offered:

Performances for K-12 audiences

After-school or weekend programs for K-12 students

Professional development opportunities for teachers

Partnerships with whole schools

Partnerships with public broadcasting

Performances/exhibits by students

Performances/exhibits by school-based teachers

Performances/exhibits by teaching artists

Technical/planning assistance

Evaluation methods

PROFILE

Education plays a vital role at the Kimmel Center, as evidenced by the creation of the 4,000 square-foot Merck Arts Education Center (MAEC) that has three areas providing opportunities for young and old to experience the arts:

• The Multipurpose Performance/Learning Space, where music, dance, and theater arts are presented

• The Interactive/Exhibit Area, which contains kiosks, costumes for children to wear, a conducting podium, a two-sided mirror, educational journals, nine-foot panels describing the nine resident companies, and models of Verizon Hall and Perelman Theater

• A Technology Lab for teaching music theory, history, and arranging/composition.

Since the dedication of the MAEC in September 2002, free curriculum-based arts classes have been taught on weekdays to fifth to eighth-grade students; they experience the arts with the aid of professional teaching artists, tour the Center, and explore the Interactive/Exhibit Area as a culminating activity. Prior to working with the classes, the teaching artists meet with members of the Center's education staff to discuss and plan the instructional program from philosophical, artistic, and pedagogical perspectives. Additionally, the instruction programs are organized to meet the National Arts Standards adopted in 1996.

KELLY AND MASSA

Under the direction of Marc D. Johnson, the Kimmel Center Youth Jazz Ensemble performs at the Martin Luther King Jr. Celebration at Commonwealth Plaza, inside the Kimmel Center.

Because the MAEC is able to arrange master classes and workshops with artists who perform in the "Kimmel Center Presents" concert series, there is an array of musical and cultural diversity: classical, world music, jazz, and pop. Artists give performances to students and adults, who often attend through the aid of a subsidized-ticket program.

Innovations during the 2002-2003 school year included the following:

• In November, the Kimmel Center created the first regional jazz ensemble composed exclusively of middle school students. Selected from public, private, and parochial schools, 33 young musicians attended six Saturday-morning rehearsals and debuted at the first anniversary of the Kimmel Center on December 15, 2002. The ensemble performed also at the Martin Luther King Jr. Tribute before an audience of invited middle school students, Kimmel Center staff members, and the general public.

• In February, the MAEC launched a Distance Learning Pilot Program with three schools selected from the School District of Philadelphia. By lending them start-up equipment and offering expertise, the education department not only provided technical assistance, but also helped to expand its cultural relationship with middle and high school students, teachers, and administrators.

• The education department plans to widen its community outreach by instituting a summer arts camp. Each week a different art form will be offered to students (ages 14-17) who wish to pursue a week of vigorous study in vocal/choral music, dance, chamber music, or jazz.

Arts Center of Coastal Carolina
Hilton Head Island, SC   www.artscenter-hhi.org

• **School districts served per year: 2**
• **Elementary schools served per year: 14**
• **High schools served per year: 3**
• **K-12 students served per year: 15,000**

Programs offered:

Performances for K-12 audiences

Short-term in-school residencies (one week or less)

Long-term in-school residencies (multiple weeks)

After-school or weekend programs for K-12 students

Professional development opportunities for teachers

Professional development opportunities for teaching artists

Partnerships with whole school districts

Programs with parents and/or other adult caregivers

Adult education opportunities

Performances/exhibits by students

Evaluation methods

PROFILE

Education programs of the Arts Center of Coastal Carolina include the following:

• *Educational Field Trips* provide performances and offer activities to more than 4,000 students each year in a variety of visual and performing arts disciplines and genres.

• The live *Matinee Performances and Gallery Walks* for young audiences offer exciting educational opportunities that enhance the goals of community educators and provide real-life reflective and interactive arts experiences for the students.

• *ArtsReach* is an arts-exposure and -enrichment program offered free to participating schools in the Hilton Head, Bluffton, Daufuskie Island, and Hardeeville areas, along with Boys & Girls Clubs of the Carolina Lowcountry region. By bringing

ARTS CENTER OF COASTAL CAROLINA

Kevin Locke with Field Trip program students

professional artists into the schools to work directly in the classrooms and on stage presentations for all grade levels, the program serves up to 10,000 students and teachers. It has four components:

–**ArtsReach/InClass** offers the services of contracted artists (who are prominently included on the South Carolina Arts Commission's Approved Artist Roster) in a residency format. The Arts Center's Education Department works with a designated coordinator at each site to determine the selection of artists based on the school's curricular needs.

–**ArtsReach/OnTour** features a select menu of presenting artists in educational, cultural, and entertaining performances for grade level or school-wide audiences. The purpose of these assembly presentations is to expose students to live performances that embrace educationally relevant themes, thereby providing pathways to knowledge through the performing arts.

–**ArtsReach/AfterSchool** offers students well organized and productive experiences beyond the scope of the normal school day. Activities include performance opportunities at the Arts Center as well as at schools and institutional sites.

–**ArtsReach/InService** is based on the principle that the professional development of teachers and community educators is a necessary component of any effort to increase the artistic literacy of young people. Workshops for educators zre offered in a variety of discipline areas.

• *The Community Education Series* includes workshops, lectures, and demonstrations that offer integrated learning experiences with theater programs as well as visual arts exhibitions. They are planned for participants of all ages and scheduled to run concurrently with events during the season in an effort to maximize the relevance and impact of the learning experiences. Each year, more than 300 individuals are enrolled in one or more of the 40 workshops and lectures of this series.

• *Professional Development for Educators.*

–The Arts Center and the Beaufort County School District offer graduate level re-certification courses that utilize the programming and facilities of the Center as seminar topics.

–In 1999, the Arts Center became a Crayola Dream-Makers program site. Since then, more than 100 educators have attended Crayola Dream-Makers workshops at the Center, subsequently integrating the program's projects into classroom curricula.

To ensure opportunities for the whole community, the Education Department also offers performance opportunities and a diverse range of arts and crafts activities at free outdoor festivals, including the Holiday Tree-Lighting Festival, GullahFest, Youth ArtsFest, and Family Fiesta Latina.

The Peace Center
for the Performing Arts

Greenville, SC   www.peacecenter.org

- School districts served per year: 22
- Elementary schools served per year: 250
- High schools served per year: 17
- K-12 students served per year: 64,455

Programs offered:

Performances for K-12 audiences

Short-term in-school residencies (one week or less)

Long-term in-school residencies (multiple weeks)

Professional development opportunities for teachers

Professional development opportunities for teaching artists

Summer institute for K-12 teachers

Partnerships with whole schools

Partnerships with whole school districts

Web-based learning opportunities

Programs with parents and/or other adult caregivers

Adult education opportunities

Performances/exhibits by teaching artists

Evaluation methods

PROFILE

The Peace Outreach Program (POP!), created by the Peace Center for the Performing Arts in 1991, touches the lives of more than 70,000 students, teachers, and community members each year in a nine-county area of upstate South Carolina, western North Carolina, and northeastern Georgia. Major programs include:

• *School Matinee Performances.* POP! presents a season of performances that are curriculum-based and age-appropriate, bringing to life the everyday subjects of the classroom. For many students, these presentations are their only opportunity to see a live professional performance. Study guides are sent to every teacher attending; together with pre- and post-performance activities, they help to enhance the students' experience in the theater.

The materials provide background information about the company and artists, as well as suggested lessons that make relevant connections to South Carolina curriculum standards.

• *Artist-in-Residence Grant Program.* During the academic year, POP! offers eight fully-funded residencies to schools seeking to incorporate the arts into their classrooms. Residencies can help integrate the arts into another area of the curriculum or offer opportunities for students to learn about a specific art form. Either way, students, teachers, school administrators, and community members get to see first-hand the impact that a professional arts experience can have on the life of a child.

Because an artist residency can profoundly affect the teacher as well the students, an important component of the program is professional development for teachers. By requiring participating educators to attend a workshop with the teaching artist, it is more likely they will continue to use the artist's ideas and methods after he or she has left the classroom. Also, all teachers who receive artist-residency grants are expected to participate fully in the planning and implementation process, which helps maximize the learning for everyone involved.

An exciting development in this area is the professional development residency created in partnership with drama specialist Sean Layne. This artist spends a week as the model and coach for a team of teachers.

• *Training Teaching Artists.* The Kennedy Center's "Artists as Educators" seminar was offered in 1998 and 2000. Participants learned how to develop high quality relationships with teachers and make the most meaningful use of their instructional time in the classroom, particularly in the area of arts integration.

• *Teacher Workshops* are held throughout the year to provide teachers with practical methods and strategies for incorporating the arts into their classrooms. The majority of the workshops are offered through the John F. Kennedy Center's Partners in Education program. Feedback from participants indicates that the quality is perceived as outstanding. Approximately 350 teachers take part each year and receive professional credit from their schools/school districts. In the past three seasons, almost every session offered has been filled to capacity. The Peace Center is frequently asked for assistance from other educational partnerships on how to effectively market workshops to teachers.

• *Summer Teacher Institute.* Each year POP! sponsors two Summer Teacher Institutes for educators who wish to integrate the arts into their classrooms. In collaboration with Clemson University, the Institute includes two graduate re-certification courses: "Integrating the Arts Across the Curriculum" and "Teaching Through the Arts." Fifty teachers participate in a series of workshops, learning about practical implementation of drama, dance, music, art, and creative writing in their classrooms, as well as integrated-curriculum design and arts assessment models.

THE PEACE CENTER
FOR THE PERFORMING ARTS

• *POP! Talks.* There has been an increase in demand recently among teachers for POP! staff members to model effective arts-integration in their classrooms. For example, a teacher who attended a creative-movement workshop might feel more confident with an education representative present on the first day he or she tries out the new techniques. This is an excellent opportunity for mentoring teachers who need more coaching in using the arts as a teaching tool. A major goal is to expand and formalize this type of "classroom consulting."

• *The Teacher Connection.* In order to facilitate communication with area teachers, representatives from more than 200 Upstate schools act as liaisons to the Peace Center, sharing information about what POP! has to offer to students and educators alike. The growing number of teachers who participate in this program has helped to increase attendance at virtually all POP! events.

Washington Pavilion of Arts and Science
Sioux Falls, SD   www.washingtonpavilion.org

- School districts served per year: 1-5
- Elementary schools served per year: 22-25
- High schools served per year: 5-7
- K-12 students served per year: 2,000

Programs offered:

Performances for K-12 audiences

After school or weekend programs for K-12 students

Professional development opportunities for teachers

Professional development opportunities for teaching artists

Summer institute for K-12 teachers

Summer institute for teaching artists

Partnerships with whole school districts

Partnerships with public broadcasting

Web-based learning opportunities

Training for school leaders, principals, superintendents, others)

Programs with parents and/or other adult caregivers

Adult education opportunities

Performances/exhibits by students

Evaluation methods

PROFILE

The Washington Pavilion of Arts and Science is a single nonprofit institution containing the Husby Performing Arts Center, Kirby Science Discovery Center, and Visual Arts Center. Its mission is to educate, entertain, inspire, and enrich the community by making arts and science important parts of its life.

The Pavilion provides learning opportunities for children and youth through numerous and diverse programs. In addition, K-12 classroom teachers are supported through the unique Teachers' Circle program. The visual arts and sciences are integrated into many of the performing arts educational activities.

John F. Kennedy Elementary School students perform their Chinese lion dance as part of their Nightingale study unit, January 2003.

Examples of student programs include:

• A lecture/demonstration was held at L.B. Williams Elementary School, where students learned about dance and showcased their own dancing abilities.

• "The Art & Science behind Dance" was held at Harvey Dunn Elementary School in conjunction with a performance by Diavolo. Collaborating with a local dance instructor, a university physics professor, and performing arts, visual arts, and science center staff, the event was created to demonstrate the scientific principles of movement through light, sound, and color. The age of the students, as well as the South Dakota Education Content Standards, were considered in choosing content.

• The Paul Taylor 2 Dance Company gave a performance/demonstration at Eugene Field Elementary School, the local A+ school. The student body gained a greater understanding of the health and training requirements for being a professional dancer.

• Ballet Hispanico participated in the Longfellow Elementary School's diversity week and then followed up with a discussion on diversity issues.

• Opera a la Carte company members came to Washington High School to discuss their performance of *The Mikado*, which students had attended the previous day.

• In 2002, the Washington Pavilion was awarded a grant from the South Dakota Department of Education to provide distance education programs through the state's Dakota Digital Network. When South Dakota teachers were surveyed, their first choice for a distance education site was the Washington Pavilion. The first season of this program included three courses—"Explosions, Implosions, and Kabangs" for 7th and 8th grade students; "Rocket!" for 4th and 5th grade students; and Dakota Time Traveler for 4th grade students—offered free to South Dakota schools.

• In February 2003, a youth symposium took place in conjunction with local performances of the Broadway musical *Rent*. The Washington Pavilion worked with numerous local agencies, such as a performing arts academy, an at-risk youth center, the City of Sioux Falls, and local hospitals. This allows area youth to take advantage of discounted tickets to the musical; attend an open-ended social play that addresses a major issue they face (HIV/AIDS); participate in a post performance discussion; gather information from booths of area social agencies; view a literary broadside gallery; watch a performance by a local hip-hop band; and enjoy pizza and pop.

The core strength of the education program lies in working closely with teachers. This program is innovative because it tailors programs to fit the specific community's needs through extensive teacher involvement in the planning and implementation process. For example, the Teachers' Circle is a group of dedicated multidisciplinary teachers who strive to utilize community resources to enhance their students' educational experience. Participants engage in the following ways:

• Attend Washington Pavilion professional development workshops (in conjunction with the Kennedy Center's Partnership in Education program)

• Learn how to integrate arts activities into standard classroom curriculums

• Select a show in the Performance Series around which they create a lesson plan or unit. These lessons and units, which meet state content standards, are published and archived so that other teachers and their students can also benefit from them.

• Bring their students to the Pavilion as audience members for a live performance

• Become advisors to the Pavilion, providing feedback about programming choices and assisting in the preparation of new teachers and their students for the arts experience.

In the past year, the Pavilion began a program to train teaching artists. Phil Baker, a local musical performer, first attended a teaching artists' workshop at the Kennedy Center and then offered his own workshop, Language Rhythm, for colleagues. Washington Pavillion also began to support in-school artist residencies.

Tennessee Performing Arts Center

Nashville, TN   www.tpac.org

- School districts served per year: 40
- Elementary schools served per year: 120
- High schools served per year: 155
- K-12 students served per year: 70,000

Programs offered:

Performances for K-12 audiences

Short-term in-school residencies (one week or less)

Long-term in-school residencies (multiple weeks)

Professional development opportunities for teachers

Professional development opportunities for teaching artists

Summer institute for K-12 teachers

Summer institute for teaching artists

Partnerships with whole schools

Partnerships with whole school districts

Web-based learning opportunities

Programs with parents and/or other adult caregivers

Adult education opportunities

Mentoring for students with community volunteers

Performances/exhibits by students

Technical/planning assistance

Evaluation methods

PROFILE

The Tennessee Performing Arts Center (TPAC) is proud to be home to one of this country's largest and most comprehensive arts-in-education programs connected to a performing arts center. Students attend outstanding performances of theater, dance, music, and opera. Artists inspire learning in classroom residencies, from preschool to high school. Adults as well as children have wide-ranging enrichment opportunities. Over the years, more than 1.25 million students and educators have participated in TPAC's programs.

• *The Wolf Trap Early Learning Through the Arts* program provides artist residencies that help pre-school children learn life and academic skills through the performing arts. During these seven-week residencies, professionally trained teaching artists engage 3- to 5-year-olds in hands-on music, dance, and drama activities that address general skills such as creativity, sequencing, listening, cooperation, self-expression, and confidence; as well as curriculum-related topics such as emerging literacy, safety, nutrition, and multicultural awareness. Wolf Trap also provides teachers and parents with training in the techniques of arts-based instruction so that they may continue to use and develop performing-arts activities for the children after the artist has left the classroom.

• *Humanities Outreach in Tennessee (HOT)* presents the Season for Young People each school year. Comprehensive guidebooks, teacher workshops, in-school visits, and post-performance seminars ensure that students who attend the season's performances return from TPAC with a memorable learning experience. Performances are presented at little or no cost, with subsidies for students and school systems in financial need.

• *ArtSmart* creates extended classroom study of a HOT performance by bringing a professional teaching artist (TA) into partnership with teachers. They work together to prepare hands-on lessons that not only prepare children for experiencing works of art, but also offer opportunities for developing higher-order thinking skills, nurturing creativity, and practicing collaboration and teamwork.

This 23-year-old teaching approach originated with the Lincoln Center Institute in New York and is now practiced by 16 sister organizations worldwide. ArtSmart has been serving Nashville teachers and children for 20 years. It was the first such program to be created outside Lincoln Center.

Classroom teachers undertake rigorous training in education-through-the-arts. They must participate in summer or winter seminars led by the best TAs and most experienced ArtSmart teachers, attend additional "refresher" workshops during the school year, contribute to collaborative planning sessions with their partner TAs, and commit themselves to integrating their chosen work of art into the general curriculum.

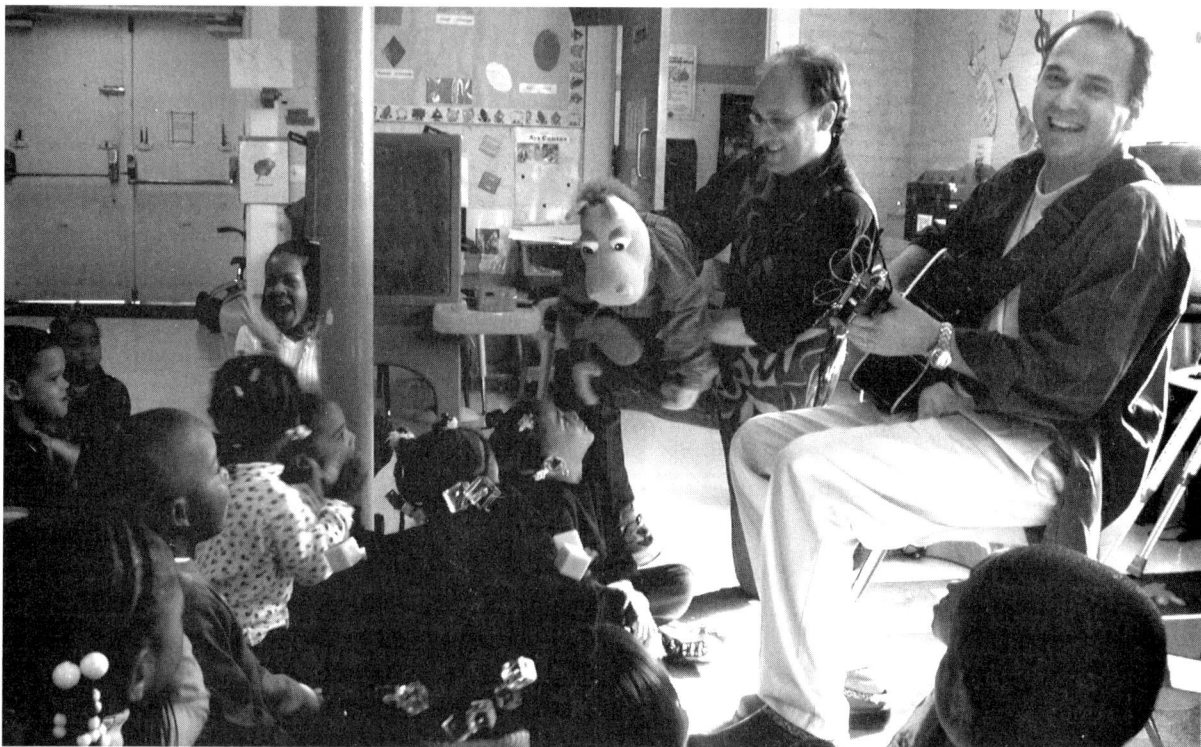

ROB STACK

For TPAC Education's Wolf Trap Early Learning Through the Arts program, teaching artists Barry McAlister and Marcus Hummon use puppets and music to help Head Start children learn about cooperation.

• *Summer/Fall/Winter Institutes* bring educators together in a relaxed camp-like setting for daily sessions over the course of a week to explore the upcoming HOT season and take part in ArtSmart seminars. During the school year, another two-day institute offers a choice of seminars on two ArtSmart "Focus Works" and opens previews to educators participating in HOT.

Teaching Artists who participate in these annual training events increase their understanding of ArtSmart teaching practices, which improves their own teaching. In particular, through this comprehensive training TAs will:

–Better distinguish ArtSmart teaching approaches from technical arts instruction. Rather than directing students to a particular outcome, TAs can present challenges that allow students to take risks, make authentic choices, and resolve challenges independently.

–Be more adept and at ease in working with audiences of learners

–Refine reflection skills

–Better understand school culture, student potential, and teacher realities

–Come away with increased joy from, love for, and commitment to aesthetic education

–Practice self assessment using a variety of tools and approaches.

• *InsideOut* is for adult learners (18 and older) who want to grow in their knowledge and enjoyment of the performing arts. InsideOut events, led by Nashville-based teaching artists, local experts, and special guests, come in many shapes and sizes and occur in many different places. The events enable adult learners to make deeper explorations of the performing arts through innovative hands-on activities that relate to artistic processes and aesthetic decisionmaking.

MSC OPAS at Texas A&M University

College Station, TX   www.mscopas.org

• School districts served per year: 12
• Elementary schools served per year: 26
• High schools served per year: 5
• K-12 students served per year: 15,000

Programs offered:

Performances for K-12 audiences

Short-term in-school residencies (one week or less)

After-school or weekend programs for K-12 students

Professional development opportunities for teachers

Partnerships with whole school districts

Partnerships with public broadcasting

Partnerships with cable media

Training for school leaders (principals, superintendents, others)

Evaluation methods

PROFILE

MSC OPAS, a 150-student committee of the Texas A&M University student union complemented by a Board of Directors that includes 30 community leaders, is the region's professional performing-arts presenter. (Originally called the Memorial Student Center Opera and Performing Arts Society, it is now known mostly by its acronym.)

OPAS's education program began as an outgrowth of its Board Audience-Development Committee's activities for extending the influence of the arts on people's lives. The major strength of the education program has since become the breadth of projects organized for the regional community and the sense of commitment and ownership among local school teachers and administrators.

Currently, the education efforts' core elements are focused on:

—Professional development workshops for teachers through MSC OPAS partnerships with local school systems and the Kennedy Center

—Study materials for classroom teachers to help prepare their students for field trips to the MSC OPAS venue for special school-day performances

—Camp OPAS, a full-day arts-immersion project for 4th graders

—The Performance Partners program, which pairs at-risk children with college mentors to attend performances and gain from pre-performance study guides.

Camp OPAS—the instrument petting zoo

The school partnerships began as MSC OPAS built relationships with the schools by giving special school performances of works relating to their curriculums. Having discovered the Kennedy Center's Partners in Education program, MSC OPAS realized that this was the perfect vehicle for growth in building arts education locally. Buy-in occurred from the independent school district (ISD) boards and superintendents, and MSC OPAS recently completed its second year as a partner. Seven professional development workshops have been presented on dance, song, playwriting, story writing, and music—and have reached approximately 175 teachers.

This past year the partnership began follow-up evaluations with the teachers some six weeks after

each workshop. To discover how much teachers were using the new methods and information they learned in the workshops, an easy-to-complete Web-based survey was e-mailed to them. The comments back were positive with teachers indicating they were utlizing many of the workshop tools.

Camp OPAS is another off-campus opportunity for elementary schools to participate in the arts. The first Camp OPAS was held last year for 4th graders in the two local ISDs. The day focused on the music of Anton Dvorak and the Marian Anderson String Quartet, which is in residency. The students were divided into four groups to move through four stations, which were:

—Storytelling about the life of Dvorak

—Choreographing and performing Dvorak's music

—An instrument petting zoo staffed by college-age musicians

—A Q&A session with the Marian Anderson String Quartet

In the last half hour of the day, the entire group came together for a concert by the Quartet on the Dvorak piece that the students had been studying.

The hope is to enhance this project in the coming years so that it will incorporate all genres of performing arts, ultimately to be a multi-day activity somewhat like science "discovery" camps.

Realizing that at-risk students often do not receive family support for attending performing-arts programs, OPAS devised Performance Partners to join at-risk students, mentors, ticket sponsors, and study materials in an effort to ensure that all children have opportunities to experience the passion of the arts. Volunteers, who are experienced in curriculum development, write study guides for mentors to use with their student partners, and each guide is tailored to the specific program that will be performed. By using the guide, mentors are able to share information with the children in a way appropriate to their ages and to the type of performing arts program they will see together. Thus the college-age mentors don't have to be experts in the particular art form being performed, and in fact they learn along with the children.

Performing Arts Fort Worth, Inc.

Fort Worth, TX   www.basshall.com

- School districts served per year: 18 public and 27 Catholic/private
- Elementary schools served per year: 138
- High schools served per year: 16
- K-12 students served per year: 86,000+

Programs offered:

Performances for K-12 audiences

Short-term in-school residencies (one week or less)

After school or weekend programs for K-12 students

Professional development opportunities for teachers

Professional development opportunities for teaching artists

Summer institute for K-12 teachers

Summer institute for teaching artists

Partnerships with whole schools

Partnerships with whole school districts

Training for school leaders (principals, superintendents, others)

Mentoring for students with community volunteers

Performances/exhibits by students

Performances/exhibits by teaching artists

Evaluation methods

PROFILE

The Children's Education Program is essential for filling the void left by the scarcity of art and music teachers in the public school systems. It provides high-quality arts education and engenders enthusiasm, motivation for learning, and creative potential. Performing Arts commitment is based on two beliefs—that the arts are critical to education, and that it is sowing the seeds to cultivate the artists and audiences of tomorrow. Long before the Nancy Lee and Perry R. Bass Performance Hall opened in 1998, Performing Arts Fort Worth

had begun planning the Children's Education Program which introduces students of all ages in the Fort Worth area to the best in music, theater, and dance.

Since the program's inception, more than 200 programs have been presented at Bass Hall, all curriculum-related, to more than 325,000 students (grades 1-12) in Fort Worth and neighboring communities, and at no charge to the students or their schools. Programs range from performances by such groups as the Cashore Marionettes to concerts by the Fort Worth Symphony Orchestra, recitals by pianists from the Van Cliburn Foundation, and dance by such world-famous troupes as the Alvin Ailey American Dance Theater and Pilobolus. Each performance includes a study guide, written by the education director that suggests ways to incorporate the program into the curriculum; these guides are distributed to teachers prior to each scheduled performance.

In addition to these specific curriculum-related activities, the master classes give high school students with serious interest and talent in the arts, an opportunity to work with artists of international renown. These classes also give teachers the opportunity to observe "master artist-teachers"—who have included Canadian Brass, jazz soloist Bobby McFerrin, Midori, Cliburn pianist Aviram Reichert, clarinetist Richard Stoltzman, the King's Singers, and Ariel Winds, among others—at work with students.

Through these classes, the next recipient of the Bayard H. Friedman Award for the Outstanding Student in the Performing Arts is identified. Four very talented young students have received this award, which is presented annually and accompanied by a $1,000 scholarship. The Bayard H. Friedman Chair for Teaching Excellence in the Performing Arts, with a $5,000 honorarium, is awarded annually to a Fort Worth ISD teacher.

An important element of the Children's Education Program is the Summer Teachers' Institute, which Performing Arts Fort Worth began offering two years ago to provide support and professional development for classroom and music teachers. Well-respected clinicians with many years of teaching experience share their expertise and knowledge of materials with local teachers attending the workshops.

This past year kindergarten, first, second, and third grade teachers were offered stipends to encourage workshop attendance. The reason for the focus on these grades is that even though they are the most

Jason Issokson, 2002 recipient of the Bayard H. Friedman Outstanding Student in the Performing Arts, works with Midori in a Master Class.

critical time to introduce music to a child, music teachers generally do not teach in those. Therefore the workshops provide techniques and help build confidence for teachers untrained in music, enabling them to introduce performing arts programs in the classrooms with some depth and authority before the students come to a performance at Bass Hall.

Society for the Performing Arts

Houston, TX   www.spahouston.org

- School Districts served per year: 54
- Elementary Schools served per year: 701
- High Schools served per year: 377
- K-12 students served per year: 40,000

Programs offered:

Performances for K-12 audiences

Short-term in-school residencies (one week or less)

After school or weekend programs for K-12 students

Professional development opportunities for teachers

Professional development opportunities for teaching artists

Partnerships with whole schools

Partnerships with whole school districts

Partnerships with public broadcasting

Partnerships with cable media

Training for school leaders (principals, superintendents, others)

Programs with parents and/or other adult caregivers

Adult education opportunities

Mentoring for students with community volunteers

Performances/exhibits by students

Performances/exhibits by school-based teachers

Performances/exhibits by teaching artists

Evaluation methods

PROFILE

The core education programs at the Society for the Performing Arts form a continuum of arts education services, including Student Matinees, $2.00 Student Series Tickets, Student Preludes, a Student Visual Art Contest, and a Master Class Series.

• *Student Matinees.* This program gives schools and community groups an opportunity to offer a culturally enriching theater experience to their students and youth at a substantial discount. In the past season, SPA presented four *The Velveteen Rabbit* matinees and three

Streb Go! Action Heroes performances; the Oberlin Dance Company brought *The Velveteen Rabbit* alive through Benjamin Britten's music and KT Nelson's choreography; ten HISD students who were selected to perform with ODC/San Francisco in *The Velveteen Rabbit* also participated in SPA's yearlong Student Mentor program; and the Streb dancers used fast "popaction" modern-dance events to redefine the boundaries of physical motion. Teacher Packets provided pre- and post-performance lessons, which were related to the Texas Essential Knowledge and Skills (TEKS) objectives. For the first time, SPA offered a Transportation Funding Assistance program that subsidized schools expenses in transporting students to performances. Additionally, a "Virtual Student Matinee" program was created to allow for two-way interactive learning without participants being constrained by the theater's physical capacity.

• *$2.00 Student Series Tickets* make it possible for local area students to attend any of six performances at a significantly reduced price. Teacher packets, which are TEKS objectives-compliant, are provided. Also, an Art Talk (pre- or post-performance lecture) is offered for each performance. Students attending these musical or dance presentations learn appropriate theater etiquette, career options in the arts, how to creatively express thoughts and feelings through music and dance, and how to evaluate performances.

• *The Student Prelude Program* offers an opportunity for students to examine the artistic style and philosophy of a particular performing arts company. First the students view a videotape or listen to an audiotape of the company's work and study additional resources provided in the teacher packet. As a follow-up, they develop their own interpretations and then share them with a live audience as they perform in a professional theater environment prior to a public performance by the company they have studied. After the show, they are invited to explore the behind-the-scenes environment and meet the professional performing artists.

• SPA sponsors a *Visual Art Contest* for all K-12 students in the greater Houston area. All submitted work is judged on interpretation of the theme and skill. Teacher packets with objectives correlated to the TEKS are provided. Participants will create art-

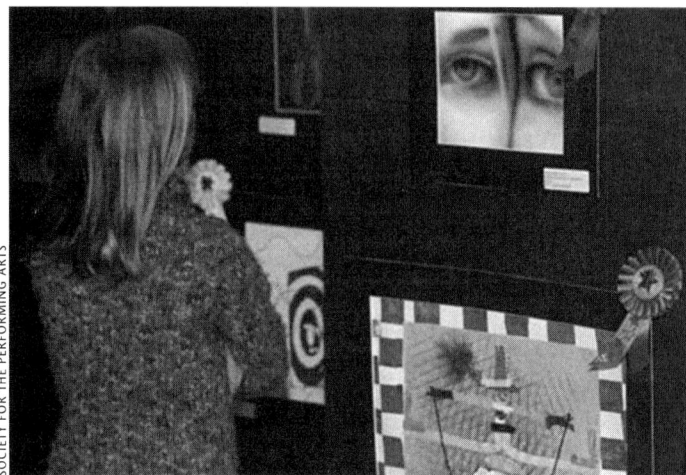

Society for the Performing Arts Annual Art contest

works using a variety of colors, forms and lines, arrange forms intuitively to create art, and develop manipulative skills needed to photograph, draw, paint and construct artworks using a multitude of materials. Grade 12 contest winners are awarded college scholarships ranging from $500 to $1,000; and winners in grades K-11 receive savings bonds ranging from $50 to $500. Additionally, SPA works collaboratively with the Texas Children's Hospital to provide a venue for display of selected art-contest entries.

• SPA offers *Master Classes* in music, dance, and theater. Experts from the companies invited to perform for SPA visit schools and serve as guest teachers. They help students develop new and innovative ways of using all of their senses to glean information about their environment and express their ideas through dance, music, or theater. Classes are free, and those scheduled to be conducted in collaboration with community organizations are open to the public. In addition, the implementation of virtual master classes enables SPA to reach large numbers of students beyond the physical capacity of master-class venues.

• SPA provides artist workshops for the Jewish Community Center, Children's Museum, public and private schools and universities, and culture-specific community centers. SPA recently held a one-week residency with the Liz Lerman Dance Company as part of the Hallelujah Commissioned evening of dance, which included more than 100 community participants on stage for the public performance of *Hallelujah: In Praise of Family Legends.*

Virginia Arts Festival

Norfolk, VA   www.virginiaartsfest.com

- School Districts served per year: 11+/-
- Elementary Schools served per year: 35+/-
- High Schools served per year: 15+/-
- K-12 students served per year: 18,000

Programs offered:

Performances for K-12 audiences

Short-term in-school residencies (one week or less)

After school or weekend programs for K-12 students

Professional development opportunities for teachers

Partnerships with whole schools

Partnerships with whole school districts

Adult education opportunities

Performances/exhibits by students

Performances/exhibits by teaching artists

Technical/planning assistance

Evaluation methods

PROFILE

Arts study has long been one of society's greatest allies in harnessing the energy of youth in a positive way. Numerous recent reports have concluded that the arts provide a unique stimulation to the mind, and offer opportunities for individual and group achievement. Public schools have continued to decrease arts education budgets, making it too expensive for students in low income schools to do such things as buy or rent instruments, purchase music, obtain private lessons, or attend concerts. In many instances the arts are becoming unavailable to many students. This challenging situation has helped to inspire the Virginia Arts Festival's education and outreach program, which has two components:

- *WorldClass®* programs encourage artists participating in the Festival to create student matinees, in-school workshops, master classes, and continuing education opportunities for educators.

- *Rhythm Project* is a year-round, after school, performance-based program that targets low-income middle and high school students by teaching African drumming and Caribbean steel-pan playing.

Established in 1997, the Virginia Arts Festival presents world-class performances in a variety of genres over a four-week period each spring. Nearly two-thirds of the artists involved in the Festival participate in WorldClass programs. Over the years, area students have worked with Midori, Dance Theatre of Harlem, Joe Burgstaller from the Canadian Brass, David Shifrin, André-Michel Schub, and the Royal Shakespeare Company. The Mark Morris Dance Group, in a five-year residency with the Festival, has established a special relationship with several of the area dance schools.

With artists who are in town for an extended residency, WorldClass works directly with educators and administrators to tailor in-school activities to their specifications. All WorldClass student matinees, and many in-school residencies, are complemented by Student Arts Information Lessons (SAILs) education guides created for educators. These guides contain background information on artists, lesson plans, Web links, Virginia Standards of Learning connections, and creative teaching aids to help integrate the arts across the curriculum. All SAILs are sent to participating schools and can be downloaded directly from the education page on the Web site.

WorldClass has set up partnerships with public and private schools and school districts to plan programming that meets specific needs, and to be an arts resource for the large and disparate community. Virginia Arts Festival strives to make the arts accessible to all students, regardless of finances, and seeks underwriting to offset artist fees.

For educators, WorldClass partners with Tidewater Community College to present a Symposium on Shakespeare. This is a mixture of scholarly presentations, hands-on workshops, and an actual Arts Festival performance for English and theater teachers. The 2001 season Symposium featured the Royal Shakespeare Company's *The Tempest;* the 2004 Symposium will be organized around the Guthrie Theater's *Othello.* In addition, arts educators can register for and receive recertification points through Old Dominion University for attending Arts Festival performances.

Rhythm Project performance, TCC Roper Performing Arts Center, Norfolk, VA, Arts Festival

A commitment to helping restore equality of opportunity for the region's neediest students led to the creation of the Rhythm Project, a program that provides positive alternatives through the arts to public school students in low-income areas. Providing all of the benefits of traditional arts study in a framework that is attractive to and respectful of the urban communities it serves, participants study African drumming and Caribbean steel-pan playing in an after school environment; all equipment, uniforms, and instruction are provided free. Students follow rigorous rehearsal and performance regimens, and they are required to meet strict standards of attendance and academic achievement at their home schools in order to maintain their standing in the ensemble. Now in its seventh year, the Rhythm Project continues to grow. It has created a college scholarship fund from performance income, recorded a CD and video, and tours and performs regularly around the state.

Wolf Trap Foundation for the Performing Arts

Vienna, VA   www.wolftrap.org

- School districts served per year: N/A
- Elementary schools served per year: 150
- High schools served per year: 8
- K-12 students served per year: 55,000

Programs offered:

Performances for K-12 audiences

Short-term in-school residencies (one week or less)

Long-term in-school residencies (multiple weeks)

Professional development opportunities for teachers

Professional development opportunities for teaching artists

Summer institute for K-12 teachers

Summer institute for teaching artists

Partnerships with whole schools

Partnerships with whole school districts

Partnerships with public broadcasting

Partnerships with cable media

Web-based learning opportunities

Training for school leaders (principals, superintendents, others)

Programs with parents and/or other adult caregivers

Adult education opportunities

Mentoring for students with community volunteers

Performances/exhibits by students

Performances/exhibits by school-based teachers

Performances/exhibits by teaching artists

Technical/planning assistance

Evaluation methods

As part of its mission to present innovative performing arts for the enrichment and enjoyment of diverse audiences, the Wolf Trap Foundation for the Performing Arts proudly offers a wide variety of education programs, both locally and nationally, for people of all ages.

PROFILE

The Foundation's premier education program, established in 1981, is the Wolf Trap Institute for Early Learning Through the Arts. Its goal is to provide professional development opportunities for early childhood educators (preschool, Head Start, and kindergarten teachers; and home care and day care providers) in the use of performing arts techniques that help young children learn basic literacy skills and meet curricular goals. With the support of local sponsoring organizations and regional programs around the country, the Institute serves more than 55,000 children, parents, and teachers in more than 1,200 classrooms annually.

At the core of the Institute's professional development program are more than 200 Wolf Trap Teaching Artists who conduct in-class residencies, professional development workshops, one-week teacher institutes, and other comprehensive training for early childhood educators and families throughout the country. Each teaching artist has a specialty—in creative drama, storytelling, puppetry, instrumental or vocal music, or dance and movement—and comes to Wolf Trap with experience in working with children. New teaching artists participate in a comprehensive training program, and all teaching artists engage in continuing in-service training.

Through a grant from the Federal Technology Opportunities Program, the Wolf Trap Institute for Early Learning Through the Arts recently initiated the stART smART Network, a unique distance-learning community that enables early childhood educators to continue receiving professional development opportunities from the Institute long after their initial work in the classroom with a teaching artist has been concluded.

The Wolf Trap Foundation for the Performing Arts has committed itself to America's Promise—The Alliance for Youth, a national not-for-profit organization (led by Gen. Colin Powell) dedicated to mobilizing the nation so that children and youth have access to the basic resources they need to become successful adults. Wolf Trap's partnership with America's Promise gives approximately 100 young people from the Boys and Girls Clubs of Greater Washington an opportunity to attend and learn about Wolf Trap performances and participate in master classes. The summer college interns (as part of their hands-on training program in arts administration, education, and technical theater) work with these adolescents, who may ordinarily have limited access to live cultural events or natural surroundings.

Master Classes are offered to people of all ages and skill levels throughout Wolf Trap's performance seasons at the Filene Center and the Barns of Wolf Trap. Professional performing artists present master classes in dance, musical theater, opera, jazz, and folk, pop, and classical music. The classes provide participants with a behind-the-curtain view of Wolf Trap's stages, as well as the opportunity to work closely with a culturally diverse group of artists.

The Wolf Trap Foundation also presents children's performances to more than 30,000 attendees each summer at the Theatre-in-the-Woods; and it houses the Wolf Trap Opera Company, where young singers of exceptional achievement and potential—who are at an interim point between academic training and full-time professional operatic careers—can experience the demands of a career in the performing arts.

ANDI KLING

David Parsons leads a master class for Wolf Trap's local community.

Broadway Center for the Performing Arts

Tacoma, WA   www.broadwaycenter.org

- School districts served per year: 12
- Elementary schools served per year: 50
- High schools served per year: 10
- K-12 students served per year: 23,000

Programs offered:

Performances for K-12 audiences

Short-term in-school residencies (one week or less)

Long-term in-school residencies (multiple weeks)

After school or weekend programs for K-12 students

Professional development opportunities for teachers

Summer institute for K-12 teachers

Partnerships with whole schools

Partnerships with whole school districts

Training for school leaders (principals, superintendents, others)

Programs with parents and/or other adult caregivers

Adult education opportunities

Performances/exhibits by students

Performances/exhibits by teaching artists

Technical/planning assistance

Evaluation methods

PROFILE

The Broadway Center for the Performing Arts has built diverse offerings around education. Its programs include the following:

• *Children's Shows.* In the past several years these shows have included the Kennedy Center's *Nightingale*, Mufaro's *Beautiful Daughters*, *Young King Arthur*, and *The Magic School Bus*. Shows are selected for their links to children's literature and the Washington Essential Academic Learnings. Along with dramas, the Broadway Center presents culturally diverse dance and music programs, including Somei Yoshino Taiko, Ballet Folklorico de VeraCruz, East Indian Orissi Dance, and many others.

• *Touring Performances.* The Broadway Center has developed tours built upon the work of local artists. In 1999, playwrights Lucas Smiraldo and Jacqueline Harmon co-wrote a show to celebrate the contributions of black women in opera and classical voice. The piece, called *Blackbird Singing*, toured more than 30 schools and other venues over the next 18 months and reached an audience of 15,000. This past year, the Center prepared another touring piece, *Edgar Allan Poe—The Poet's Journey*, which was written by local playwright Bryan Willis. The show debuted at the Broadway Center in October of 2002 and toured in the fall of 2003.

• *After School Programs Culminating in Performance: Page to Stage and Foot to Footlight.* The Broadway Center has developed an extended after school performing arts program that prepares youth to perform for the community on the Rialto stage. Now in its third year, youth from the Spanaway Learning Center (a semi-rural district in the South Sound) have learned traditional Senegalese dances from dance artist Franchesska Berry, along with West African drumming to complement the dance program. The culminating performance also toured local schools and the Boeing Corporation. Similarly, youth performed Asian folk tales and dances from China, Japan, and Korea after working with Asian-American storyteller and performer Nancy Calos Nakano.

• *Year-Long Teacher Training and Mentoring.* In collaboration with the Cultural Council of Greater Tacoma, the Broadway Center co-hosts an intensive training program for teachers that helps them introduce performing arts into daily classroom activity. Teachers receive 30 hours of training from a skilled drama or dance mentor, and then another 9 hours of mentoring support during the school year. The program, now entering its sixth year, recently received a one million dollar expansion grant from the U. S. Department of Education.

• *Cultural Building Through Festivals.* The Broadway Center features festival and community events around performances that reflect diverse cultures and traditions. Over the past several years, the Center has worked with numerous community partners to present Latino, Hawaiian, and Gospel festivals. These events, often free to the public, have featured local stand-out artists, nationally touring artists concurrently performing at the Center, other entertainment (such as an evening of salsa dance), and ethnic food appropriate to the occasion.

- *Literacy and Performance Outreach Through Poetry.* This past year the Broadway Center partnered with poets from the South Sound Poetry Slam to introduce spoken-word and poetry skills into South Sound classrooms. They performed in their characterically animated style, and sessions were often supplemented by day-long workshops to teach the students how to develop and publicly perform their own works.

- *Extended Residencies of Nationally Touring Artists.* The Broadway Center schedules residencies in schools with visiting artists whenever possible. This past year it hosted Ruby Nelda Perez of *Dona Rosita's Day of the Dead.* Ms. Perez did Latino theater residencies at schools throughout the South Sound, which included her own mini-performances and collaborative performances with youth.

- *Partnering with the Tacoma School of the Arts (TSOTA).* The Broadway Center is a major cultural partner with this first arts high school in Tacoma. The Center provides performance space, staff support, and links visits from touring artists to school curriculum in order to enhance the performing arts education of TSOTA students.

University of Washington World Series

Seattle, WA   www.uwworldseries.org

- School districts served per year: 6
- Elementary schools served per year: 17
- High schools served per year: 9
- K-12 students served per year: more than 5,300

Programs offered:

Performances for K-12 audiences

Short-term in-school residencies (one week or less)

Partnerships with whole schools

Partnerships with whole school districts

Adult education opportunities

Performances/exhibits by students

Performances/exhibits by teaching artists

PROFILE

The University of Washington (UW) World Series' comprehensive education program allows it to provide many different types of learning opportunities to K-12 students. Each season, the UW World Series offers three or four daytime performances at Meany Hall for the Performing Arts to local schools and community centers. These free interactive presentations expose underserved students to the highest quality performing arts, while providing them the opportunity to visit one of the nation's leading public universities. For many of these students, it is their first encounter with either experience.

Through a strong partnership with the Ladies Musical Club, an advocate for music education since 1891, the UW World Series brings renowned musicians into local schools for workshops and lectures. These classroom experiences allow children to interact with dedicated performers in a non-threatening and familiar setting, thus maximizing the potential for learning. Schools selected to participate in the Music in Schools program serve mainly low-income students and lack a music program of any type.

The UW World Series frequently engages visiting artists for three- to five-day residencies, allowing for greater impact as students interact with the artists in classroom workshops or master classes and then watch them perform in an evening presentation. The UW World Series also works to support teachers as they integrate these programs into standards-based curricula. Study guides are provided to teachers, including background information on the artists and art forms, vocabulary terms, classroom activities, and more.

The core strengths of the education program are the diversity, quality, and professionalism of the visiting artists, who enable the UW World Series to offer insights into cultures and performing-arts traditions unavailable elsewhere in the region. Children from all backgrounds are able to see performers on our stage who represent their own culture, history, and possible future. Students are encouraged to open their minds both to the beauty of art and music, and the incredible diversity of peoples around the world.

Students are introduced to internationally known artists such as the Emerson String Quartet, as well as artists from countries as far-ranging as Mali, Brazil, Turkey, and China. More than 200 of these artists have made their Seattle debuts at Meany. UW World Series visiting artists also display a consistent teaching skill in the classroom; those who participate in residencies often have extensive experience working with children.

These programs provide valuable examples of creativity, teamwork, professionalism, and discipline, while giving students the opportunity to witness living cultures too often relegated to textbooks.

Washington Performing Arts Society (WPAS)

Washington, DC   www.wpas.org

- School districts served per year: 7
- Elementary schools served per year: 170
- High schools served per year: 30
- K-12 students served per year: 50,000

Programs offered:

Performances for K-12 audiences

Short-term in-school residencies (one week or less)

Professional development opportunities for teaching artists

Summer institute for teaching artists

Partnerships with whole schools

Partnerships with whole school districts

Performances/exhibits by students

Performances/exhibits by teaching artists

PROFILE

The Washington Performing Arts Society (WPAS) provides school systems in the metropolitan DC area with high quality opportunities for teachers and students to interact with the performing arts.

WPAS's flagship education program, Concerts In Schools, brings local artists into schools to give performances, complemented by interactive lectures and demonstrations that conform with national learning standards. Roster artists include jazz musicians, classical ensembles, storytellers, dance companies, and other cultural arts presenters. To further enrich students' learning experiences, guides and posters are distributed prior to the performance to build background knowledge. In 2001 02, Concerts In Schools worked with 186 schools in the metropolitan DC area, reaching approximately 48,000 students.

Violinist and composer Daniel Bernard Roumain conducts a series of week-long residency activities with school and community students.

WPAS encourages all local artists to participate in professional development sessions held throughout the year. These workshops, which build on participants' skills and knowledge, are led by touring artists or WPAS staff.

Since 1974, the District of Columbia Public Schools and WPAS have jointly sponsored the Embassy Adoption Program, an award-winning multicultural enrichment activity designed for sixth graders. Using the unique resources of embassies in Washington, DC, the program allows teachers and students to increase their knowledge and appreciation of the geography, culture, and government of other nations. Each year, 50 classrooms are teamed with 50 embassies. Students then have the opportunity to work with embassy officials to build a presentation—in the style of the partnered country—which is then given at a later embassy visit. To date, more than 30,000 children have partnered with 98 embassies of countries ranging from Australia to Zimbabwe.

In 2001-2002, WPAS developed programming that linked educational programs with particular themes concurrent with the performance season. For example, Yo-Yo Ma's Silk Road Project was integrated into the Embassy Adoption Program. Through collaborations, teachers who were teamed with Silk Road countries, such as China and India, were given opportunities to expand content with the aid of an artist-in-residence; the artist conducted workshops that built students' knowledge of the performing arts of the Silk Road, and helped prepare them for their embassy presentation. Students also had the unique chance to perform for Mr. Ma as the finale of the project.

In addition, WPAS recently partnered with the DC Arts and Humanities Education Collaborative to provide free arts events, from a variety of DC arts venues, to schools.

The utilization of local artists lies at the core of WPAS's mission. In order that they stay up to date with educational methodology and artistic trends, and thus better serve the community and schools,

In 2002-2004, WPAS is continuing its linkage of educational programs with particular themes—specifically, Arte America (Hispanic culture) and the influence of the African Diaspora—leading up to residency and performance events by the Lincoln Center Jazz Orchestra and Orquestre El Arranque. Throughout this initiative, students will not only learn about these performing arts of the Americas but also engage in them. Teachers will also benefit from a workshop on how to implement the Jazz for Young People curriculum, developed by Jazz at Lincoln Center. And the artists themselves will further their own professional development as they integrate their art forms into the the public schools' curriculum.

WPAS's strength and diversity in arts programming also includes training. For example, its Children of Mass Choir, in operation since 1993, illustrates the Society's commitment to gospel music in the Washington area. The program's objective is to showcase the talents of local youth selected through community-wide audition, provide them with discipline and artistic skills in putting together a professional production, and create an environment that heightens self-confidence, self-image, motivation, and respect for others. In an effort to improve the musicianship and overall artistic excellence of the group, WPAS sponsors an annual summer camp/vocal workshop for the gospel program.

In a similar spirit, WPAS's annual Feder String Competition has encouraged study and artistic achievement among District of Columbia string players since 1971. Open to students in grades 6 through 12, the competition awards cash prizes for instrument purchase or private lessons as well as scholarships to summer study programs such as Tanglewood and the Interlochen Center for the Arts. With more than 600 participants to date, accomplished alumni can be found in music organizations all over the country.

Madison Civic Center

Madison, WI   www.madcivic.org

- **School districts served per year:** 72
- **Elementary schools served per year:** 500
- **High schools served per year:** 85
- **K-12 students served per year:** 60,000

Programs offered:

Performances for K-12 audiences

Short-term in-school residencies (one week or less)

After school or weekend programs for K-12 students

Professional development opportunities for teachers

Professional development opportunities for teaching artists

Partnerships with whole school districts

Programs with parents and/or other adult caregivers

Adult education opportunities

Performances/exhibits by students

Evaluation methods

PROFILE

The Madison Civic Center believes that the arts are essential to children's development; and its arts education program reflects its commitment to act on this belief. The Civic Center engages children in the arts and enhances their classroom curriculum. It leverages partnerships with schools, and it works with local, regional, and national cultural and social service organizations to help breach the barriers to arts participation. The arts education program strengthens the links among children, parents, teachers and the community with the following activities:

• *The Pleasant Company OnStage! Performing Arts Series for Children* provides Dane County teachers and students at all grade levels with access to high-quality performing arts of virtually all disciplines.

Since 1987, this series of daytime performances—featuring a diverse list of approximately 20 dance, music, and theater companies—has exhibited high artistic, educational, and cultural standards. Study guides, provided for each performance, help teachers and students link the educational and artistic content of the performances to classroom curriculum. Currently, this series serves more than 40,000 students and teachers.

• *The Kids in the Crossroads and ArtsAlive!* programs reflect the goal of eliminating financial barriers to the arts by providing free performances and workshops to area youth. "Kids in the Crossroads" is a series of free daytime performances for children and families held every Saturday during the academic year for the past 19 years. Performances feature local and regional storytellers, musicians, jugglers, puppeteers, theater companies, magicians, and dance troupes in an interactive atmosphere. Also throughout the year, "ArtsAlive!" places local artists in not-for-profit organizations throughout Dane County to give free performances and workshops to youth who are unable to attend events at the Civic Center. For both programs, local artists are chosen based on quality, age-appropriateness, potential for audience participation, educational content, cultural diversity, and artistic variety.

• *Educator Workshops in the Arts.* Since 1993, the Madison Civic Center and the Madison Metropolitan School District have presented this series of three-hour and day-long programs to area educators. These workshops, designed in association with the Kennedy Center, give teachers tools for increasing student participation and integrating the arts into daily classroom teaching.

• *Artist Outreach Series.* Each season, the Madison Civic Center arranges several residencies during which visiting artists conduct performances, workshops, lecture-demonstrations, and master classes at local schools and neighborhood centers. Nearly a

thousand schoolchildren and adults participate in these activities annually. This past spring, the Artist Outreach Series featured the companies of Lula Washington, Percussion de Guinée, and Urban Bush Women.

• *Family Programming.* As part of the public performing arts series, the Madison Civic Center schedules evening and matinee performances for children and families in the Oscar Mayer Theatre. Family outings to Civic Center performances reinforce the importance of arts in children's lives and encourage lifelong participation in the arts.

• *The Community Ticket and Transportation Voucher Programs*, in partnership with 110 social service organizations, distributes thousands of ticket vouchers to individuals and families every season. When customers redeem these vouchers for the price of $1, they receive the best available seat, often worth $30 or more. Similarly, the Transportation Voucher Program is a partnership with Union Cab of Madison and Madison Metro that provides transportation vouchers to members of the Community Ticket Program for whom transportation is a barrier.

• *The Children's Arts Festival* is a mix of national, regional, and local theater, music, dance, and literary and artistic activities for and by children. This day-long annual event began in 2001 and attracts approximately 1,800 visitors to the Madison Civic Center.

Clay Center for the Arts & Sciences-WV

Charleston, WV   www.theclaycenter.org

- School districts served per year: 20
- Elementary schools served per year: 10
- High schools served per year: 10
- K-12 students served per year: 1,600

Programs offered:

Performances for K-12 audiences

Short-term in-school residencies (one week or less)

After school or weekend programs for K-12 students

Professional development opportunities for teachers

Summer institute for K-12 teachers

Partnerships with whole schools

Partnerships with whole school districts

Partnerships with public broadcasting

Web-based learning opportunities

Adult education opportunities

Mentoring for students with community volunteers

PROFILE

The Clay Center's arts education programs include:

• *Partners in Education Teacher-Training Program.* The Clay Center and Kanawha County Schools have partnered (under the Kennedy Center's Partners in Education program) to train teachers, with the help of arts specialists, to integrate the arts with all areas of the K-12 curriculum. Teachers learn how to use the arts to teach other core subjects, as well as innovative techniques and strategies to teach their own subject areas; and new ways to address the WV Education Content Standards and educate the whole child.

• *Professional Sabbatical Module.* The Clay Center has developed a year-long sabbatical program to offer teachers an opportunity to refresh their skills. This program also provides the Clay Center itself with the direct experience necessary to ensure that its workshops and other activities support the Department of Education's Instructional Goals and Objectives. From one to four teachers spend 20 hours per week developing a project that will be presented by the Clay Center. The remainder of their time is devoted to a range of duties as these professionals engage in other Center educational programs.

• *Residency Activities.* The Clay Center has sponsored five school residencies since 1999, with artists in theater, jazz, storytelling, classical guitar, crafts, folk music, and dance, that resulted in concentrated workshops, performances, and special projects for the schools, both in-class and after school. Each residency involved a partnership with several school systems and arts groups (such as Carnegie Hall, Museum in the Community, and Charleston Stage Company).

• *Distance Learning.* The Clay Center's educational programs will use several technologies, such as Web-based and Microwave, to deliver: pre- and post-educational materials to prepare students and teachers for residency projects; online courses or units of study; live artist chats; walk-throughs of exhibitions; and lectures, workshops, and experiments. The Clay Center is in discussions with West Virginia Public Broadcasting to see how they might work together to produce content and deliver programs.

MICHAEL KELLER

Aquila Theatre, Movement in Shakespeare Workshop at Capital High School, Charleston, WV

Advisory Committee

Dana is grateful to the *Acts of Achievement* Advisory Committee for its conscientious review of the individual profiles submitted by performing arts centers nationwide during the winter of 2003. The committee examined each profile for the quality of its content, the breadth and depth of the described K-12 program offerings, and the clear identification of the institution as a performing arts center. Based on the Committee's recommendations, 8 institutions were selected for featured case studies in this publication, and 66 additional performing arts centers were chosen for profiles.

The Advisory Committee provided insights that informed the development of the Lynne Silverstein essay on artist residencies, and the recommendations included in Jane Polin's executive summary and observations statement.

We thank the Advisory Committee for its valuable contributions to *Acts of Achievement.*

Jane Bonbright
Executive Director
National Dance Education Organization
Bethesda, MD

W. Robert Bucker
Dean, Peck School of the Arts
University of Wisconsin-Milwaukee
Milwaukee, WI

Kim Chan
Vice President of Programs
Association of Performing Arts Presenters
Washington, DC

Janet Eilber
Principal Arts Consultant
The Dana Foundation
Los Angeles, CA

Derek E. Gordon
Senior Vice President
The John F. Kennedy Center for the Performing Arts
Washington, DC

Hollis Headrick
Executive Director
The Center for Arts Education
New York, NY

Richard Kessler
Executive Director
The American Music Center
New York, NY

Larry Scripp
Director, Research Center for Learning Through Music
New England Conservatory of Music
Boston, MA

Additional Resources

Artistic Talent Development for Urban Youth: The Promise and the Challenge by Barry Oreck, Susan Baum and Heather McCartney, published by The National Research Center on the Gifted and Talented (2000); see www.gifted.uconn.edu/ncrgt

The Arts and School Reform: Lessons and Possibilities from The Annenberg Challenge Arts Projects, published by the Annenberg Institute for School Reform at Brown University (2003); see www.annenberginstitute.org

Arts Education in the News, a free publication of the Dana Foundation focusing on the intersect of the fields of arts and education, highlighting best practice initiatives around the country; see www.dana.org/books/press/artsnews

Arts Education in Public Elementary and Secondary Schools: 1999-2000, published by the National Center for Education Statistics (2002); see www.nces.ed.gov

Arts Survive: A Study of Sustainability in Arts Education Partnerships, by Steve Seidel, Meredith Eppel, and Maria Martiniello, published by Project Zero at the Harvard Graduate School of Education (2001); see www.pz.harvard.edu

The Capacity of Performing Arts Presenting Organizations by Mark A. Hager and Thomas H. Pollak, published by the Center on Nonprofits and Philanthropy, The Urban Institute (2002); see www.urbaninstitute.org

Champions of Change: The Impact of the Arts on Learning, edited by Edward B. Fiske, published by the Arts Education Partnership and The President's Committee on the Arts and the Humanities (1999); see www.aep-arts.org

A Community Audit for Arts Education: Better Schools, Better Skills, Better Communities, published by the Kennedy Center Alliance for Arts Education Network, The John F. Kennedy Center for the Performing Arts (2001); see www.kennedy-center.org/education/kcaaen

Creating Capacity: A Framework for Providing Professional Development Opportunities for Teaching Artists, prepared by The National Conversation on Artist Professional Development & Training and published by The Kennedy Center for the Performing Arts (2001); see www.kennedy-center.org/partners

Critical Links: Learning in the Arts and Student Academic and Social Development, published by the Arts Education Partnership (2002); see www.aep-arts.org

Gaining the Arts Advantage: Lessons From School Districts That Value Arts Education, published by the Arts Education Partnership and The President's Committee on the Arts and the Humanities (1999); see www.aep-arts.org

Handbook of Research on Improving Student Achievement, second edition, edited by Gordon Cawelti, published by Educational Research Service (1999); see www.ers.org

How the Arts Can Enhance After-School Programs, published by the U.S. Department of Education and the National Endowment for the Arts (2000); see www.ed.gov and www.arts.gov

Measuring What Matters: Using Assessment and Accountability to Improve Student Learning, published by the Committee for Economic Development (2001); see www.ced.org

National Arts Education Public Awareness Campaign Survey, research monograph published by Americans for the Arts (2001); see www.americansforthearts.org

Planning an Arts-Centered School: A Handbook, edited by Carol Fineberg, published by The Dana Press (2002); see www.dana.org

Promising Practices: The Arts and School Improvement, published by The Center for Arts Education and The United Federation of Teachers (2000); see www.cae-nyc.org

Teaching Artist Journal, a quarterly publication, edited by Eric Booth and published by Lawrence Erlbaum Associates; see www.erlbaum.com

Toward Cultural Interdependence: The Fourth Phase of the Performing Arts in America, paper issued by the Association of Performing Arts Presenters (2002); see www.artspresenters.org

Young Achievers: A National Summit on Learning, Excerpts and Commentary, published by Young Audiences (2002); see www.youngaudiences.org

Contributors

Janet Eilber was principal dancer with the Martha Graham Dance Company. She soloed at the White House, was partnered by Rudolf Nureyev, and starred in three segments of Dance in America. She danced many of Graham's greatest roles, had roles created for her by Graham, and since has directed Graham ballets internationally. Eilber has also performed in films, on television, and on Broadway, directed by Agnes deMille, Bob Fosse, and Tommy Tune. As co-founder of the American Repertory Dance Company, she has received four Lester Horton Awards for her reconstruction and performance of seminal American modern dance. Eiber is current artistic advisor to the Library of Congress Martha Graham Collection, artistic director of Martha Graham Resources, and a Trustee of the Interlochen Center for the Arts. She is the principal arts consultant to the Dana Foundation and guides the Dana initiatives in arts education.

Jane L. Polin brings more than twenty years of innovative leadership experience within the nonprofit and private sectors in developing and investing philanthropic resources. She is now serving as a philanthropic advisor, principally in the arts, education, and public policy. Previously at The GE Fund, Polin led various education grant programs and financial administration for GE's $60+ million annual philanthropic support, and created "Tools for Change," a program that brought proven change processes to community-based nonprofit leaders. She also designed and grew The GE Fund's award-winning arts education and research initiatives, including *Champions of Change: The Impact of the Arts on Learning, Gaining the Arts Advantage: Lessons from School Districts That Value Arts Education,* and other efforts to advance the role of the arts in learning. Polin earned a B.A. in music from Wesleyan University and holds a M.B.A. in marketing from Columbia University.

Lynne Silverstein has more than 30 years experience in arts education, arts administration, and teacher education. From 1993 to the present, Silverstein has provided extensive consultation to the Kennedy Center's Education Program. She has written publications, designed curriculum resources, developed more than 100 performance guides, conducted arts education-related research, designed summer institutes for teachers, and taught numerous seminars to artists and educators. From 1980-1993, Silverstein initiated and directed the Kennedy Center's national Partners in Education Program and directed the Kennedy Center's local Professional Development Opportunities for Teachers program. Previously, Silverstein directed a teacher education center in aesthetic education for CEMREL, and was an art specialist in Prince William County Schools, VA. Silverstein earned a B.F.A. from Cornell University and an M.A. in Curriculum and Instruction from Virginia Tech.

Editors

Barbara Rich, Vice President of the Dana Foundation, is responsible for the News and Internet Office and helps oversee arts education at the Foundation. Rich's background in communications and education includes posts at Rutgers University and Marymount Manhattan College, where she was a Dean and then a Vice President. She earned a B.A. from City College of New York and an Ed.D from Teacher's College, Columbia University. Rich has published many articles on science and education and has served often as a discussant on media.

Jane L. Polin (See "Contributors")

Steven J. Marcus is a freelance editor and writer whose clients include the National Academies, Howard Hughes Medical Institute, the Dana Press, Mayo Clinic, Harvard University, BioMedNet, and *Science* magazine. He was editor of *Technology Review,* MIT's national magazine of "technology and its implications," from 1991 to 1997; a decade earlier, he served as its managing editor. He was editor of *Issues in Science and Technology,* executive editor of *High Technology,* and a business reporter for *The New York Times.* Most recently, he was science/medicine editor of the *Minneapolis Star Tribune.*

Acknowledgements

Dana Foundation:

Special thanks:

Janet Eilber,
Principal Arts Consultant,
The Dana Foundation

Jane Nevins,
Editor in Chief
The Dana Press

David Balog
Tamina Davar
Rebecca Luib
Barbara Peterson
Rachel Postman
Isaac Sashitzky

Association of Performing Arts Presenters:

Sandra Gibson
Kim Chan
Brandon McWilliams

John F. Kennedy Center for the Performing Arts:

Derek Gordon
Darrell Ayers
Amy Duma
Barbara Shepherd

Internet Computers, Inc.

Mario Arce

Index

Index continued

Index continued

Notes